AHMAD CHALABI, BAGHDAD, MAY 2010

ARROWS

of the

NIGHT

ARROWS
of the
NIGHT

. . . .

Ahmad Chalabi's Long Journey

to Triumph in Iraq

RICHARD BONIN

DOUBLEDAY

New York   London   Toronto

Sydney   Auckland

www.doubleday.com

DOUBLEDAY and the portrayal of an anchor with a dolphin
are registered trademarks of Random House, Inc.

Book design by Michael Collica
Jacket design by Emily Mahon
Jacket photograph by Goran Tomasevic © Reuters/CORBIS
Frontispiece photograph is by courtesy of Associated Press/Karim Kadim

Library of Congress Cataloging-in-Publication Data
Bonin, Richard, 1957–
Arrows of the night : Ahmad Chalabi's long journey to triumph
in Iraq / Richard Bonin.—1st ed.
        p.   cm.
Includes bibliographical references and index.
1. Chalabi, Ahmad, 1944–   2. Politicians—Iraq—Biography.   3. Iraqis—
United States—Biography.   4. Iraq War, 2003—Political aspects.
5. United States—Politics and government—2001–2009.   I. Title.
DS79.66.C45B56   2011
956.7044'3092—dc23
[B]   2011031208
ISBN 978-0-385-52473-5
EBOOK ISBN 978-0-385-53503-8

MANUFACTURED IN THE UNITED STATES OF AMERICA

1 3 5 7 9 10 8 6 4 2

First Edition .

To my Olivia and Abigail

CONTENTS

ARROWS
of the
NIGHT

ONE

A hmad Chalabi was in Washington, D.C., on Inauguration Day, 2001. He had chosen his favorite double-breasted Ermenegildo Zegna suit and a bright orange tie to celebrate opening day of the George W. Bush presidency. With his mischievous smile and aristocratic bearing, the fifty-six-year-old Iraqi-born Chalabi made his way from one inaugural bash to the next, gliding among the crowds of Bush partygoers. A Muslim who neither smokes nor drinks, he took it all in with the eye of an exile and the soul of a schemer. What would the Bush era mean for him? he wondered. How could he make the most of it?

The day after Bush's swearing in, Chalabi took a car to Chevy Chase, Maryland, just outside the nation's capital. He was invited to a meeting at the two-story home of Richard Perle, a leading figure in the neoconservative movement, which advocated using American military power to promote democracy abroad. Among those present, Chalabi said, were Paul Wolfowitz, Douglas J. Feith, Zalmay Khalilzad, and John P. Hannah. Within a few months, they all would hold influential positions in the new administration—with Wolfowitz and Feith landing the number two and number three positions at the Pentagon and Perle becoming a top adviser to Secretary of Defense Donald Rumsfeld, Khalilzad a special assistant to Bush and ambassador at large for Iraqi exiles, and Hannah a national security adviser to Vice President Dick Cheney. But on this brisk and sunny afternoon, January 21, 2001, they were just a handful of like-minded civilians who saw the charting of U.S. foreign policy as both their dominion and their duty.

Everyone came casually dressed, some in blue jeans, sweaters, and polo shirts—except for Chalabi, who, as always, chose his outfits with care. In this case, a beige sports coat with blue pinstripes, a pale blue shirt, and a wide navy tie. Casual was not his way. They gathered in a small salon near the front of Perle's house, seated around a glass coffee table atop a red-and-black Turkish rug and beneath a portrait of Arthur Rimbaud, the influential eighteenth-century French poet who was as famous for his scandalous behavior as he was for his groundbreaking and revolutionary writings.

"Well, we have won." Perle beamed as he opened the meeting. "And now we have to get our policy objective adopted by the administration."

That policy objective was both simple and audacious: to get Bush to back Chalabi in his long quest to overthrow Saddam Hussein.

"We were sympathetic to what Ahmad was trying to accomplish," Perle later explained matter-of-factly. But more important, the group believed that Chalabi was the missing piece in their own strategy for engineering a post-Saddam Iraq. To them, Chalabi was a modern-day Charles de Gaulle, someone "who shared our values" and who could be trusted to carry U.S. national interests to the most vital of regions, the Middle East.

"I believed at the time that we didn't know enough about Iraq to go in there and remake the place," Perle recounted. "We had to work with some-body, and I thought that he was the right person."

So, over the next two hours, as they snacked on cold cuts and salad, they sketched out their agenda. Chalabi mostly listened. It was, in his estimation, a crucial meeting.

"Of course, none of these people had jobs in the administration," Chalabi noted. "But it was important that they would be mobilized early to move the agenda for the liberation of Iraq." The primary objective was to get "ideas through to the people who would be in a position to do things." The ideas, he said, included "that Saddam was dangerous to U.S. interests in the Middle East. He was bent on revenge [over losing the 1990–1991 Gulf War]." Another objective was "to brush up and revive the arguments that would make it in the U.S. interest to help us overthrow Saddam."

By "us" Chalabi meant the Iraqi National Congress (INC), the frac-tious umbrella group of Iraqi exiles—composed of Shiites, Sunnis, and Kurds—that he led. Chalabi was under no illusion about the enormity of the INC's challenge, especially given the roster of enemies he had amassed over the years inside the U.S. foreign policy establishment, which preferred to maintain the status quo in Iraq.

"I didn't know how they were going to outmaneuver the State Department," Chalabi said of his neoconservative supporters. Or how they might neutralize the Central Intelligence Agency (CIA), where senior officials detested Chalabi, viewing him as a charlatan and an opportunist.

Then there was the question of Bush and where he stood on regime change. After a meeting with him in 2000, Perle had come to believe that Bush had "the temperament" to finish the job his father, George H. W. Bush, had begun. But Chalabi and his supporters gathered at Perle's house that afternoon realized they would have to persuade the new president to make a U-turn on his campaign pronouncements denouncing nation building.

Perle, who had spent a quarter century in government—first on Capitol Hill as a Senate staffer and later as a senior Pentagon official in the Reagan administration—knew from experience that the fate of their agenda would most likely boil down to what he called "the battle of the memos." He advised the group in his sitting room that while he expected many of them to land senior positions in the new administration through which they could promote their cause, they would still face formidable opposition from the career professionals in the State Department, the Department of Defense, and the intelligence community. He called members of that permanent bureaucracy "mattress mice" because of their skill in quietly and anonymously gnawing away at policy initiatives they opposed. As one of the participants at the meeting described it, "Just when you think your bed is all made up and your policy is securely in place, along come these mattress mice with their nay-saying memos and, before you know it, you're lying on a bed of shreds."

To counter the mattress mice, Perle advised that they preassemble their own stack of memos to answer the likely arguments opposing regime change: that the United Nations' trade sanctions against Iraq, though imperfect, were working well enough; that Saddam was safely contained and posed a minimal threat to the United States; that whatever the upside of removing the dictator might be, it was not worth the inevitable empowerment of neighboring Iran; that because Iraq is so ethnically divided, toppling Saddam could lead to a dangerous and uncontrollable explosion in ethnic and religious violence among its people; that without a strongman the country could break up into separate Shiite, Sunni, and Kurdish enclaves, igniting an ethnic war so chaotic and violent that it would destabilize the region. There was much work to be done.

Even still, an epochal shift in U.S. foreign policy had begun. From day two of the Bush presidency, the push for a new Iraq was on—and Ahmad Chalabi was smack in the middle of it.

Who was this Iraqi exile?

I first met him a year after the Bush inauguration on behalf of CBS News' *60 Minutes*, where I have been a producer since 1988. At the time, I knew nothing of the meeting at Perle's house. All I knew was that Chalabi was a leading figure in the Iraqi opposition movement and that he was campaigning hard for the overthrow of Saddam. The prospect of regime change in Baghdad was far from certain then, and the notion that the straight-talking former Texas governor would saddle up with this Iraqi blue blood with a taste for designer suits seemed far-fetched at best—especially to the executives at *60 Minutes* in New York. But when I visited Chalabi that first time—at the Iraqi National Congress's office in London near Hyde Park—I was struck by the nonstop frenzy of backroom meetings and cross-Atlantic cell phone calls I observed between him and the clique of neoconservatives working inside and outside the Bush administration. Chalabi was no mere dandy, I realized. This was a well-connected man of action who should be taken seriously. I called Lesley Stahl, the *60 Minutes* correspondent, to propose our doing a story on him and the potential policy change afoot in the Bush administration, and she agreed. The result was the first of several stories she and I did together on Chalabi—and the beginning of a ten-year-long association with him in which I got a glimpse into just how wily he was, and how well positioned to maneuver the United States toward war.

I also knew that there was much more to this man and his story than I could document on a deadline or report in a television news segment. Chalabi had secrets to tell; it was a matter of prying them out of him. So I approached him in 2007 about sitting down with me and filling in the unexplored crevices of recent history—both his and that of the Bush administration's decision to topple Saddam Hussein. Chalabi took several months to reply but eventually agreed, and since then I've traveled back and forth to Baghdad, where he now lives, interviewing him for more than sixty hours about his life and machinations. These include a larger-than-life résumé of triumphs and scandal: a degree in mathematics from the Massachusetts Institute of Technology (MIT) and a doctorate from the University of Chicago, stints as university professor and banker, a conviction for embezzling. And that was all before he became a CIA operative and decided to devote his prodigious intellect full-time to what had always been his true obsession: overthrowing the murderous Ba'athist regime in Baghdad and returning home to Iraq in a blaze of glory.

Often the fate of an exile is to see his dreams dim and then die before ever making it home again. But throughout the 1990s and early 2000s, Chalabi skillfully, fanatically, and sometimes ruthlessly orchestrated a uniquely different course for himself. Depending on whom you ask, he is either the Great Liberator of Iraq or the Great Seducer of America. Either way, there has never been a foreigner more crucially involved in a decision by the United States to go to war than Chalabi. He is one of the titanic figures to emerge from the U.S. adventure in Iraq, and the meeting at Richard Perle's house that January 21, 2001, proved to be a turning point in his long journey home.

TWO

There was nothing distant or unfamiliar to Ahmad Chalabi about the world in which he was now operating—that of coups d'état and political intrigue conducted at the highest levels of government. It was what he knew. It was the world he had been steeped in as a child growing up in Iraq.

Chalabi was born in Baghdad in 1944, the last of nine children and a scion of one of the country's most eminent families dating back to the days of the Ottoman Empire. It was during the reign of the sultans in the seventeenth century that his ancestors first achieved financial and social distinction as landowners and administrative rulers for the empire, implementing its decrees in a province located in the northernmost part of then Baghdad. The Ottomans bestowed on the family the rare designation of *Chalabi*.

"It's a very honorific title that means, 'Close to God,'" Chalabi told me with pride. "The sons of the sultan were called 'Chalabi.'"

The family converted to Shiism in the eighteenth century, something that a fair number of Sunnis did back then to gain access to the local water supply, which was controlled by the Shia clerics. But since the Shiites shared the same faith as the Sunni Ottomans' erstwhile enemy, the Persians, the Shiites were generally mistrusted and feared—sometimes persecuted. They were also prevented from participating in the government. The Chalabis, however, continued to thrive and prosper.

With the collapse of the Ottoman Empire at the end of World War I, the British redrew the map of Iraq, giving the country its present-day borders and creating a new political order that once again empowered the Sunnis at the expense of the Shiites, despite the Shiites' roughly three-to-one preponderance in numbers. The British established a monarchy, handpicking the country's first Hashemite king, Faisal I, who—along with his fellow Arab Sunnis—ran the new parliament, bureaucracy, police, and army. Shia religious leaders rebelled, urging their followers in 1920 to rise up against their occupiers. When the revolt was suppressed, many Shia religious leaders were forced to flee the country. On their way out, they called on their adherents to boycott the new government, which many of Iraq's leading Shiites did—and the rift between the country's Sunni and Shia communities only deepened. Chalabi's grandfather, Abdul Hussein, however, navigated his own course, maintaining sometimes difficult yet intimate relations with the Shia clergy while also joining the new government's cabinet, becoming its sole Shia face for much of the next two decades. From 1922 until his death in 1939, he served as minister of education nine times. One of his sons, Chalabi's uncle, was put in charge of the state bank and, through that position, came to rule what was called Bank Street, old Iraq's financial hub.

But it was Chalabi's father, Abdul Hadi Chalabi, who rose to the pinnacle of economic and political standing in the *ancien régime*. He did so thanks to not only an uncanny acumen for business and management but also a strategic friendship that he forged with the future regent of Iraq, Crown Prince Abd al-Ilah. The regent-to-be, it turned out, had passions for whiskey and—more to the point—the ponies, gambling on races that he lost far more often than he won. Chalabi's father helped out in 1938 with loans that the crown prince never repaid. The following year, after the king died in an automobile accident, the crown prince assumed power and ruled the country for the next fourteen years. During that time, he showed his gratitude to Abdul Hadi in many ways, for instance, by making him a minister of public works and eventually the president of the Senate.

Abdul Hadi's fortunes soared as his natural entrepreneurial flair, alongside the growing connections and opportunities his government positions afforded him, helped him expand his business interests throughout the country. He became the principal agent for a British company that dominated the barley trade in Iraq and had a monopoly on date exports. He handled 90 percent of the country's grain exports and moved much of the cotton that was grown on the land between Iraq's two great rivers, the Tigris and the Euphrates. He also dived into land speculation, buying up some 160,000 acres of property in old Baghdad and beyond. He owned a flour mill, acquired a majority stake in the country's largest cement company, and in the spring of 1936 became the first president of the newly created Iraqi stock exchange. In short, Abdul Hadi had mastered the art of transforming economic power into political influence and vice versa. By 1958, the year in which the monarchy was overthrown, Abdul Hadi had become the country's single wealthiest individual, with a net worth of about 9 million Iraqi dinars (or $36 million). At the time, average Iraqi workers—most of them Shiites—earned roughly 1 to 2 dinars a week, while a comfortable home in Baghdad went for about 500 dinars.

In 1950, when Ahmad Chalabi was six years old, the family moved into a suburb of Baghdad called Adhamiyah. Located near the banks of the Tigris River, it was a predominantly Sunni enclave where many of Iraq's most prominent politicians and intellectuals lived. Even among the homes of these elite, the Chalabi manor, which took two years to build, stood out: an eleven-bedroom residence resplendent with large French windows, crystal chandeliers, tiled walls, and sumptuous teakwood furniture. To get to his room, the young Ahmad walked up a wide flight of stairs made of expensive Italian marble. On hot summer nights, he and his brothers—there was a nine-year gap between him and his next-oldest sibling—used to sleep on the roof under the stars as a breeze rustled through a thicket of palm trees in the distance. Back then, Baghdad was a small and gentle city for those of the upper class—quiet, simple, even graceful. Ahmad often walked down to the river—less than a hundred yards from his house—to swim and play. Every Thursday, a driver and an escort took him and his friends to the movies. He traveled abroad for holidays, dressed in European-made clothes, and was cared for by a kindly and loving woman named Saeeda, a former African slave who had been the nanny to his mother. Saeeda lived in a small but comfortable room in the basement of the house. She catered to his every need, overseeing a team of servants who prepared his meals, helped comb his hair, and even sometimes peeled off his sweaty shirt after a raucous game of basketball. When Ahmad was nine, his father gave him his very own swimming pool, a near Olympic-sized amenity located at one of the family's other homes, the Sif, a large palm-tree-studded estate on the west side of the Tigris. The singular condition of wealth and privilege in which he was reared was as intrinsic to Ahmad Chalabi's state of mind as his state of material comfort.

But as much as he pampered his son, Chalabi's father was an aloof and largely remote figure. He was so consumed with his political and economic designs that he had little time for his children. He did, however, allow young Ahmad to sit in on his dealings and observe the life he led, giving him an education in the ways of old Iraq. In that era, Iraq's elite conducted business and politics on a highly personalized basis, and Ahmad was enthralled by the give and take of it. A stream of prominent personalities and foreign dignitaries passed through the Chalabi household, among them Harold Macmillan, the future prime minister of England; the president of Turkey; the shah of Iran; and Iraq's preeminent political figure at the time, Nuri al-Said, Iraq's prime minister. At dinner parties and over afternoon tea, alliances were cemented, cabinets formed, and opponents co-opted and if necessary crushed with the ruthless use of force. In 1957, the crown prince gave Chalabi's father $150,000 to squirrel away on behalf of the royal family in a numbered bank account abroad. On another occasion, senior Iraqi officials came to the Chalabi residence to discuss a coup plot that the government was supporting in neighboring Syria. The officials wanted to funnel money to the Syrian conspirators but feared disclosure of Baghdad's involvement, so they asked Chalabi's father to help out. He agreed to put up the equivalent of about $25,000 of his own money. He stuffed the cash into small cardboard boxes and then had one of Ahmad's brothers, Hazem, hand-deliver the boxes to the coup plotters in Beirut.

Nothing ever came of the intrigue, but such was the milieu of Chalabi's youth. Another twelve- or thirteen-year-old might have been bored by it. But not Chalabi. He was an unusual young man: not just smart but cerebral. When he thought of his grandfather, for example, he tried to think of him not from a personal perspective, but in the context of history: that he was of Winston Churchill's and Virginia Woolf's generation, born in 1875 when Victoria was queen of England, Ulysses S. Grant was president of the United States, and Abd al-Aziz was sultan of the Ottoman Empire. He was also deeply perceptive—perspicacious in fact. He soaked up and intuitively grasped the world of his father as much as he did the algebra and Euclidean geometry he studied at Baghdad College, the Jesuit-run preparatory school that he attended along with the other sons of Iraq's most prominent citizens. As he sat in on his father's various meetings, he never said a word. He just listened and analyzed, often wondering what he would do if he were in his father's shoes.

Growing up, Chalabi was acutely aware of his Shia identity. His grandfather was buried inside the shrine of Imam Ali in Najaf, the third holiest site for Shia Muslims, while his father was a respected and generous patron of the Shia clergy. His mother, Bibi Hassan al-Bassam, often spoke of her faith and the vivid drama surrounding the slaying of its saint, Husayn. She abstained from alcohol, she prayed daily, and she fasted during the holy month of Ramadan. But by no means was she a traditional Muslim woman. She also liked to gamble and loathed the *abaya*, the long, loose overgarment worn by women in public. Her tastes ran more naturally to Parisian haute couture, which she liked to adorn with large ruby rings, diamond brooches, silk scarves, and crocodile handbags. She and the rest of the Chalabis were, in the words of a close family friend, quintessentially secular. They were Shia to the core in the way that secular Jews can be culturally and psycho-logically Jewish without being observant, and, as such, they were keenly aware of the political and social disenfranchisement of their fellow Shiites, their own success and privilege notwithstanding. The treatment of Shiites as second-class Iraqis was a topic of frequent and bitter conversation in the Chalabi home. Young Ahmad's oldest brother, Rushdi—twenty-six years his senior and a figure of reverence—was particularly resentful, often com-plaining of the prejudice suffered by Iraqi Shiites at the hands of the coun-try's Sunni minority and their British keepers.

Chalabi's father often remarked that there was a reason for the Shi-ites' lack of influence: they weren't nearly as well educated or worldly as Sunnis were. Chalabi's father believed that if Shiites were to embrace modernity—in particular, education and an openness to Western ideas and culture—then in time the playing field would even out and their lot in Iraq would improve. And to a limited degree the process was already under way, as the 1950s in Iraq saw a budding of opportunity for Shiites. The younger generation, educated in technical and professional subjects, moved increas-ingly into the medical and legal fields, while the exodus of 100,000 Jewish Iraqis to Israel left a vacuum in the business world that many enterprising Shiites filled. In addition, Shiites were integrated into the upper echelons of power unlike ever before. Between 1921 and 1947, the first twenty-six years of the monarchy, there was not a single Shiite prime minister and only a sprinkling of Shiite cabinet members. In the last eleven years of the mon-archy, however, there were four Shiite prime ministers, and in 1954, when Ahmad was ten years old, the top three government positions below the king were all held by Shiites for the first time: prime minister, speaker of the parliament, and president of the Senate. It was, in many ways, a golden era for Iraq's Shiites, an awakening of sorts for the perennial stepchildren of Arabia. At least in the Chalabi household there was the hope that the monarchy was developing in a way that would eventually give Shiites a share in the political and economic life of the country commensurate with their numbers. But the Chalabis also were angrily aware of the one place where Shiites still could not make inroads or have an impact: the army. While its lower ranks were largely made up of Shiites, the officer corps was almost solely dominated by Sunnis. So, no matter how influential Shiites might become, real power eluded them. That type of power resided, Chalabi's father used to say, with those who controlled the guns, and they—the army's top officers—increasingly resented the growing influence of Shiites and felt threatened by it.

The Chalabis came to believe that this fear lay at the heart of the 1958 coup that overthrew Iraq's monarchy. Historians hold that more critical forces were at play, as powerful social and political currents were roiling not only inside Iraq but also across the Middle East as a whole. One of those currents was the surging popularity of Arab nationalism, with its followers demanding faster movement on Arab unity and greater independence from Great Britain. Another was the call from social reformers for more rapid change to address the gaping disparities between Iraq's landed aristocracy and its vast majority of people. For example, about 3 percent of the country's largest landholders, among them Chalabi's father, controlled roughly 70 percent of the land, while running water was available in less than half of the country's municipalities and most people had no electricity or sewage control. But to the Chalabis it was fundamentally the Sunni army's fear and resentment of the Shiites' growing influence that triggered the unrest. So when street demonstrations led by students and workers erupted, the Chalabis saw them primarily through the prism of their Shia identity rather than as a product of Iraq's internal inequities or epochal movements convulsing the Middle East as a whole.

Throughout the mid to late 1950s, public protests in Iraq became an almost daily occurrence. They often turned violent, and young Ahmad Chalabi grew increasingly apprehensive. Sometimes the demonstrators seized control of the local radio station and shut it down. Whenever the radio in his house stopped broadcasting, Ahmad immediately took notice, worried that a coup was under way.

That day was not long in coming. On July 14, 1958, a battalion of sol-diers commanded by the Free Officers of Iraq rolled into the capital and executed a classic coup d'état. They seized all the strategic buildings in Baghdad, including the radio station, where one of the leaders, General Abd al-Salam Arif, announced the overthrow of the monarchy. From there, the insurrection quickly turned into a bloodbath. King Faisal II and a number of other members of the royal family—all well known and beloved by the Chalabis—were rounded up and shot dead in front of the palace fountain. The crown prince, who had once borrowed money from Chalabi's father to pay off his gambling debts, was also killed. His body was taken from the palace and dragged through the streets by a frenzied mob of protesters who swarmed over his corpse, hacking at it with knives and tearing off his hands, feet, and head. His body—or what remained of it—was strung up at the gate of the Ministry of Defense. Another close friend of the family, Nuri al-Said, the prime minister, met a similar fate. Initially, he fled to the home of Chalabi's sister Thamina. The next day, however, he was brought to the hometown of Chalabi's mother, where he was spotted trying to escape while cloaked in a black *abaya*. He was shot on the spot. After he was buried, another angry crowd dug up his body, dragged it through the streets, and then tore into it with knives and their bare hands as though they were trying to kill him all over again.

News of the carnage quickly reached the Chalabi household in Adhami-yah, where the family had gathered and was now reeling from a profound sense of both sorrow and panic—even terror.

"I was aware of the danger, very acutely aware of it," Chalabi recalled. "We expected to be butchered next."

Chalabi's father, who was president of the Senate at the time, was out of the country on state business when the coup occurred—which is why he survived the events of that day. But it meant his wife and children were trapped in Baghdad without their patriarch. The family decided it was too dangerous to stay in their main residence in Adhamiyah, so they fled to one of their farmhouses, located north of Baghdad. But within minutes of arriving, young Ahmad heard the rumble of armored trucks rolling up to the house and, as he looked out the front door, saw a platoon of some sixty soldiers jumping out of their trucks and surrounding the house. The soldiers were all wearing helmets and carrying rifles with fixed bayonets. Some set up heavy machine guns mounted on tripods. The commander, an army lieutenant, promptly marched into the house and walked up to one of Chalabi's brothers, Talal, and pointed his Webley revolver directly at him, demanding, "Are you Rushdi?" He was referring to Chalabi's oldest brother, who was a prominent member of the newly deposed government.

"No," Talal said.

Then the lieutenant turned to Chalabi's mother, Bibi, and pointed the revolver at her head. "Where is your son Rushdi?" he barked.

"I don't know," Bibi said.

"Then we will look for him," the lieutenant said. He took Talal by the arm and walked up to another of Chalabi's brothers, Hassan, and shouted, "Stand up." Realizing just then that Hassan was blind, the army officer huffed, "You're no good to me," and pushed Hassan away.

"At that point," Chalabi remembered, "I was so angry I said, '*I* will go with you.'"

But Chalabi's mother became frightened, beseeching the soldiers to leave her thirteen-year-old son alone. "He's young," she implored. "Don't take him."

Upon hearing his mother's cries, Chalabi said, "I immediately became very scared. But I said, 'I will go.'"

The lieutenant then marched Talal and Ahmad outside and threw them into the family's green 1954 Chrysler sedan and, along with a carful of armed soldiers, drove down to where the farm's five large irrigation pumps were housed. Rushdi was not at the farm at all. But, no less dangerous for the Chalabis, the foreign minister of Iraq was—and he was holed up in one of the very irrigation sheds the soldiers now wanted to inspect.

"This officer stopped at the first shed, the third, and the fifth," Chalabi recalled. "The foreign minister was hiding in the second. So the lieutenant didn't find him. He would have killed him, and us, right then and there if he had."

Immediately after abandoning the search, the soldiers returned to the Chalabi farm, where, remarkably, they were all served lunch. While they were eating, Rushdi, even more remarkably, appeared out of the blue, unaware of the soldiers' presence. He was promptly arrested and taken to jail.

When Ahmad attempted to visit his big brother at the Abu Ghraib prison a few days later, the sergeant on duty told him, "If you move beyond that door, I'll make your back like a sieve with my machine gun."

Ahmad didn't blink. He wasn't afraid so much as he was furious. He felt that his family was being punished because the army hated what they stood for. To many in Iraq, the Chalabis symbolized the injustices of Iraq's old order. But in young Ahmad's mind, his family embodied what he believed the Sunni army feared and resented most: the empowered Shiites.

Ahmad's fury persisted and intensified over the next several months. It led him to defy the teachers and local government officials who extolled the new order and got him into fistfights with fellow students who were now calling him the son of traitors.

It took several months and what remained of the family's residual influence, but by the end of the year the Chalabis were finally able to get Rushdi released from jail and to have their travel ban lifted. In October, Ahmad left for London, where he met up with his father and began his life in exile. Three months later, in January 1959, Ahmad's mother joined them, as did eventually most of his brothers and sisters. The Chalabis were now together again. But they were unhinged, as one family member described it, by the abruptness with which the coup had turned their lives upside down—financially, socially, politically, and personally. Everything was different, their deep roots in the country of their ancestors severed. Immediately, the Chalabi men gathered together and began to plot their return home to Iraq.

THREE

In London, a defining paradox—advantage and anxiety—took hold for the now fourteen-year-old Ahmad. His father had managed to sock away some money outside Iraq before the revolution, so the family remained financially comfortable. But they had lost much—houses, businesses, and real estate totaling about $1 billion in today's currency, according to family estimates. Whereas in Iraq he had presided over a vast empire that included 160,000 acres of property, in England Abdul Hadi was the lord of a two-bedroom London flat whose walls were adorned with only a handful of black-and-white photographs of his children and his beloved homeland. He once had considered purchasing *all* of London's Dolphin Square, a block of 1,250 private apartments near the river Thames; now he was a mere tenant there. Gone were the tea boys, manservants, cooks, and bodyguards who had hovered over him as though he were the king himself. Abdul Hadi now had to prepare and serve his own meals. The fall from prominence, along with the loss of prestige, was as stark as it was profound.

So was the pain of exile. It was a pain in Abdul Hadi's heart for which there was no medicine—an emptiness he could not fill or put straight. From the time he woke each morning, Abdul Hadi spoke of little else except the politics of Iraq and how to restore the Hashemite monarchy the usurpers had overthrown. He ate and drank to Iraqi politics and the notion of returning to his lost paradise. And he spent many afternoons and late evenings plotting with his sons and fellow exiles their triumphant return. But it didn't take long for him to realize there was no constituency inside Iraq for a countercoup—at least not anytime soon—as Arab nationalism and other currents of history sweeping the region held more sway for Iraqis than a return to prerevolutionary Iraq. Abdul Hadi's dreams quickly gave way to reality and then to melancholy.

Ahmad Chalabi has rarely spoken about the toll of exile on his father. One of the few times he has mentioned it was to a fellow exile, Entifadh Qanbar, who has been one of his close political lieutenants for more than a decade. "Ahmad told me that his father in London cried every day," Qanbar recalled. "They were still wealthy, but Ahmad's father could not adjust to the change. . . . He was depressed." Seeing his father like this, Qanbar believes, was psychologically searing for Ahmad: "It's not easy on a boy to see this great man—charismatic, very successful, wealthy, you admire him—it's devastating to see him brought so low."

Another longtime friend of Chalabi's, Tamara Daghistani, agrees. She saw the effect of Abdul Hadi's humiliation from the vantage point of Arab culture. "To Middle Easterners, the family name and honor is more important than life itself," she said. "So losing face in the Arab world—you do anything to avoid it. And if you think you've lost honor, you are duty-bound to avenge your family honor. Otherwise, it will remain a black mark on your life and your family name."

Daghistani, now sixty-five, has known Chalabi longer and perhaps better than almost anybody else. Two years apart in age, they grew up together—down the street from each other—in old Baghdad, and have remained close friends ever since. The fact that he so rarely talks about the trauma of 1958 and its aftermath suggests to her how deeply and strongly this great assault on the family honor must still affect him.

Chalabi himself is not inclined to self-analysis. But he acknowledges the shock of seeing his father in diminished circumstances. "When I got to London," Chalabi said, "I realized how much things had changed. My father always had a lot of people around—guards, servants, and so forth. He was now living in a small apartment in London with none of that. I actually saw him cooking rice. It was a strange experience, my father cooking rice. I thought to myself, 'What's this? What's happening?'" The sight struck Chalabi with the force of revelation. "I said to myself," Chalabi recalled, "'That's it. I have to bear everything. I must not be a burden on anyone, and I must do the best I can on my own.'"

And, indeed, within days Chalabi was on his own, for his parents enrolled him in an upper-crust boarding school for boys, Seaford College. Founded in 1884, the school was located in West Sussex, some sixty miles south of London, amid four hundred acres of green rolling hills. The fall and winter days there were filled with gray, foggy skies—a far cry from the palm trees and desert sun of Iraq. Chalabi had never lived away from home before, and he didn't want to now, especially not in a place where he would be just one of a handful of Arab boys among the fair-skinned children of England's upper middle class. But he swallowed his apprehension and decided to make the best of it. As it turned out, he had both the brains and the moxie to quickly master his new environment—much in the way that he had learned at his father's side.

First, there was the matter of his placement. When Chalabi arrived on campus, he was assigned to the least-demanding academic track possible, the one in which students destined for trade school were placed. To Chalabi, it seemed that Seaford reserved that track for Arabs—and he took note of the slight, real or otherwise. However, it took all of two days for the headmaster to figure out that Chalabi was exceptionally bright; he was quickly bumped up to the "A" track for college-bound students, then to the fast track, and finally to what was called the transitional level, where the cleverest of students were placed.

Chalabi knew he was smart and took great pride in that fact. But he also was something of an intellectual exhibitionist, wanting everyone else to know it. If rugby players liked to flex their muscles, he liked to flaunt his intelligence. In a geometry class, for example, he presented a proof for Pythagoras's theorem that was so unconventional that his professor was skeptical of it. Chalabi was not only right, but he took an unseemly self-satisfaction in proving the professor wrong—and doing so in front of the whole class. The teacher didn't appreciate it, but Chalabi didn't care. There was now no doubting just how smart this young Arab was.

Or how crafty. Chalabi would arrange elaborate schemes to get what he wanted at Seaford. For example, he hated the cafeteria cuisine, so he got his parents to send him a fresh parcel of delicacies every week, a special shipment that included six boiled eggs, two tins of corned beef, several slices of cheese, two loaves of bread, six fresh oranges, two containers of mandarin oranges, and three packets of Cadbury biscuits with orange filling. There was just one problem: the school required that students eat together. Three times a day, the boys from his house were loaded onto a bus and driven across the school's sprawling campus to the cafeteria, where they ate breakfast, lunch, and dinner together as a group; there was no way Chalabi would have been permitted to bring his own spread. The prefects, or upperclassmen, of each house were charged with ensuring that the younger students obeyed the rules, and they were allowed to flog those who didn't. Chalabi had to figure out how to get the prefects to agree to look the other way while he stayed back at the dormitory and ate his smuggled-in smorgasbord. So he engaged them and charmed them and got them to like him—and, finally, he bribed them with cigarettes. But that cost money, requiring Chalabi to get around another rule, the one limiting how much money students were allowed to keep on them. The school permitted a weekly allowance of 5 shillings, or about 40 cents. That wasn't nearly enough money, however, to purchase all of the cigarettes Chalabi needed to buy off the prefects, so Chalabi got his parents to pitch in again. They sent him an envelope every week containing an extra £2—nearly $6. They gave him another £20 cash to keep stashed in his room and deposited £100 in a safe-deposit box at the local post office. Chalabi then befriended the proprietor who ran the campus concession stand and got him to agree to give free cigarettes to the designated prefects, with Chalabi later reimbursing the proprietor. In the end, the proprietor made money, the prefects got cigarettes, and Chalabi got to eat his own food on his own schedule back at the dormitory without any of the noise or commotion of the cafeteria. The scheme worked so well that Chalabi decided to sidestep some of the other aspects of campus life he didn't like, such as the Seaford tradition that allowed prefects to order lowerclassmen like Chalabi to iron their pants and polish their boots. Chalabi thought that such acts were undignified and refused to do them. He hired other students to press and polish not only the prefects' uniforms but also his own. He paid 2 shillings for the pants, and another 2 shillings for the boots if their tips were properly shined. By the end of his first year, Chalabi had settled nicely into the ways of Seaford, a pasha in the making.

The following year, 1959, his family moved back to the Middle East while Ahmad remained in West Sussex. His father, Abdul Hadi, bought a house in Beirut, Lebanon, where he was able to resurrect much of his old life, surrounding himself with a retinue of servants and drivers, and holding court with those of his fellow exiles who had also migrated to Lebanon. From Beirut, it was also easier for Abdul Hadi to extract more of the wealth he had still tied up in Iraq. He plunged back into business—most notably, banking—and quickly arranged to have two of Ahmad's older brothers marry into the Lebanese Shia aristocracy, bolstering the family's economic and political status in their new homeland. Ahmad spent his summer breaks in Lebanon, swimming at the beach, going to the movies, and learning how to drive. He liked the country very much, but he never abandoned the idea of returning to Iraq. To the contrary, that idea gnawed at him throughout his years at Seaford, and even while still a teenager he presumed a role for himself in what he regarded as the righting of Iraq.

"I must prepare myself," he thought. "I must work to get home." But how? What could he do? He decided that at that stage of his life the only answer was to develop himself intellectually. He vowed to do what his father once told him the Shiites must do to level the playing field with the Sunnis: embrace modernity, seize education—inside the classroom and out—and take advantage of Western ideas and culture. Chalabi therefore came to devote himself to learning. He made that decision in a conscious and deliberate way. The restlessness of his mind was such that arguably he would have immersed himself in the world of ideas anyway, but now he went about it with a passion.

Initially, he delved into books. At age fifteen, Chalabi became enthralled with Dostoyevsky. Every night, when the lights in his dormitory went out, he crawled under his blanket and switched on a flashlight to read *Crime and Punishment*. He found it so compelling that he decided to read another one of Dostoyevsky's tomes, *The Possessed*. In his spare time he taught himself calculus. And with the Soviets' launching of *Sputnik* in the late 1950s, he decided to look into satellites, which led him to read up on Newton and Kepler and their observations on gravity and planetary motion. He also studied English history, taking special note of the Tudor dynasty and the story of its first monarch, Henry VII, who enlisted the aid of France in an intricate web of co-conspirators to usurp the crown despite a tenuous claim to the English throne. And this was all before the end of high school. In 1961, when he moved to the United States to attend college, it was more of the same. While obtaining his undergraduate degree in mathematics at MIT, for example, he traced the intellectual genesis of Marxism, which had become an important ideological force in Iraq. While immersing himself in the subject, he was struck by how Lenin had managed to overthrow the government of Russia while sitting in Switzerland. Lenin did so, Chalabi noted, with the help of the German government, exploiting history to his own advantage—in this case, Germany's desire to defeat Russia on its eastern front during World War I.

While at MIT, he also kept a close eye on events inside Iraq, reading a wide range of American newspapers and subscribing to BBC Monitoring, the news service that reported (and still reports) on mass media worldwide, including government propaganda. During World War II, it provided the British government with valuable information about military, security, and economic developments globally, particularly in countries where foreign journalists were banned. Chalabi figured what was good enough for Winston Churchill was good enough for him. And so once a week a package from BBC Monitoring in London arrived at his doorstep in Boston full of news reports that Chalabi scoured for information about Iraq.

What he found was a country in constant turmoil, with countless changes of government and failed coups. The first leader of postrevolutionary Iraq, General Abd al-Karim Qasim, ended the political order Chalabi's father had long dominated, the one in which the urban wealthy and the landed class called the shots. At the same time, Qasim rejected the Arab nationalist ideology, with its pro-Sunni sentiments, that was so dominant throughout much of the Middle East and, under his rule, Iraq's Shiites continued to participate in governmental and economic affairs much as they had before. Encouraged by that development, Chalabi's father in 1962 decided to travel to Baghdad to explore the possibility of ending his exile. Had Adbul Hadi been permitted to return to Iraq, Ahmad would have joined him after finishing his studies in the States, he believes, and lived out his life there as a mathematics professor. But the Qasim regime sent Chalabi's father packing back to Lebanon.

The following year, Saddam Hussein's Ba'ath Party staged a coup and executed Qasim. The 1963 Ba'athist reign, which lasted for only nine months before being brought down itself in a coup, was characterized by a fervent embrace of Arab nationalism. It was also noteworthy for its singular brutality. While few of its opponents were spared, it was the hundreds of Shiites who were hanged in the public square that caught the Chalabi family's attention, prompting two of Ahmad's older brothers to join a brewing conspiracy to overthrow the Ba'athists. Working with disaffected members of the military, they hoped to midwife a new sort of government, one neither communist nor Ba'athist. When Ahmad, then eighteen, finished his second year at MIT and visited Lebanon that summer, they approached him about joining their cause, which he readily embraced. Ahmad facilitated contact among some of the officers, helping them move around safely inside Iraq and organizing clandestine meetings. He also did some press work in Lebanon, talking to reporters and editors working for *Al Hayat*, a leading and widely respected daily regarded as the newspaper of record for the Arab diaspora. The coup, however, ultimately collapsed, and many of the military officers involved were arrested and executed. As for Ahmad Chalabi, though his role was limited, he had his first taste of conspiracy—and it suited him.

Over the next several years, he continued to straddle the two worlds of America and Arabia. In February 1965, he graduated from MIT—a semester early. With his mathematics degree in hand, the twenty-year-old Chalabi then traveled to Mecca, fulfilling his religious obligation of making hajj—the holy pilgrimage. He went with his father and, like all pilgrims to Mecca, shaved his head and dressed in sandals and the *ihram*, a garment of unhemmed white cloth that is draped over the torso and secured at the bottom by a white sash. He observed all of the rituals, from animal sacrifices to walking counterclockwise seven times around the Kaaba, the holiest site in Islam, in whose direction all Muslims face when they pray. It was a spiritually fulfilling time for young Chalabi. In Mecca, he met King Faisal of Saudi Arabia and the grand mufti of Jerusalem, the cleric in charge of Jerusalem's Islamic holy sites. He met leaders of Morocco's resistance movement and Ayatollah Muhammad Baqir al-Hakim, one of Iraq's foremost Shia Muslim leaders, who cofounded the country's modern Islamic political movement. He met Yemenis, Turks, Chinese Muslims, and a distinguished-looking Nigerian who first caught Chalabi's eye from afar.

"In the shrine, I saw a very impressive man, a black man, sitting," Chalabi recalled. "He was big, and he had white flowing robes and a white turban with a lot of people sitting around him. He was speaking English. Curious, I went and introduced myself to him. It turns out, the man was a prince from northern Nigeria. And he, actually, was one of the last people to do conquests for Islam in Nigeria."

The encounter made a lasting impression on him, he says, as he came to understand the extent of the Islamic movement and appreciate the wisdom of the hajj experience—how it brought Muslims together from diverse parts of the world and different cultures, all unified by Islam and the geographic location of the religion's origin. It deeply affected him, Chalabi told me in a rare discussion of his faith. "It cemented my identity as a Muslim and an Arab, and made me very proud of being part of this historical and religious continuum."

Hardly skipping a beat, Chalabi departed the birthplace of Islam for the University of Chicago, where he would obtain his doctorate in mathematics. His advisers there regarded his dissertation, "On the Jacobson Radical of a Group Algebra," as both original and insightful. But as hard as he worked on his dissertation, he was not immune from what was going on around him—in Chicago, in the late sixties. He took up with a girlfriend, bought himself a brand-new 1966 Ford Thunderbird with black leather interior, and went on a twenty-day road trip across the American South, retracing the route of General William Tecumseh Sherman's Atlanta campaign during the Civil War. Chalabi even tried drugs, popping Dexedrine, a stimulant, to help him cram for a test in Galois theory. He failed the exam, however, and never experimented with that aspect of sixties counterculture again.

Chalabi also continued his practice of roaming the library stacks in search of new books and ideas that he hoped would prepare him for his eventual return to Iraq. But it's what he saw unfold on the front pages of the *New York Times* that was the most instructive to him—in particular, the impact of the newspaper's increasingly critical coverage of the U.S. war in Vietnam. When Lyndon Baines Johnson was forced to withdraw his bid for reelection in the 1968 presidential race because of Americans' growing opposition to the war, Chalabi first grasped the power of the press.

"I was there when the press knocked out Johnson," Chalabi told me. "I saw what the *New York Times* could do to a sitting president of the United States on foreign policy." It was a lesson that he would remember and later employ not to end a war, but to help start one.

In July 1968, the Ba'ath Party and one of its rising forces, Saddam Hussein, returned to power in Iraq. The following summer, within days of donning a Renaissance scholar's cap for the University of Chicago's graduation ceremonies, Ahmad Chalabi was back in Lebanon arguing with his mother over his intention to participate in yet another attempted coup against the Ba'athists. She thought it was too dangerous for him to get involved. But Chalabi would hear none of it, handing her his newly minted diploma as he and his blind brother, Hassan, set off for Iran. Another brother, Jawad, also pitched in, but Abdul Hadi Chalabi was completely uninvolved; the zeal for rebellion had deserted him.

Once in Iran, Chalabi joined up with a small group of Kurdish rebels and their hosts from SAVAK, the Iranian intelligence service under the shah. Together, they crossed through the mountains into Iraq and proceeded directly to the guesthouse of Mustafa Barzani, the legendary Kurdish rebel leader, where they all bedded down for the night. The next morning, the diminutive but charismatic Barzani met with them and discussed his alliance with a group of mutinous, anti-Ba'athist military officers in Baghdad—most of them Shiites (who were now permitted to hold officer rank, albeit in nonessential commands).

Over the next several months, Chalabi acted as both a courier and a mediator, traveling to London, Spain, Jordan, and elsewhere to deliver messages and negotiate on behalf of the conspirators. He also attended a series of secret meetings in Tehran, where he plotted with SAVAK's top official, Nematollah Nassiri, as well as two former prime ministers of Iraq, a former Iraqi general, and leading figures from Iraq's Shia community. The plot ultimately failed, but the experience was a seminal one for Chalabi. At age twenty-four, he was already operating at the highest levels—and with the mind-set that his background and intellect entitled him to be there and that the spoils of war would be divided from the top down. Chalabi was also introduced to Iran's intelligence service, a relationship that would continue—indeed thrive—after the shah of Iran was deposed in 1979. But, most important, Chalabi met the Kurds. They were central to a way forward that he began to think about while he was still a student at MIT.

Basically, his approach to overthrowing the Ba'athists ignored the ideological trend of the day—whether it was communism, Arab nationalism, or Nasserism—and instead focused on the age-old Sunni/Shia split among Muslims. In his view, it was Iraq's army—not its politicians—that was responsible for perpetuating Sunni dominance over Iraq's majority Shiites. If change was to occur in Iraq, if the Shia awakening his father and brothers used to talk about in Baghdad was to flourish, he believed, then Iraq's army would first have to be dealt with. That's where the Kurds came in. Chalabi envisioned establishing a provisional government in northern Iraq where the Kurds controlled a large swath of territory, an arsenal of artillery and antiaircraft weapons, and an army of battle-tested fighters who had more than held their own against Iraq's army during their periodic revolts against

Baghdad for Kurdish independence. Under the umbrella of the Kurds' Mustafa Barzani and his Peshmerga, Chalabi hoped to establish an alternative Iraqi government that would be ready to take over should Baghdad fall. It was essentially the same plan Chalabi would get Richard Perle and the neoconservatives to embrace many years later.

Following the failed 1969 coup, for which scores of Iraqi officers were executed, Chalabi joined his family in Beirut. It was the first time since the 1958 revolution that he had lived in an Arab country full-time. He was twenty-six years old. He taught advanced mathematics at the American University of Beirut, where he was regarded as a mathematical wizard. But politics were his passion. Lebanon in the early seventies was rife with exiles—Iraqis, Syrians, and Palestinians—all dreaming and plotting to get back home. But something else took hold of Chalabi. As in Iraq, the Shiites of Lebanon were the most numerous yet least powerful. But, unlike in Iraq, the Lebanese Shiites were beginning to organize and lay down the roots of what would become in the space of thirty years the most significant political community in the country. Lebanon was a place where the Shiites would shed their political timidity and attain power at the highest levels of government. Chalabi saw it happening—and it captivated him.

In early 1972, Chalabi married Leila Osseiran, the daughter of Adel Osseiran, a founding father of modern Lebanon and one of the Lebanese Shiites' most distinguished politicians. It was a highly strategic arranged marriage, one that immediately catapulted Chalabi to the apex of the Lebanese Shiite world. Over the years, Adel Osseiran had been speaker of the parliament, the highest office in the land open to Shiites, and had been minister in numerous other cabinets. He was wealthy, well educated, and, something of a rarity for a Lebanese Shiite: powerful. And he happily extended to his new son-in-law unfettered access to the political life of the country, showing him how a Shiite politician in Beirut could have entrée to the great powers of the world—the French, the Russians, even the Americans.

Chalabi's wedding was officiated by Musa al-Sadr, the great spiritual leader of Lebanon and a close friend of the Chalabi family. Al-Sadr was the flip side of the power coin from Adel Osseiran—a turban-clad but worldly wise activist cleric who led the Shia faithful of Lebanon until his disappearance in 1978. The Iranian-born mullah represented a new kind of leader in

Arab politics, one as conversant with Western thought and culture as with Shia theology. He embraced modern technology and understood both the power of public opinion and the tools of popular mobilization in the modern world. He fought tirelessly for the downtrodden and disenfranchised of his community—and, most significantly, he succeeded, becoming a seminal figure in the Shiites' rise from the fringes of power in Lebanon. Chalabi spent time with al-Sadr, observing his formidable skills in organizing the men and political institutions that in later years would come to play a central role in Lebanon's Shia awakening.

To Chalabi, these men—Osseiran and al-Sadr—and this place—Lebanon—all spoke to the possibility of a new order in his own homeland, an Iraq free of the so-called Sunni Pact, which had prevailed in the Middle East for centuries. They gave sustenance and direction to his growing ambition for family redemption.

Chalabi's yearning for restoration came into slightly sharper focus in the spring of 1974. At the time, Thomas J. Carolan Jr. was the acting political officer at the U.S. embassy in Beirut. While sitting at his desk one afternoon, he received a call from the receptionist downstairs at the main entrance.

"Mr. Carolan," the receptionist said, "there's a gentleman down here who insists on seeing somebody in the political section. He won't take no for an answer."

"What's his name?" Carolan asked.

"Ahmad Chalabi."

Carolan decided to see what was on the mind of this pushy walk-in. As he descended the flight of stairs from his second-floor office past the U.S. Marine guard post, Carolan saw a dapper, anxious-looking young man. He greeted Chalabi, who got right to the point. Chalabi said he had come to the embassy in desperation on behalf of Mustafa Barzani, the Kurdish leader. War had broken out between Barzani's fighters and the Ba'athist regime in Baghdad, and Chalabi urgently wanted the United States to step up its support of Barzani. The shah of Iran was already helping arm the Kurds, while the U.S. government was funneling millions to them through Tehran. But Chalabi complained that the shah was untrustworthy; he wanted the Americans to cut out the shah as the middleman and deal directly with Barzani instead. Carolan invited Chalabi up to his office to discuss the issue and for the next two hours listened to one story after another about the Kurds' longtime struggle for independence and the heroism of its leader, Mustafa

Barzani. Carolan was mesmerized. "I found him not only very, very interesting, but inspiring," Carolan recalled.

Immediately following the meeting, he cabled Washington, laying out Chalabi's argument on behalf of the Kurds. Carolan also walked across the hall from his office and spoke to the CIA station chief. In both instances, Carolan was told to mind his own business. Normally, he would have done just that—dropped the matter—but he had taken an immediate liking to the young Iraqi and found himself wanting to help him, wanting to press his case again and again with Washington. It was as if he had been seduced, intellectually speaking.

Chalabi pursued a friendship with Carolan, often inviting him to lunch or to his upscale home near the Mediterranean Sea. Over dinner, Chalabi introduced the American diplomat to Kurdish rebels who happened to be passing through Beirut. Other times, Chalabi would simply transfix him with his storytelling. If he had perfected the art of listening as a child, Chalabi had become a raconteur par excellence as a young man. It was as if Carolan had walked into a real-life version of *One Thousand and One Nights*. He was almost helpless.

"When Ahmad really wants to turn it on—the persuasion, the charisma, the flattery—it's amazing," Carolan recalled. "But it's not just charm. It is a personality that is at once complex and attractive because of his knowledge of the world, his knowledge of history, his knowledge of science, his curiosity and thoughtfulness. It's all there. He used to hold me spellbound sometimes in the things he knew about that I didn't know anything about."

For all Chalabi's passion on behalf of the Kurds, however, it was clear to Carolan that Chalabi's support of the rebels was rooted in his hatred of the Ba'ath Party and its then fast-rising star, Saddam Hussein. "Almost from the very first day I met him," Carolan recalled, "Ahmad was on a crusade. He had an obsession, and the obsession was to bring about by whatever means he could the downfall of Saddam Hussein and the Ba'ath Party. He wanted them wiped off the face of the earth, and he was gonna do everything in his power, somehow, to accomplish that. He didn't say 'by hook or by crook.' But it was clear that he had an all-consuming ambition to do whatever it took. He would sup with the devil."

Chalabi used to tell Carolan lurid tales of Ba'athist atrocities, from the torturing of Iraqi citizens to the gunning down of Iraqi exiles living in London and Rome. " 'They'd be at home and the doorbell would ring,' " Carolan said, recounting Chalabi's words. "'They'd open the door and then, bang, a hail of machine-gun bullets would mow them down.' The killers, of course, were never found. But it was Saddam Hussein, and Ahmad made sure I understood that so that I could see what evil and despicable characters Saddam and the Ba'athists were."

In his conversations with Carolan, Chalabi seemed to equate the fate of his family with that of Iraq. They were one and the same. Chalabi spoke of his father and other family members reverentially, as enlightened figures akin to the country's founding fathers—leaders who could have shepherded Iraq into a modern and more prosperous era if not for the 1958 revolution and the Ba'athists who followed. "He certainly made clear that his family had been cheated of its influence and its destiny in Iraq," Carolan said. Chalabi confided that even as an adolescent he was "filled with intense anger at what had happened in '58, and with this burning vision, determination, obsession—whatever you want to call it—he would somehow turn the clock back, or right what he perceived to be a terrible wrong and a terrible mistake."

And the Kurds were central to his aspirations, Carolan related. If their rebellion could succeed in overthrowing Saddam Hussein, Chalabi believed, it would open the door to a new and better Iraq in which his family would recover a key role in the country.

Carolan continued to write dispatches to Washington—but always to no avail. Eventually, Chalabi decided he would try to employ the power of the press he had witnessed as a student in the United States during the time of the Vietnam War, asking Carolan to introduce him to any American reporters he might know. The political officer happily obliged, facilitating meetings with, among others, Jim Hoagland, the Pulitzer Prize–winning foreign correspondent for the *Washington Post*. Hoagland would remain a key and influential outlet for Chalabi throughout his decades-long campaign against Saddam Hussein. While in Beirut, Chalabi also met Peter Jennings, then a young reporter for ABC News, and David Hirst, the chief Middle East correspondent for the British *Guardian*. They, too, would provide important platforms for Chalabi in the years to come.

But at the moment Chalabi was concerned only with the Kurds' cause. While he managed to get some stories published on the subject, they never led to the change in U.S. policy he wanted. For much of 1974, however, it didn't seem to matter much. With the strong backing of Iran and the

United States, Barzani and his Peshmerga were able to exact a heavy toll on the Iraqi army. The tide of war looked promising. But by early 1975, secret negotiations between Baghdad and Tehran had begun and, largely on the initiative of Saddam Hussein, Iraq accepted all of the shah's territorial claims. In exchange, Tehran agreed to cease all support for Barzani and his Peshmerga. The United States did as well, accommodating the abrupt about-face of its ally, the shah, without a word of protest. The CIA also terminated its covert program for the Kurds, which included $16 million in aid. As a result, the revolt quickly collapsed.

Chalabi didn't know of the backroom details at the time, but he knew the facts on the ground—and they were devastating to the Kurds and, therefore, to his own objectives. Thousands of Peshmerga surrendered, while Barzani was granted safe passage to the United States, where he died a broken man in 1979. Meanwhile, upward of half a million Kurds were forcibly relocated from their villages to new settlements closer to the big cities.

The U.S. and Iranian betrayal of the Kurds became public knowledge long ago. Henry Kissinger, the U.S. secretary of state at the time, famously quipped, "Covert action should not be confused with missionary work." But to Chalabi, the treachery toward Barzani was more than a lesson in the cold-blooded calculations of realpolitik; it was unconscionable. "The CIA," he fumed years later in an interview with me, "is completely prepared to burn down your house to light a cigarette. That's the lesson I learned." And it's one that he apparently took to heart, for he would soon light up a few houses himself.

FOUR

In 1978, Ahmad Chalabi moved to the kingdom of Jordan. His venture there began (and would end) with the help of his childhood friend and neighbor Tamara Daghistani. She was the daughter of a prominent Sunni army general who opposed the 1958 coup. After the revolution, her parents—like the Chalabis—fled to London, where the two families were thrown together; they have remained close ever since. Also like the Chalabis, the Daghistanis were one of old Iraq's most important and well-known families. As a child, Tamara all but lived in Iraq's royal palace, regarding the king, Faisal II, and other members of the royal family as her extended family. In exile in Jordan, the Daghistanis became just as close to the other Hashemite king, Hussein bin Talal. When Tamara's brother married King Hussein's sister, she became an extended member of that royal family. This proved to be a crucial connection for Chalabi.

In the summer of 1977, when she was thirty years old, Tamara was staying in London and hosted a small get-together for Chalabi and two of his older brothers, Rushdi and Jawad. As they were sipping tea and snacking on cookies, King Hussein's brother, Hassan bin Talal, dropped in. Next in line to the throne, the thirty-year-old crown prince was a man of consequence. Jawad Chalabi mentioned to him that the family was looking for a new place to start a bank. "Why don't you open one in Amman?" Prince Hassan suggested. "You will be welcome." And just like that, Jawad was off to Amman applying for a license. After his third visit, however, Jawad called Tamara to say that it wasn't going to work. His application had been rejected, he told her, and there was no hope of budging the chairman of Jordan's central bank. Tamara told him to stay put. She hung up the phone, called Prince Hassan, and told him of the situation. "Within minutes," Tamara recalled in an interview, "Jawad called me back and said, 'What did you do?! The whole thing has changed.' It was that quick."

What had changed was that the head of Jordan's central bank, Dr. Muhammed Saeed el-Nabulsi, had received a phone call from a senior official at the royal palace, advising him to rethink his decision. "King Hussein of Jordan was very close to the Hashemite King of Iraq, who in turn was close to the Chalabi family," was how it was explained to Nabulsi. The central banker understood that the palace official was speaking on behalf of Prince Hassan, and the thrust of his message was crystal clear. Nabulsi immediately reversed himself and approved the Chalabi application.

License in hand, the Chalabis quickly raised about $9 million in start-up capital (some $1.8 million of their own money, the rest from outside investors) and decided to put Ahmad in charge. So in 1978, at age thirty-three, the young mathematics professor left his classroom in Beirut for a new life in Amman, where he opened the doors to Petra Bank, named after the famous cultural and archaeological site in Jordan that a poet once described as "a rose-red city half as old as time."

Chalabi arrived in Amman at a propitious time. Following the 1973 oil embargo, the Middle East was awash in petrodollars, with rivers of oil money flowing from the Gulf states into stable countries nearby, like Jordan. Add to that the civil war in Lebanon, which prompted businesspeople there like the Chalabis to move large chunks of capital to Jordan as a safe alternative, and the result was a Jordanian economy poised to explode. Jordan's banking industry was also ripe for the taking, especially for someone as shrewd as Chalabi. For one, there were only a handful of banks in the country then, and their practices were primitive compared with those of Western banks. None of them, for example, extended loans without heavy collateral or offered electronic banking, automated teller machines, or credit cards. Ahmad Chalabi introduced all of these innovations to Jordan. Chalabi also invested his Petra Bank capital in large-scale projects, another novelty for Jordanian banks in those days. He opened the country's first supermarket, a Safeway, invested in a local hospital (which he later sold to Jordan's army), and financed the construction of Amman's first townhouses. It was as though Chalabi had stepped into the past with all the financial weapons of the future and taken over. Indeed, in a mere two years Petra grew to be the country's second-largest bank, a position it held even after the number of banks in the country swelled to seventeen. Between 1978 and 1982, its assets multiplied tenfold, from $40 million to $400 million. In the next five years, they more than doubled again—to nearly $900 million. It was an eye-popping sprint to the upper rungs of Jordan's financial world.

For a banker, Chalabi was extremely unconventional. He had long sideburns and rarely wore a tie, usually opting for an ascot or the high-collared Nehru jacket that the Beatles popularized in the sixties, though Chalabi's buttoned diagonally across the chest. He also had an odd penchant for small knives. He always had one in his hand, clicking away, opening and closing it and scraping his cheek with the blade as he spoke. He didn't even know he was doing it, Daghistani noted. It was just a tic, his razor-edged equivalent of worry beads. Chalabi liked to be chaperoned around town in a bank-owned Range Rover, and he surrounded himself with a small entourage of bodyguards. He had truly become his father's son.

Chalabi also liked to live well, extravagantly well. He built what neighbors called a grandiose mansion, distinctive for its multimillion-dollar price tag and its historic Islamic architecture—three courtyards, wind towers, looming arches, intricate wood moldings, and heavy stonework. He lived there with his wife and four children, two girls and two boys, and the house served as the hub of his social circle, where he entertained almost nightly, enthralling guests with his detailed knowledge of everything from philosophy and politics to phosphates. Chalabi liked the company of people, and he took delight in holding court. His guests in Amman basked in his presence as much as he did in all the attention. Jordan had never seen anyone quite like him before.

But what really set him apart were his thirst for power and his modus operandi for getting it. Nabulsi, the central bank's former chief, was typical in his comments: "In Jordan, bankers sought first and foremost to be successful as businessmen and, to the extent that they became influential, it was as a result of that success—as a secondary by-product. Chalabi, on the other hand, did the opposite. His objective was not success, but influence. To him, banking was merely the means to that end. He targeted specific influential people, eminent people who had the keys to—I don't want to say the palace—but, shall we say, houses of power."

Actually, those Chalabi homed in on had the keys to both, and he was so brazen about it that everyone knew what he was up to—from King Hussein to people like Osama Sha Sha'a, the owner of Amman Bookstore and a highly sought-after fixture on the city's social circuit. When Chalabi first arrived in the country, Sha Sha'a says the young banker came to his shop every day searching not just for books, but for the kind of information Sha Sha'a kept only in his head. "He wanted to know everything," Sha Sha'a recalls. "He wanted to know who was important and who was not. Who was smart and who wasn't."

When Chalabi was a fourteen-year-old student at Seaford College in London, he identified the school's levers of power—the prefects—and bribed them with cigarettes to get what he wanted. In Jordan, he updated that approach. He targeted military officers, intelligence officials, and ex-politicians and put them on the bank's board. He loaned money abundantly to soldiers, members of the elite royal guards, journalists, and government ministers. And, according to Tamara Daghistani, he did so on exceptionally lenient terms. "They didn't have collateral," Daghistani said. "Ahmad guaranteed the loans personally. If they couldn't pay an installment, Ahmad would say, 'Don't worry. It's a gift.'"

He gave what amounted to a seven-figure gift to the government's minister of media, executing a $1.5 million contract for public relations services never performed. He gave a Visa card to the country's prime minister to use at his pleasure. And he extended hundreds of loans to royal family members. In all, they borrowed, without ever repaying, some $60 million from Petra Bank, according to a former senior central bank official.

One of those borrowers was Prince Hassan, the man Tamara Daghistani called when the Chalabi family's bank application seemed dead in the water. Prince Hassan and his wife built the highly regarded Amman Baccalaureate School with a $6 million loan from Petra Bank, a credit that was never repaid. Just as his father had once bailed out the crown prince of Iraq, Chalabi is said to have frequently helped out Jordan's crown prince with such loans and gifts. Prince Hassan was saddled with many official duties but had a paltry budget to pay for them, friends in the royal court explained. Regardless, Chalabi says that he extended more than $28 million in advances to the heir apparent to King Hussein's throne, and that they became close friends. The prince, who oversaw Jordan's economy in those days, made Chalabi one of his principal economic advisers. And the two men socialized frequently. To be sure, they had much in common: they were close in age and had both been educated in the West. But they also had much to offer each other.

"I learned very well how the Jordanian system works," Chalabi said with a laugh, "and I worked it. I reached the top." In fact, you could count on one hand the number of people in Jordan with more influence than Chalabi. As his friend Tamara Daghistani said, "On feast days and other important occasions, people would go to His Majesty first and then come to Ahmad's house to greet Ahmad and give him well wishes." When asked if he used the bank as a vehicle to make himself powerful, Chalabi replied, "That's interesting. Can you not say the same of Bill Gates, for example?"

Surely Chalabi was not the only man on the make in Jordan. But, by all accounts, he took the tried-and-true methods of power seekers and employed them to an extent rarely seen before. But Chalabi was also willing to put it all at risk. When it came to Iraq and Saddam Hussein, he went against the grain in Jordan and worked counter to his own interests—commercial and otherwise. He did so during the brutal and bloody war between Iraq and Iran, which broke out just two years after Petra Bank opened its doors.

On September 22, 1980, Saddam Hussein invaded his neighbor Iran, in large part out of fear that Ayatollah Ruhollah Khomeini's 1979 Islamic Revolution would galvanize the Shia majority in his own country. King Hussein of Jordan immediately backed Saddam, for his own political and security reasons. But war and profit go hand in hand, and Jordan prospered handsomely from the conflict. Throughout the eight-year battle, the kingdom served as Iraq's main supply line for everything from beans and baby formula to bullets, superguns that could supposedly fire payloads into orbit, and the component parts necessary for manufacturing and stockpiling chemical and nuclear weapons. Much of the military hardware entered Jordan through the southern port of Aqaba, from where it was loaded onto trucks and driven overland into neighboring Iraq. In return, Jordan received oil from Iraq at prices far below market value—and Jordanian businessmen profited handsomely from the around-the-clock war economy that took root.

Members of Jordan's establishment, most of whom are Sunnis, also felt a special kinship toward Saddam. They saw him as a fellow Arab taking on the Islamic Shia radicals of Iran. That affinity remained steadfast even as the war dragged on, with estimates of 500,000 to 1 million killed and twice that many injured and maimed; that support held firm even when Saddam employed chemical weapons against Iranian forces in the south and mustard gas and nerve agents on the Kurds of Halabja in the north, killing 5,000, and disfiguring and debilitating 10,000 more.

But Chalabi—even as he flattered princes and other Jordanian notables with his charm and guile—risked alienating them with his open disdain for Saddam Hussein. He was famous for boasting of Iran's battlefield successes to anyone who would listen, unfurling maps at his afternoon parties and dinner soirees to show where the Iranians had dealt a blow to Saddam's forces. Once, while he was attending an outdoor luncheon at Osama Sha Sha'a's house, a fellow guest was so offended that he grabbed Chalabi's knife and threw it into the ground between Chalabi's legs, pinning the hem of his *abaya* into the grass. "Aren't you ashamed?" the man yelled at Chalabi.

During this time, Chalabi said he funneled money through Petra Bank to some of the Iraqi Shia opposition groups based in Iran and Kurdistan. His office, moreover, became a way station for international bankers heading to Iraq. He would give them advice on doing business with Iraq. "I would persuade them that they would not collect on their loans," he said, "and would show them examples of where others had lost theirs."

Chalabi's campaign against Saddam reached its peak with his efforts to expose what he calls Saddam's plan to subvert the international banking system to finance his illegal weapons program. Chalabi learned through his position at Petra that Iraq and its suppliers were receiving billions in loans through the Atlanta, Georgia, branch of Italy's largest bank, the Banca Nazionale del Lavoro (BNL). U.S. investigators eventually would trace the loans to the development of Iraq's nuclear, chemical, and biological weapons. But at the time, the Reagan and George H. W. Bush administrations, which tilted toward Iraq over Iran, turned a blind eye to the illicit financing, even though nearly a billion dollars of the credit was guaranteed by a U.S. Department of Agriculture program that was supposed to sell food and other such products to Iraq.

Though Chalabi takes more credit than he deserves for exposing the scandal, he did help journalists at the *Financial Times*, the *Washington Post*, *ABC News*, and elsewhere publicize what became the signature scandal of that war, the so-called BNL affair. He also helped congressional investigators in Washington, D.C., get to the bottom of it. At the invitation of Peter Galbraith, then a senior staff member for the Senate Foreign Relations Committee, Chalabi traveled to Capitol Hill several times a year throughout the late 1980s to meet with U.S. congressional aides to explain how Saddam was misusing the Department of Agriculture's loan program and to provide evidence of specific transactions.

As the war between Iran and Iraq ground to a bloody stalemate, Chalabi's efforts against Saddam Hussein did not go unnoticed by the dictator in Baghdad. It was his banking practices, however, that would draw the most unwelcome attention. Soon he would be toppled from the pinnacle of Jordanian society and thrust into the white light of scandal, his descent into disgrace as steep and swift as his rise to prominence had been. Chalabi's downfall would reveal both the contradictions of his character and the pattern of his life: attaining power, provoking controversy, and then turning adversity into advantage.

FIVE

Ahmad Chalabi's father died on March 7, 1988. Though expected, Abdul Hadi Chalabi's passing was a particularly heavy blow to the family, unleashing an outpouring of grief and anguish among the Chalabis, not only for the loss of their beloved father and husband but also for the way that loss underscored their fate as exiles. Ahmad flew to London, where his father had succumbed, and observed the Islamic ritual of purification, personally washing the face, arms, head, and feet of his father. Then, with quiet deference, the family patriarch's honored remains were loaded onto a plane for Syria and brought to a Shia shrine located on the outskirts of Damascus. There, Chalabi climbed down into the grave and laid his father's body to rest among a gathering of friends and family from all over Europe and the Middle East.

During the wake, Chalabi listened intently as the imam recounted the storied martyrdom of the Prophet Muhammad's grandson Husayn, who was killed and beheaded at the siege of Karbala in AD 680. Husayn led seventy-two men into battle against the much larger Syrian army and held them off for six bloody days before he and his men were cut down and slaughtered. Husayn's courage, born of desperation and an unwavering belief in the rightness of his cause, is legendary among Shiites—and a galvanizing force among the faithful. During the cleric's telling of the story, one of the guests in attendance, Tamara Daghistani's husband, Nasser al-Sadoun, looked over and saw Chalabi nodding his head up and down, transfixed—tears trickling down his cheeks. It was a rare exhibition of emotion by the otherwise self-contained Chalabi. His father, whom he had revered growing up, had lost everything when the 1958 revolution forced him into a thirty-year exile. Now, even in death, the elder Chalabi was unable to return to his homeland. That thought pained Ahmad deeply, and he was as determined as ever to do something about it. But first family history would repeat itself. One year later, everything Chalabi had built in Jordan during the past decade would collapse amid allegations of corruption and criminality. He would be forced to flee the country and become an exile for the second time in his life.

The story of Chalabi's undoing is obscured by the absence of transparency and the abundance of self-serving memories on the parts of both Chalabi and the government of Jordan. Thus, no accounting can ever hope to be complete. But based on interviews with independent parties familiar with Petra Bank's internal records, an understanding of what came to be known as the Petra affair can be pieced together.

The trouble for Chalabi began in the early 1980s, when some of the fiercest fighting of the Iran-Iraq War was under way. Chalabi saw an opportunity to help the Islamic Republic of Iran while also turning a nifty profit. He wanted to extend loans and letters of credit to the cash-starved government in Tehran. But because of Jordan's close relationship to Saddam Hussein, Chalabi was unable to use the Petra Bank. He therefore arranged for another of the family-owned banks, MEBCO Geneva in Switzerland, to do it for him. Over the next several years, MEBCO Geneva extended huge amounts of financing to companies controlled by a Jordanian businessman and accused arms trafficker named Taj Hajjar. His firms, in turn, financed large exports of wheat and, some say, weapons to the Iranian government. By 1989, Chalabi once boasted, Hajjar had transacted $29 million in various business ventures with Iran. But at the same time, Hajjar's companies and the government of Iran together owed MEBCO Geneva more than the bank's entire capital base of some $21 million, putting the bank's shareholders and its depositors at great risk. The loans violated Swiss regulations limiting a bank's exposure to a single borrower—in this case, two borrowers: Hajjar and the Central Bank of Iran. So, on April 27, 1989, MEBCO Geneva's license was revoked, forcing the bank to file for bankruptcy and, in the process, igniting a worldwide run on all the Chalabi family-owned banks. To stave off a total collapse, Chalabi put up about $25 million in cash and collateral—much of it from Petra Bank's coffers. But just as it seemed that he had weathered the storm, Jordan's economy coincidentally suffered a near collapse. The value of the Jordanian dinar plunged, inflation raged, and food riots broke out in the cities. In addition, the country's foreign currency reserves had all but dried up, with Jordan owing $60 million in U.S. currency alone to foreign banks. To salvage its financial system, Jordan's central bank ordered the country's banks to transfer 35 percent of their foreign currency assets to its accounts.

"All the banks of Jordan complied except Chalabi's," says Dr. Muhammed Saeed el-Nabulsi, the head of the central bank at the time. "I called him to come to my office and asked why he hadn't given the central bank 35 percent of the foreign currency assets he listed on his books." Chalabi had reported $200 million, so he should have put $65 million in foreign currency with the central bank. But by now, of course, he was totally tapped out. He couldn't tell Nabulsi why, so he came up with a cover story. "Chalabi told me that his foreign currency assets were all tied up in long-term foreign bank accounts and therefore he couldn't give me anything. Not a penny," Nabulsi says. "I said to him, 'Are you serious? You're trying to tell me that all $200 million is tied up? This is bad banking!'"

During the encounter, Chalabi did little to conceal his disdain for the dowdy and diminutive Nabulsi. He thought, Who was this third-rate civil servant to question the man who revolutionized banking in Jordan? More to the point, what mischief could Nabulsi possibly make for the infinitely more clever and powerful Chalabi? It was a grave miscalculation on Chalabi's part. Nabulsi not only was prone to resentment but also was a bureaucrat with a badge. Right after the meeting, he ordered an emergency audit of Petra's books and discovered there were no major Petra Bank deposits in any of the overseas banks Chalabi had listed. "In fact," Nabulsi told me, "a couple of the banks we checked with said that Petra Bank owed *them* money."

Nabulsi requested an audience with King Hussein of Jordan, the only person in the royal family who outranked Chalabi's close friend Prince Hassan. Nabulsi told His Majesty that Petra Bank's books were a sham and that he wanted to take drastic action. The king assented, giving Nabulsi his full blessing. And so, on August 2, 1989, the banker-bureaucrat whom Chalabi had so contemptuously underestimated dropped the hammer, ordering Petra Bank and its books seized and posting a contingent of armed guards outside the bank's doors, inside the building, and in front of Chalabi's personal office.

In conversations with Nabulsi, Chalabi insisted that there had been no criminal wrongdoing and that whatever financial irregularities might exist were innocent and could be resolved—with no loss to depositors or the central bank. But by now Nabulsi—who more than ten years earlier had sought to deny the Chalabi family a bank license—neither trusted Chalabi nor thought he could rein him in. He ordered a thorough, top-to-bottom audit of Petra's operations. He also issued a decree mandating that the bank merge with a smaller one and be placed under government control. Travel bans were issued against a dozen of Petra Bank's executives, including Chalabi, and Jordan's internal security ministry, the General Intelligence Directorate (GID), put Chalabi under 24/7 surveillance.

Remarkably, Chalabi still thought everything would work out. "I didn't really bother very much about it," he told me. "It was possible to get people involved and form alliances." But the environment for Chalabi grew more and more hostile. Many of the well-wishers who came to look in on him were actually keeping tabs for the GID. There was talk of an impending arrest. And Chalabi's ace in the hole, Prince Hassan—the recipient of some $28 million in Petra Bank loans—sent him a message via a third party. "My heart is with you," the message said. "But don't involve me." For Chalabi, it was time to slip away.

His wife, Leila, and their four children were in London on summer holiday. He sent word to start looking for schools there for the children. He also arranged to get some cash to his wife. Then he began to make plans for his own departure. Initially, he sought to procure a false passport from a currency smuggler he did business with occasionally. "He would give me the passport of his brother with my picture on it," Chalabi explained to me. "I put this plan into process in July." But Tamara Daghistani persuaded him that with around-the-clock surveillance he would surely get arrested once he stepped foot in the airport. She considered staging a wedding party in Syria and smuggling Chalabi across the border disguised as a woman in a head-to-toe *abaya*, much as Iraq's prime minister, Nuri al-Said, had been in 1958. But she remembered all too well how that had ended (with al-Said unmasked and gunned down on the street). Finally, she came up with a plan to sneak Chalabi into neighboring Syria in the back of a car. It was about a fifty-five-mile drive to the border. The challenge was to lose the GID surveillance in Amman and somehow get Chalabi past Jordan's customs and border police. No easy feat. But she and Chalabi agreed that it offered the best chance for a getaway.

The night of his escape, Chalabi kept to his usual routine, hosting a get-together with about fifty guests. At one point, Daghistani and Chalabi slipped away from the party. "He walked around the house and pointed to three or four Persian rugs to smuggle out and sell," Daghistani recalled. "They were probably worth about ten thousand Jordanian dinars each [$30,000 each in U.S. currency]. When there was a lull in the activity at Ahmad's house, we rolled up the carpets and snuck them out the kitchen door and put them in my car. The kitchen was in the back of the house. The GID guys who had Ahmad under surveillance were parked in front of the house, so they couldn't see what we were doing." Daghistani then drove off to her home, where she unloaded the carpets and waited.

Shortly after two in the morning, just as the last of his guests were leaving, Chalabi walked through the back door of his house, climbed into his nephew's car, and lay down on the floor in the backseat area. His nephew then pulled out and drove right past the unsuspecting GID officers. Once at Daghistani's, Chalabi got into a Saab sedan newly registered in Daghistani's maiden name. "I had him lie down again on the floor in the backseat area of the car," Daghistani said, "and then I draped a long black cloak over him so he couldn't be seen." Accompanying them was a third accomplice, whom Daghistani had enlisted to the cause—a nephew of King Hussein. Thus, the prince, the banker, and the banker's friend set off for Syria. Chalabi was calm in the midst of crisis. Daghistani didn't realize just how calm until they were well into the seventy-five-minute drive. "Ahmad remained on the floor in the backseat area the whole time," she recalled. "It was as tense as hell because this man's life was in my hands. Suddenly, I hear this funny noise, and it's Ahmad snoring. He fell asleep!"

When they finally arrived at the border, she says the plan worked exactly as they had calculated: when the prince pulled up, with his personal military escort traveling in a trail car, Daghistani was waved through with no inspection at all of her car. She said the king's nephew hand-carried her passport to the customs official to be stamped, while she and Chalabi, who remained hidden under her black cloak, remained in the car. From there, she drove Chalabi into Syria, with the prince staying behind.

By time the GID figured out what happened, Chalabi was long gone—and Daghistani was back in Jordan. She was immediately arrested and held in custody for twenty-eight days for aiding and abetting Chalabi's flight from the country. During her incarceration, she told her GID interrogators essentially the same story she told me—with one exception, according to a former senior Jordanian government official who oversaw the questioning of Daghistani in 1989 and who reviewed the transcripts of her statement: by the time they had reached the border, Chalabi was hiding in the trunk of the prince's car. "At both the customs security station and the police checkpoint," the official told me, "the guards saw the prince's military escort and immediately knew he was a VIP. They presumed everything was approved out of the palace beforehand, so they waved him through."

Daghistani, meanwhile, got her passport stamped like anyone else would. Then, according to this account, the young prince stopped the car before the Syrian checkpoint and Chalabi jumped out of the trunk and sidled into the Saab next to Daghistani. The prince and his military escort turned around and drove back to Jordan while Chalabi and Daghistani went on to Syria. Either way, in the trunk of a car or lying on the floor of the backseat area, Chalabi made it out of the country—a fugitive, but a free man.

News of his disappearance broke on August 11, 1989. Renda Habib, the Barbara Walters of the Middle East, reported from Amman that the GID had lost sight of Chalabi and that "the chairman of Petra Bank is nowhere to be found and he seems to have sneaked out of the country." Her broadcast on Radio Monte Carlo was heard throughout the region. At three the next morning, she was awakened from a sound sleep when her phone rang. An operator on the other end of the line said she was calling from the Sham Palace Hotel in Damascus and was connecting Ahmad Chalabi. "He told me, 'I want you to know I did not flee Jordan,'" Habib recalled. He lied to her, saying that he had left legally from the airport and that the Jordanian authorities had never asked him not to leave the country. After that call, Chalabi continued to phone Habib at least two or three times a week. "He told me that he helped finance projects for Crown Prince Hassan and that he helped two other princes buy their homes. Chalabi definitely gave a lot of money to members of the royal family. He gave the open Visa credit card to the prime minister. He was lashing out, and said all of those things on the phone full well knowing that the phones in Jordan are tapped." Then Chalabi came right out with it, throwing down the gauntlet. "If they want to have a trial, fine!" he screamed to Habib. "I will talk!"

Chalabi then published his account of the Petra Bank affair. "I have decided to provide Arab readers with this booklet," he announced in the introduction. Chalabi maintained that he had done no wrong, and he accused Nabulsi, the governor of Jordan's central bank, of trumping up the case against him. Nabulsi "was utterly driven by grudge," Chalabi wrote. "He was driven by his complexes and hatred of me." In the booklet, Chalabi accused Nabulsi of pressuring investigators to "conceal information, forge records and act selectively" against him.

About five weeks after he fled Jordan, Chalabi surfaced in London with another explanation for his dead-of-night departure. He laid it out in an interview with his friend Jim Hoagland, the influential *Washington Post* columnist whom he had met years earlier in Beirut. Chalabi told Hoagland that the Petra affair, as he came to call it, was actually a political frame-up orchestrated by his archnemesis, Saddam Hussein. Leaflets had begun to appear in Amman accusing Chalabi of supporting Iran against Iraq. He also said Saddam was demanding that he be turned over to Iraqi security, which would then torture and kill him. The Jordanians were willing to go along, Chalabi explained, because they needed the cheap oil and other economic assistance Saddam was supplying.

The essence of Chalabi's account appeared in the *Washington Post* in a September 14, 1989, column entitled "Hussein Needs All His Survivor Skills Now." To this day, it's the story Chalabi swears by. "The banking stuff could have been contained," he said to me recently. "But the Saddam thing was uncontrollable. [Jordan's] King Hussein was so dependent on Iraq at that time, he couldn't say no to Saddam." Chalabi said he never steered any loans to Tehran and that any capital extended to Taj Hajjar was merely a routine transaction between a bank and a businessman. His only "transgression," he said, was to try to block credit from international banks to Baghdad. And that, he explained, is why Saddam wanted him dead.

But in Jordan, officials scoffed at Chalabi's claim of political intrigue. "The only word to describe this accusation is 'bullshit,'" said a former senior government official who worked closely with King Hussein. "If Chalabi was someone we wanted to eliminate politically, even permanently, I'm sorry to say, why fabricate a bank scandal? How difficult would it have been to throw him in the trunk of a car and send him to Saddam? Or imagine how easy it would've been to whisper to the interior minister, 'He's a foreigner,' which he is, and deport him?"

In addition, the official points out, shutting down Petra proved costly for the government of Jordan, which assumed the bank's debts of approximately half a billion dollars. That's to say nothing of the $60 million King

Hussein personally kicked in to cover the uncollateralized loans Petra Bank had extended to members of the royal family. "Look, Petra Bank was the country's second-largest bank," the former official noted. "Its collapse nearly crippled the economy. It doesn't stand to reason that King Hussein would go to such lengths if all we wanted to do was railroad Chalabi or run him out of town because Saddam asked us to. And then, to top it all off, we let him escape right under our noses. It makes no sense."

Nor does it explain the evidence of fraud and embezzlement that Nabulsi says his investigators turned up, including the doctoring of Petra's books to make them appear balanced and the $250 million in bad loans Chalabi gave himself, his friends, and his family-owned companies—among them, a $2 million loan to a Swiss software company run by Chalabi.

Chalabi dismissed the evidence as fabricated. There is no doubt, however, that Chalabi had indeed landed on Saddam's radar. Even Nabulsi says that Iraq's ambassador to Jordan complained to him about Chalabi. At the height of the Iran-Iraq War, personal emissaries of Saddam Hussein complained at least twice about Chalabi's support of Iran to a former member of King Hussein's staff. That's a significant event, the former aide said. "But Saddam wanted only to contain or control Chalabi, not kill him," he clarified.

In a final, surprising twist to the tale, after the war ended Petra Bank took a new tack toward Saddam in 1988 and 1989, going into business with his regime, affirming the old Arab proverb "Money has no religion"—and offering up, perhaps, a window into Chalabi as the consummate opportunist. The whole Petra mess stemmed from Chalabi's principled opposition to Saddam, whom he still hated. But with the war over, there was money to be made. Thus, Chalabi—who once warned other businessmen about the perils of investing in Iraq—poured money hand over fist into the banks and other financial institutions belonging to the devil incarnate. Chalabi authorized letters of credit totaling millions to Jordanian businessmen trading with Baghdad. He set in motion at least $20 million in loan guarantees from the Export-Import Bank of the United States. He also dispatched a loan and marketing officer to Baghdad to meet with top banking officials there about establishing a relationship with Petra. All systems were go five months later when the Petra Bank scandal erupted and Chalabi went on the lam. All of which raises the question: How afraid of Saddam could Chalabi truly have been if he was nurturing a multimillion-dollar relationship with him?

In Jordan the interpretation of Chalabi's sudden flight from Amman was, and remains, an admission of criminal wrongdoing: Chalabi was guilty as charged, pure and simple. Chalabi's response, however, was "It's better to leave that impression and fight another day than to be dead." He has said that on the night of his escape as he lay crumpled on the floor of Daghistani's car like a common thief, he thought of the flight of Muhammad, the Hijra. In AD 622, the Prophet and his followers escaped persecution in Mecca by fleeing to Medina. "The Prophet did it, so there's no shame in Hijra."

On April 9, 1992, a military tribunal in Jordan convicted Chalabi in absentia of thirty-one counts of fraud, forgery, embezzlement, theft, and related charges. He was sentenced to twenty-two years in prison. The conviction was a stigma Chalabi would never shake or overcome. And yet it was the ignominy of the Petra affair that set in motion his long-yearned-for return to Baghdad. This second exile, from Amman, led Chalabi into a series of bold and escalating gambits that propelled him onto the world stage, from London and Damascus to Tehran and, ultimately, Washington, D.C.

SIX

Ahmad and the rest of the Chalabi clan took a major hit from the Petra affair—both personally and financially. According to one family estimate, when their cash investments in Petra Bank, in the Safeway in Amman, and elsewhere were all added up, the family lost about $50 million. Add to that the loss of the bank licenses in Geneva, Amman, and eventually Beirut. Having them revoked—rather than sold—cost the family another estimated $250 million. On the personal side, the toll was also severe. It struck the Chalabis in the place that Middle Eastern men value most, their honor. Arab society is very much an honor society, and one's name—the family name—is treasured like an ancient artifact. It is a fragile and priceless link to one's ancestry, and a solemn duty is owed to preserving it. It goes to the core of a man's identity and his self-esteem, no matter who he is or how modest his lot in life. One crack and it is shattered.

The more exalted the stature, the greater the fall, and so for a man of Chalabi's pride and pedigree the consequences were severe. His résumé—scion of one of old Iraq's most prominent families, holder of degrees from MIT and the University of Chicago—was now eclipsed by a rap sheet that included such scarlet-letter entries as "embezzlement," "fraud," and "fugitive." It was beyond humiliating; it was scarring. And since the taint encompassed the *family's* business—with financial institutions founded in his father's good name and spread out over three continents, from Europe to America and the Middle East—the blow could not have been more punishing or all-pervasive.

It was, in the words of a nephew, Mohammad Chalabi, worse than death itself. It was a "living death," a sense of shame so profound that, for anyone else, it would have been unbearable. It was exactly that for Mohammad's father, Rushdi, Ahmad's oldest brother. Rushdi maintained a largely peripheral and ceremonial position in one of the family's financial companies and therefore bore little or no culpability for any of the financial legerdemain beyond perhaps failing to rein in his younger brother. But as the eldest son and inheritor of the family mantle after the passing of their father, Rushdi was deeply affected by the disgrace. The fact that many of the depositors were fellow Iraqi exiles who had entrusted their life's savings to the Chalabis made the shame that much more painful for Rushdi.

"He maintained his dignity throughout," Mohammad said of his father. "But he became silent and withdrawn. He lost his energy. He cut himself off socially." The burden of infamy drove him "into a depression that I think ultimately caused his death," Mohammad added. The other brothers—Talal, Hassan, Hazem—all took it nearly as hard as Rushdi did, chastened by the blot on their reputations and the family name.

There's no doubt in Mohammad's mind that his uncle Ahmad also bore the weight of his ignominy. But Ahmad showed no outward signs of it—no sense that he was either humbled or even shaken by the crisis. To the contrary, he was roused to action. For Chalabi, the response to this crisis was not to slink in the shadows, let alone assume responsibility for it. It was to double down and change the story line of his life—to obscure and redeem opprobrium through triumph—with bolder and grander feats. Until the Petra affair, the main driving force in his life had been the feeling that his family had been robbed of its destiny and that his role was to regain what the family had lost. Now that impetus was inflamed by the need to cleanse the stain of the Petra affair. So while his brothers spiraled into melancholy, Chalabi sought opportunity in the chaos, ramping up for action in a most deliberate and analytical fashion. "Whenever I face mortal danger," Chalabi explained to me, "I immediately become calm and I think clearly. I become not agitated or hostile, but focused and unemotional, very much logical. It's as if I'm outside of myself observing the crisis. So when this crisis happened in Jordan, I felt that way."

He quickly devised a course of action, focusing on the avenues still available to him. They were obviously greatly circumscribed now that he was a disgraced banker. But the family still retained a number of businesses into which he could throw himself. There was, for example, Card Tech, a burgeoning and lucrative credit card systems provider located in the Knights-bridge section of London. A stellar business success might rehabilitate his lost luster, and that of the family's. But the prospect of running a company hardly stirred the passions of his soul, nor did it seem to fit the need for redemption. What he sought, what was required to clear the slate and deal with the self-reproach gnawing away at his psyche, lay elsewhere. It lay in Iraq, in overthrowing Saddam Hussein.

Chalabi understood instinctively that just as a man is bound to his past, he is also defined by his enemies. If he could pit himself against the especially ruthless Saddam Hussein, he could redefine his reputation from that of a fugitive to a freedom fighter. But he was motivated by other factors as well—in particular, a patrician sense of duty toward his fellow Iraqi Shiites. They had long been the downtrodden and disenfranchised of Iraq, but under Saddam Hussein they had become the victims of relentless deprivation and violent, systematic terror. Chalabi felt a genuine calling to ease their suffering. If he could rid them of the Ba'athist tyranny, he could assuage both the onus of his dishonor and the obligation he felt to help his own people. Undertaking the removal of Saddam Hussein was where everything came together for Chalabi, the perfect confluence of personality and patriotism, narcissism and nationalism, retribution and rehabilitation.

What Chalabi was contemplating, however, went far beyond simply deposing Saddam Hussein. That was only part of the scheme coalescing in his brain. What he envisioned was replacing Sunni minority rule—Saddam was a Sunni—with Shia majority rule. It was a truly radical proposition, this notion of a Shia-run Arab country. Ever since the rise of the Ottoman Empire in the thirteenth century, Sunnis have dominated the lands of Arabia—even where Shiites enjoy a large majority, as they do in Iraq. Chalabi would seek to overturn nearly a thousand years of history. In this he would be tilting against the prevailing interests of most of the Arab and Islamic world, as well as those of the great powers—the United States, England, even the Soviet Union. Their foreign policies were rooted in perpetuating the "Arab way" of the authoritarian, Sunni-dominated state.

To anyone else, the prospects of success would have seemed so improbable that the idea would have amounted to a fleeting fantasy. But not to Chalabi. It was partly the gambler in him; he liked the thrill of the high-stakes gambit. But there was also the sense that everything he had done in his life led to this point. He even came to view the Petra affair in this light. The collapse of the bank was a blessing; it freed him from the tiresome responsibilities of operating a billion-dollar business. If in Jordan he could afford to devote only a fraction of his time to unseating Saddam Hussein, now he could commit himself to it fully. He was unshackled, completely free to engage the crusade that had long captured his imagination. It was now his avowed mission in life, and his path to salvation. And if he could pull it off—this Shia awakening that his father had yearned for and that men like the great imam Musa al-Sadr had devoted their lives to achieving—he would not only free his people but also transform himself from a man *with* a history to a man *of* history. Chalabi would never put it so bluntly, but he clearly understood, and relished, the consequences of his ambition.

What's amazing is how quickly he arrived at his decision. "Immediately!" he yelled when asked. Actually, it took about three months after his escape from Jordan to chart a course of action. During that time, he settled his wife and children in Mayfair, a fashionable and exclusive residential district in central London. He also traveled to the United States, visiting his old stomping grounds in Boston and Chicago—all the while studying from every angle the endeavor he was contemplating and eventually coming to peace with it. "I was gonna do it. Finish it," he remembered. "I knew what I had to do."

When he returned to London at age forty-five, he did not fear failure. At the very least, there would be redemption in the act of trying. But he also felt good about his prospects for success. "I had a chance," he said. "I was probably the most successful Iraqi at that time outside of Iraq in running a business and in having influence in other places. And I was thought of as an important player in all this region at that time. As for those who would condemn me for Petra Bank, I was very much uninterested in their good opinion. The various commentators and critics who would write damning things about me in the papers made no difference to me. I was liberated, and I moved forward."

His next step was to analyze and understand Saddam Hussein. What resulted was a set of basic premises that would guide Chalabi's actions from that point forward. One was that Saddam's power rested on three pillars: terror, money, and the support of foreign governments. He concluded there wasn't much he could do about the first, terror, since Saddam was already well on his way to applying the final touches to his notorious "republic of fear"—the systematic use of ruthless repression and relentless organization to cement the Ba'ath Party's authority and to transform Iraq into a personality cult around Saddam. But Chalabi felt he could do something about the latter two, so he set out to undermine Saddam's access to international financing and to chip away at the support he was receiving from other governments, particularly from the United States.

America was the key. It was not only the source of billions of dollars in economic aid to the Ba'ath regime but also Saddam's trump card. If there was any doubt about that, one need only look at U.S. policy toward Iraq during its eight-year war against Iran. Washington had no illusions about what a brutal and repressive dictator Saddam was; however, as Chalabi understood, Iraq served as a bulwark against the Islamic Republic of Iran and the spread of its anti-American zealotry throughout the oil-rich Persian Gulf. The memories of the Iranian hostage crisis, together with Iran's support for Hezbollah, the militant Shia Muslim group based in Lebanon, only reinforced the inclination to keep the mullahs penned in. So when Saddam ordered his unprovoked, surprise invasion of neighboring Iran in 1980, and his forces seized large chunks of territory deep inside the country, the Reagan administration took a basically hands-off approach to the conflict. And when in 1982 Iraq's assault stalled and Khomeini's forces went on the offensive, recapturing lost territory and using young Iranian volunteers seeking martyrdom in human-wave attacks to push inside Iraq itself, it set off alarm bells at the State Department and the White House. If Iraq were to collapse, U.S. allies in the Gulf—Saudi Arabia and Kuwait, both rich in oil reserves—would be threatened by pro-Iranian Shia extremists. It would be an unmitigated disaster for U.S. strategic interests. So Reagan dispatched Donald Rumsfeld, his special envoy to the Middle East, to Baghdad for a meeting with Saddam Hussein.

What followed was a limited but decidedly pro-Iraqi tilt in U.S. policy that included economic aid and the sharing of crucial battlefield intelligence. In coming to Saddam's aid, Reagan, the ultimate cold warrior, was willing to overlook Iraq's alliance with the Soviet Union, which included a friendship treaty between Baghdad and Moscow. The Reagan administration was also willing to tolerate Saddam's support for various Arab and Palestinian militants who engaged in anti-Israel terrorism and sought to torpedo the peace process. The White House even stood by in 1988 as Saddam unleashed massive chemical-weapons attacks against his own Kurdish citizens in the northern Iraqi town of Halabja, attacks that included the use of the nerve agents tabun, sarin, and VX and that resulted in the deaths of nearly five thousand civilians, including women and children. That was how far the U.S. was willing to go to deny Iran a victory over Iraq. And therein lay the scale of Chalabi's challenge. How could he ever persuade the United States to pull the rug out from under Saddam's regime when doing so would threaten the United States' own strategic interests in the region?

Chalabi's other main premise was that since neither Iran nor the organized Iraqi opposition was able to defeat Saddam during the war, they would never be able to do so now that a cease-fire was in effect. The Iraqi opposition was a highly disorganized and fractious amalgam of Shiites, Kurds, Arab nationalists, Ba'athists allied with Syria, socialists, and communists. They had spent the war allied with Iran, armed and financed by the mullahs in what was one of the most deadly and savage conflicts since World War I. Tehran had expended more than half a billion dollars waging the war and lost upward of a million lives—civilian and military. And all to no avail, as the conflict ended in August 1988 in what amounted to a stalemate. There needed to be a third way, and again Chalabi returned to the idea of America. It was the only country in the world with the military and political presence to tip the balance against Saddam. So Chalabi once again concluded that he had to enlist U.S. support in the overthrow of Saddam. But again, given American interests, how?

There was another daunting challenge: Iran and its interests. Tehran would insist on having sway over any opposition group attempting to take power in Iraq. During the war, Tehran had organized the waves of Iraqi refugees who streamed out of the country into an umbrella group, the Supreme Council for the Islamic Revolution in Iraq (SCIRI), and a military wing, the Badr Brigade. Iran would want a successor government to be too weak to pose the kind of military threat that Saddam's did. Ideally, the new regime in Baghdad would fall into Tehran's orbit of influence, supporting the mullahs' aspiration to become the region's preeminent power.

Thus, as Chalabi summed up the challenges before him, he reached two fundamental conclusions. First, the road to Baghdad went through Washington. That was an astonishingly original stroke of insight on his part. Before Chalabi, the organized opposition mostly lived and operated in Damascus and Tehran and, to a lesser degree, in London. They interacted only with one another and the intelligence agencies of their host countries, rarely swimming outside those waters. Their contact with the United States was, for all intents and purposes, nonexistent. The reverse was also true: Washington—the State Department and the CIA—shunned the Iraqi resistance as a matter of policy, deeming them irrelevant proxies of Tehran. It took Ahmad Chalabi—the worldly, U.S.-educated son of privilege with a bank fraud conviction—to change all of that.

Second, Iran's concerns and aspirations could not be ignored. "After the Iran-Iraq War," Chalabi said, "it was clear to me that the Iranians held strong cards in Iraq and while they couldn't overthrow Saddam, they could thwart a U.S. effort to oust him. So I thought the only way to move forward was to get the U.S. to help us overthrow Saddam with the Iranians agreeing not to oppose this effort." That, in a nutshell, became Chalabi's grand stratagem, one that would guide him for the next fifteen years: to simultaneously gain the support of these two implacable enemies. Step one was to get Washington on board; then he'd deal with the mullahs. It was both a straightforward yet daunting formulation, elegant in its simplicity but implausible in its chances of success. Chalabi, however, brimmed with enthusiasm, confident in his ability to shape international policy according to his designs.

In Washington, he turned his brilliant mind to the issue of changing America's definition of its national interests in the region. He approached the problem like the mathematician he is, seeking out patterns, formulating conjectures, and arriving at judgments based on rigorous deductions and analyses. And what he boiled it all down to was the one simple, American axiom made famous by Speaker of the House Thomas "Tip" O'Neill from Boston: In the United States all politics is local. Translated for Chalabi's purposes, this meant that, to succeed, he would have to make Iraq a domestic political issue. He would have to make Saddam Hussein a problem and a concern for the American people and their representatives and senators in Washington. He had witnessed the role the nation's press and its intellectual elite played in turning public opinion against the Vietnam War. Therefore, Chalabi set his sights on harnessing those two forces, the news media and the American intelligentsia, in the service of his agenda. With his Rolodex of contacts already well stocked with the names of American reporters, he had a leg up on that score.

Chalabi also took for a model the success of the American Israeli Public Affairs Committee (AIPAC), the powerful Jewish-American lobby group that advocates pro-Israel policies to both the Congress and the White House. It is the single most effective advocacy group in Washington influencing U.S. policy toward Israel. AIPAC is renowned for its bipartisan courtship of the executive and legislative branches of the U.S. government. Chalabi decided he would similarly build up his contacts on both sides of the aisle in official Washington.

Chalabi recognized that he was looking at a long-term horizon and that there were many forces beyond his control. The key would be to capitalize on opportunities when they presented themselves, to float on the high seas of history and, if possible, navigate them to his advantage. As it turned out, he didn't have to wait long. On August 2, 1990, one year after the collapse of Petra Bank, he got just the break he needed when Saddam Hussein invaded Kuwait. It took Iraq's armed forces less than two days to secure the capital, and it took just a few days longer for Saddam to announce that Kuwait no longer existed. It had been annexed and was now the nineteenth province of Iraq.

The strategic implications for the United States were enormous. Not only had a close ally fallen victim to Saddam's naked aggression, but Saddam's elite Republican Guard was now sitting within easy striking distance of Saudi Arabia, America's most crucial Arab ally of all. If Saddam were to move against Riyadh and lay claim to its oil fields, then, along with those of Iraq and Kuwait, he would be in control of the vast majority of the world's oil reserves. That prospect was so unnerving to American president George H. W. Bush and his advisers that Saddam Hussein catapulted to the top of their list of regional threats, alongside Iran. In speeches and interviews, Bush began to refer to America's erstwhile ally as the latter-day incarnation of Adolf Hitler. In short, the invasion of Kuwait broke the bond between Iraq and the United States—and provided Chalabi with exactly the opening he needed. History had intervened on behalf of his ambition.

Chalabi still had his work cut out for him. As U.S. and other forces were dispatched to the region to deter further aggression against Saudi Arabia—in an action called Desert Shield—Chalabi and his fellow Iraqi exiles convened meetings in the late summer and fall of 1990 in London, Beirut, and elsewhere to arrive at a united strategy for overthrowing the Ba'athist regime. They were all members of a newly created organization called the Joint Action Committee, a group of Iraqi opposition political parties that came together after the invasion of Kuwait at the urging and behest of Syria and Iran. The group's goal was to set up a provisional government that would midwife a Shiite-led government after the U.S. defeat of Saddam.

Chalabi was new to the organized political opposition and eager to get going. But the committee's meetings only served to confirm his view of the resistance as utterly feckless. Many of the delegates showed up late or not at all. They issued nice-sounding pronouncements about human rights and democracy that were nothing more than words on paper. There was much internal jockeying for power. And the leadership skills necessary for an effective movement were sorely lacking. In one instance that was particularly telling for Chalabi, the committee organized a meeting for seventy people in London to coincide with the end of a Muslim fast, but someone failed to guarantee either the meeting location or the food. "The kebab never came, so we ended up eating stuff from a supermarket—cookies and milk," Chalabi recalled in exasperation. "They couldn't organize a dinner party for seventy people. How are they going to organize the overthrow of Saddam?" Worst of all, the opposition members were working in a vacuum, shunned by the United States as a dubious adjunct to Iranian plans and objectives. They couldn't even get in to see a low-level official at the U.S. embassy in London.

So, while Desert Shield was giving way to Desert Storm in January 1991, the Iraqi exiles of the Joint Action Committee sat on the sidelines, arguing among themselves. It was driving Chalabi crazy. He knew that a U.S. victory was inevitable and that it would be swift; therefore, it was time to act, to launch his foray into America just as he had outlined it in his head months earlier. In late February he boarded a plane in London for Washington, with three of his fellow exiles in tow and his sights set firmly on the D.C.–New York City axis, where the majority of the country's writers, politicians, policy makers, and intellectuals resided.

As he flew at thirty-nine thousand feet over the Atlantic Ocean, Operation Desert Storm—the one-hundred-hour U.S.-led war against Saddam Hussein—was just getting under way. In the Situation Room at the White House, Bush and his top advisers were already meeting to thrash out the endgame. One of the main points of dispute was what Saddam had to do to conclude the conflict now that coalition forces had ousted his troops from Kuwait and were rolling toward Baghdad. Some argued for Saddam's total surrender. But the consensus view inside the president's war cabinet was to stop the advance short of Iraq's capital and leave Saddam in power. To do otherwise, they feared, would turn the United States into an occupying force in a hostile land with no exit strategy.

They all had watched that movie before; it was called *Quagmire*, and they wanted no part of it. The outcome they hoped for, and predicted would occur, was the collapse of Saddam's rule from within. They believed that his own generals would turn against him for the stupendous blunder of having invaded Kuwait in the first place—and for having done so on the heels of his previous act of recklessness, invading Iran. Having deposed Saddam, the generals, not the United States, would then be responsible for the governance of Iraq. In addition, such a scenario would achieve what one top Bush adviser, Richard N. Haass, called the Goldilocks outcome: a weakened Iraq that was still strong enough to balance Iran and offset its desire for regional supremacy. The strategic concern about the Islamic Republic of Iran remained paramount.

Bush gave voice to the emerging strategy during a February 15, 1991, address on Voice of America, telling his listeners inside Iraq, "There is another way for the bloodshed to stop: And that is for the Iraqi military and the Iraqi people to take matters into their own hands and force Saddam Hussein, the dictator, to step aside." Two weeks later, on February 28, 1991, the cease-fire ending hostilities went into effect. The very next day, the Iraqi people—though not its generals—took heed of what they believed was Bush's invitation to an insurrection and staged a series of demonstrations that exploded into a full-fledged uprising in all the largest Shia cities across southern Iraq: Basra, Najaf, Karbala, Nasiriyah, and so on. Unrest then broke out in Saddam City (now Sadr City), the Shia slum on the outskirts of the capital. And on March 4 armed rebellion erupted in the north in Iraqi Kurdistan. It looked like Saddam just might fall after all.

The question now for Bush and his advisers was this: What would the United States do? General Colin Powell, chairman of the Joint Chiefs of Staff at the time, was Bush's top military adviser. He strongly opposed getting involved in the uprising, fearing the operational nightmare his soldiers would face in trying to tell friend from foe. Among the president's other advisers there also was a deep concern about the political goals and orientation of Iraq's Shiites. Were they Arabs first, or pro-Iranian? What was Tehran's sway over them? The fact that posters of the Iranian ayatollah Khomeini began to appear on the streets of southern Iraq heightened the

presidential advisers' apprehension and echoed evidence of Iranian meddling that had been detailed by U.S. intelligence. The president didn't send
half a million troops to Iraq just so that he could hand that country over
to Iran. With those considerations in mind, Bush made his decision: the
United States and its coalition partners would not get involved. Saddam,
in turn, wasted no time crushing the revolt. In a matter of days, tens of
thousands of civilians and lightly armed rebels were slaughtered by Iraqi
helicopter gunships and indiscriminate artillery barrages—all while U.S.
soldiers in Iraq stood by and watched.

As the rest of the world reacted in horror, the State Department explained
that it was not the United States' place to interfere in the internal affairs of
Iraq, Bush's earlier remarks notwithstanding. As for Bush, he said in an
interview that it was never his objective to overthrow Saddam Hussein. In
no time the Iraqi rebellion was quashed—and the great and often raucous
debate over U.S. policy toward Iraq was born. It would play out over the
next twelve years, culminating in the 2003 invasion of Iraq. But in early
1991 the issue roiling the body politic was the president's decision not to
protect the Iraqi Shiites and Kurds from the barbarous retributions of Saddam Hussein. The president was being hammered in the press and by his
Democratic opponents on Capitol Hill. For Bush, Operation Desert Storm
had been transformed from a triumph into a growing political liability.

It was into this flow of events that Ahmad Chalabi touched down in
Washington, D.C. His timing could not have been more propitious, or his
bearing more audacious. Over the next several months he bore into the
important centers of power: government, the news media, and the nation's
foreign policy establishment. One friend arranged for him to address a
group of senators and representatives, among them Senator John McCain,
the influential Arizona Republican, and Senator Claiborne Pell, the Democrat from Rhode Island. At the time, Pell chaired the Senate Foreign
Relations Committee. Chalabi's columnist friend Jim Hoagland set up
an editorial board meeting at the *Washington Post*. Chalabi addressed the
editorial-page writers, whose commentaries on national policy were read by
just about every politician, academician, and journalist in the Washington–
New York corridor. In addition, Chalabi gave interviews and wrote commentaries for the *New York Times* and the *Wall Street Journal*, identifying
himself as a businessman living in London who was active in the Iraqi
opposition.

In a column for the *Washington Post* on March 12, 1991, he took a jab at the president personally, writing

President Bush has called on the Iraqi people and army to rid themselves of Saddam; they are attempting to do so now. The ambivalent attitude of the United States toward the uprising against Saddam cannot have a creditable reason. De facto, the United States, covered by the fig leaf of noninterference in Iraqi affairs, is waiting for Saddam to butcher the insurgents in the hope that he can be overthrown later by a suitable officer.

He went on to evoke the memory of the Warsaw ghetto uprising during World War II, equating the struggle of his Arab brothers in Iraq with that of the Jewish resistance fighters in Poland who took up arms against the Nazis in a futile attempt to stop the deportation of Jews to extermination camps:

Forty-five years ago, the Red Army waited at the gates of Warsaw for the SS to smother the uprising in the ghetto before going in to take control. The world has surely learned some lessons since that time. Let us see them applied in Iraq now.

Chalabi was succinct in attacking the Achilles heel of Bush's policy: its focus on securing U.S. interests and the oil fields of the Middle East while ignoring questions of morality and principle. Bush's strategy may have been effective, but it was difficult to swallow as images of Saddam's ruthless repression appeared in the nation's newspapers and television news reports. Chalabi was by no means the only critic to pound at this fault line, but he was especially resonant in that he was an Iraqi, and a particularly articulate one at that.

In another editorial, for the *Wall Street Journal*, Chalabi argued that Iraq was "ripe for democracy," with a political opposition committed to the creation of a parliamentary, constitutional government. "If little is known about the political opposition to Saddam Hussein," Chalabi wrote, "that is in part because the West has long ignored it," preferring the political stability of a dictatorship.

That was Chalabi's first salvo fired at the administration's policy of barring all U.S. government contact with the Iraqi opposition. The next one came in a meeting with Representative Stephen J. Solarz of New York, a respected and influential member of Congress in matters of foreign policy. Solarz had been the Republican president's strongest Democratic ally in Congress on the war, but now he was exhorting Bush to seek a United Nations resolution calling for the resignation of Saddam Hussein and authorizing the use of force to back up the demand. "It is morally and politically unacceptable to stand by and do nothing while Saddam brutally crushes a revolt we helped inspire," Solarz told reporters. "We need to act in ways that will bring the killing to an end. There is no way to do this while Saddam is in power."

Chalabi contends that he first met the congressman years earlier in Jordan when Chalabi was still a banker there and Solarz was passing through Amman on a congressional junket en route to Israel. Solarz has no recollection of the encounter; if they met, Chalabi did not leave an impression. That was not the case, however, in the spring of 1991. Solarz was most impressed this time around. "He struck me not simply as smart, but as brilliant," Solarz recalled. The more he got to know the Iraqi, the more Solarz liked him, eventually coming to rely on Chalabi for much of his understanding of Iraq.

In their encounters, the two men mostly discussed their mutual desire to rid Iraq of Saddam. But Chalabi also spoke to another issue that was dear to the congressman's heart: Israel. Like much of his constituency, Solarz is Jewish. "The impression Ahmad left me with was that in a post-Saddam Iraq, certainly if he were in a position of leadership, Iraq would be friendly to Israel." Such was his regard for the Iraqi that Solarz invited Chalabi to celebrate a Passover seder at his house. "The celebration includes dipping your pinky in wine ten times for each of the plagues visited upon the pharaohs of Egypt," Solarz explained. The first plague was turning the Nile River into blood, the second was a horde of frogs that overran Egypt, and the third was a mass of gnats that enshrouded Egypt. As Chalabi and his hosts recounted each of the plagues, Solarz said, they dipped their pinkies into the wine. "After the tenth plague, we added an eleventh plague," Solarz told me as he dunked his finger into an imaginary cup of wine. "Saddam!" Solarz agreed to open some doors for his new friend.

While he waited for the Solarz connection to bear fruit, Chalabi flew to New York City to participate in a panel discussion on Iraq. The symposium was being held at the Council on Foreign Relations, the nonpartisan foreign policy think tank that had been on Chalabi's "hit list" of stops because of its

stature and influence. It was the heart of the American foreign policy establishment, with "an arsenal of talent," to paraphrase Arthur M. Schlesinger
Jr., that has long furnished a steady supply of experts to Republican and
Democratic administrations. It has counted among its members more than
a dozen secretaries of state, former national security officers, politicians,
bankers, lawyers, professors, CIA officials, and senior members of the
news media. Seven American presidents have addressed the council, two
while still in office.

Landing a speaking engagement before this most august of bodies was a
big opportunity for Chalabi. He got right to the point: Bush had miscalcu-
lated. Saddam had survived his darkest moment, the intifada. He would not
fall, there would be no coup, and as long as Saddam remained in power he
would continue to pose a serious threat to vital U.S. interests in the region.
Yet, Chalabi asserted, because Saddam was so unpopular with his own people, he could still be toppled. All that was needed was another push, one that
would never come from his generals, who, he pointed out, were complicit in
Saddam's terror and torture. Then Chalabi called on those assembled at the
council, and on the U.S. government, to support a democratic Iraqi political
movement that would provide that push.

Chalabi was just one of many speakers that day, but it was his appearance that caught the attention of Bernard Lewis, the white-haired, British-
American professor emeritus of Islamic and Near Eastern studies at
Princeton University. Lewis, a widely read expert on the Middle East, was
regarded as one of the West's foremost scholars on that region. In 1990 the
National Endowment for the Humanities selected him for the Jefferson Lec-
ture, the U.S. government's highest honor for achievement in the humanities. But Lewis's influence extended far beyond the walls of academia and
into the world of politics and current affairs. Diplomats, policy makers, and
members of the news media frequently sought his advice and gave it great
weight. In 1991, there was no more influential historian of Islam and the
Middle East than Lewis.

His encounter with Chalabi occurred just a few months after he had
published an essay in the *Atlantic* entitled "The Roots of Muslim Rage."
In it, Lewis argued that the Muslim world was on a collision course with
Christendom. It was this article (and not a later one by Samuel Huntington)
that first introduced the phrase "clash of civilizations," and it expanded
on his long-held view of the Arab world as a civilization in retreat from

modernity, a retreat that was inspiring a strain of hatred and violence toward the West, especially the United States. "This is no less than a clash of civilizations—the perhaps irrational but surely historic reaction of an ancient rival against our Judeo-Christian heritage, our secular present, and the worldwide expansion of both," Lewis wrote in the September 1990 article. Unless something was done to catalyze its entry into the modern world, he wrote, the Muslim world's revulsion against America and its twin progeny of modernism and secularism would foster what Lewis called "a new era of religious wars." It was a striking forecast, coming eleven years before the attacks of September 11, 2001.

Such was Lewis's mind-set as he attended the conference that day. And as he listened to the articulate and urbane Ahmad Chalabi, it was as though he had stumbled upon the very embodiment of modernity he felt the Muslim world lacked. The notion of democracy was anathema to the U.S. allies in the region, Saudi Arabia and Egypt. But it flowed with apparent conviction from the lips of this Western-educated Iraqi. Intrigued, Lewis introduced himself to Chalabi.

"Bernard was very impressed with me," Chalabi recalled with pride. And vice versa. Chalabi was well aware of the historian's academic reputation before meeting him. What he didn't realize was the unique role Lewis played in bridging the chasm between academia and government and the status he enjoyed as the intellectual godfather and éminence grise of the small and insular—but highly placed—group of neoconservatives in Washington. These policy makers revered Lewis and relied on him to guide them through the thicket of Middle East politics and culture. They shared his concerns about the Middle East and his faith in the power of American values to transform the region.

Lewis decided to introduce Chalabi to some of these acolytes. The result was meetings that spring with three leading neoconservatives: Zalmay Khalilzad, Paul Wolfowitz, and Richard Perle.

At the time, both Wolfowitz and Khalilzad were working in the Pentagon—Wolfowitz as the undersecretary of defense for policy and Khalilzad as one of his top deputies. They were in charge of coordinating and reviewing the U.S. military strategy for the 1990–1991 Gulf War. When the Iraqi uprising failed to produce the coup they were expecting, Wolfowitz became sick to his stomach, saying to colleagues, "We made a huge mistake. We had Saddam. We need to restart the war." Khalilzad had long maintained that Iraq, and not the Iranians next door, posed the more immediate threat to U.S. national interests in the region. Richard Perle, who had been the assistant secretary of defense in the Reagan administration, largely saw it the same way and was one of the few Reagan administration officials who opposed the U.S. tilt toward Saddam during the Iran-Iraq War.

When Chalabi left Manhattan and returned to Washington, D.C., that April, he was first introduced to Khalilzad, then Wolfowitz, and finally Perle, working his way up the neoconservatives' chain of eminence. Each of them was taken with the Iraqi. Perle says he found Chalabi to be someone "who shared our values and who was obviously deeply devoted to a campaign to rid Iraq of Saddam Hussein and who was traveling the world looking for support to do that."

As for Chalabi, he immediately recognized his good fortune. These three men not only shared his abhorrence of Saddam Hussein but also had first-rate minds, and Chalabi was certain they would influence U.S. foreign policy for years. Chalabi was most impressed by Perle, of whom he said, "I saw that Richard is a man who has a rare combination of qualities. He has an incisive mind, which goes straight to the heart of an issue. He has an ability to mobilize people and assign them tasks to achieve the purpose to deal with the issue that he has identified. And he also was courageous. And is loyal to a cause that he believes in. And is loyal to his friends. I could tell that quickly." Chalabi realized that Perle could be his ticket back to Baghdad. He also appreciated his utility to Perle. "When he met me," Chalabi said of Perle, "he believed that he saw the way ahead and the people who would do it."

After that meeting, Chalabi returned to London a happy man, satisfied with the inroads he had made. Meanwhile, Saddam had completed his bloody crackdown on the rebellion, prompting ever-mounting criticism of the Bush administration. In April, the president announced that the United States would establish no-fly zones in northern Iraq, where the Kurdish population was concentrated. At about the same time, Bush also signed a top secret presidential finding authorizing a covert action program that was designed to do what some 700,000 U.S. and coalition forces in theater had failed to do—create the conditions in Iraq that would result in the overthrow of Saddam Hussein. In reality, the program was nothing more than political cover for the White House, allowing the president to tell his increasingly numerous and vocal critics on Capitol Hill that he had a plan to deal with the Saddam menace. But for Chalabi this new "fig leaf" of a policy, which called for reaching out to Iraqi opposition figures, proved to be yet another opportunity.

Just a few months earlier, Chalabi couldn't get inside the U.S. embassy compound in London for a cup of coffee. But all that changed on May 11, 1991. Whitley Bruner, a career operations officer and Middle East specialist at the CIA, entered the American embassy in London, picked up a phone, and dialed the home of Ahmad Chalabi in Mayfair. When Chalabi answered, Bruner identified himself only as a U.S. government employee. "You don't know me," Bruner said rather mysteriously, "but I've heard about you, and I wonder if I can come over and talk to you." There was a long pause on the other end of the line. Finally, Chalabi said, "Why don't you come over to my house."

SEVEN

It was a brisk five-minute walk from the U.S. embassy in Grosvenor Square to Ahmad Chalabi's flat in Mayfair. When Whitley Bruner arrived, he was greeted at the front door by Chalabi and escorted through a long, curving hallway to a large sitting room where château-style French windows overlooked the wooded meadows of Green Park, one of London's royal parks. Middle Eastern and European paintings lined the walls. The two men crossed silk Persian rugs and sat down at a small table where a maid served tea. After a brief exchange of pleasantries, the career CIA case officer got to the point: "The United States government—you can imagine which part—has been tasked to set up a broad political opposition front to counter Saddam Hussein."

It was Bruner's job to find the Iraqi exile who had the skills and force of personality to bring together and mobilize that front. Bruner had been looking for nearly a year, combing through Europe and the Middle East in search of the right man.

"I felt like Diogenes with the lantern," Bruner recalled of the search.

In May 1991, when Bruner first heard of Chalabi, the CIA was completely in the dark about the Iraqi opposition. It had been a decade since Bruner had last been to Iraq; that was in 1981, when he wrapped up a two-year stint as the chief of station in Baghdad. And it had been just as long since the United States had unilaterally cut off all contact with the Iraqi opposition, after the Iran-Iraq War broke out in 1980.

"We didn't like Saddam," Bruner said of the Reagan administration, "but we didn't want to see the Iranians on the Jordanian and Saudi borders, either. So we didn't get involved with the Iraqi opposition at all."

Thus, when Saddam's tanks rolled into Kuwait ten years later, on August 2, 1990, the CIA had no inroads or insight into the Iraqi diaspora or any of its leaders. It had to start from scratch. The agency's newly created Iraq Task Force (ITF) quickly threw together the Iraqi Opposition Branch and put Bruner in charge of it, handing him a lantern and shoving him out the door. Bruner reached out to Amman, Cairo, Riyadh, London, and elsewhere, reestablishing contact with the legions of long-eschewed Iraqi exiles. He limited his search to Sunnis, but they were a strikingly unimpressive lot. Some showed up to meetings drunk—at nine o'clock in the morning—or their organizations were penetrated by Saddam's intelligence agency, the Mukhabarat. "The minute we talked to them, it'd be reported right back to Saddam," Bruner recalled.

Eventually, the Iraq Task Force at CIA headquarters in Langley, Virginia, went back to the drawing board, scouring the CIA's computer records for any Iraqi exile—Sunni or Shiite—that anyone in the U.S. intelligence community had ever tripped over or talked to. Ahmad Chalabi's name popped up and went onto a master list of names that Bruner then worked his way through. The list was simply a place to start, with no qualifying information about anyone on it. But once Bruner began to ask around about Chalabi, he realized he was on to a completely different category of person.

"He has a lot of the skills you would want if you're creating a new political organization," Bruner discovered. "He has a near-photographic memory. He's effective at public relations. He's a master backroom operator who's good at getting people to do what he wants and therefore what the U.S. government would want." In short, Bruner said, Chalabi had the ideal blend of Western know-how and Arab sensibility.

He also had charges of massive bank fraud hanging over his head, but that was neither a red flag nor an operational impediment as far as the agency's deputy chief of the Iraqi Opposition Branch, Linda Flohr, was concerned. In fact, she viewed it as a big plus. "It costs a lot of money to set up and operate a political opposition group," she explained to colleagues, "and we don't want people to think it's being funded by, or in any way connected to, the U.S. government. That would be the kiss of death. So Chalabi's reputation of corruption—the image that he has stolen all that money—is a good cover. We want people to believe he's financially independent."

In his conversation with Chalabi, Bruner was pretty straightforward, telling the Iraqi exile that the U.S. government was beginning the process of trying to put together a coherent opposition movement. He explained why the government had not dealt with the Iraqi opposition during the Iran-Iraq War, but said the effort now was well funded and serious. As for Chalabi, he was cordial throughout the meeting but noncommittal. He said he would think about Bruner's invitation to participate, and he proposed they meet again soon. Indeed, they did, a couple of days later. Chalabi took Bruner out for lunch at an Italian restaurant in Mayfair; as Bruner recalls, "he was bubbling with ideas, proposals, and schemes. It was classic Chalabi. The relationship had begun."

Chalabi was now part of a $100 million, highly classified covert action program that had as much to do with the politics of Washington as it did with the geopolitics of the Middle East. Bush authorized it on May 5, 1991, in a formal "finding," which actually was a letter that worked its way from the Oval Office to the National Security Council and, finally, to CIA headquarters. There it landed on the desk of Frank Anderson, a tall, hulking, sandy-haired senior official in the agency's clandestine services. He had just been appointed chief of the Near East Division and, as such, was the man tasked with carrying out the finding. As he read it, he sank deeper and deeper into his chair, thinking to himself, "I don't like it."

The finding was essentially calling for regime change. But as far as Anderson was concerned, that opportunity had come and gone three months earlier, when Bush decided to limit the military's mandate to the liberation of Kuwait. Now the White House was tasking the CIA with the job of pushing Saddam over the edge? Anderson was incredulous. "Give me a fucking break," he would later say. To him, it was all too familiar: cloaking policy failure in the trappings of a hush-hush covert operation. "In Washington," Anderson told me, "when an administration realizes that it can't stay in power if they tell the truth, that they can't make something happen, they come up with this as an option. It fit into the pattern of what I call political masturbation characteristic of most covert actions programs, and that is 'We can't do anything about Saddam, so we're gonna do some covert thing that accomplishes nothing but makes us feel good.'"

It's not that Anderson believed covert operations were useless. From 1987 to 1989, he played an integral role in perhaps the agency's most successful covert operation in history, helping the Afghan Mujahideen drive the Soviets out of their country. As head of the Afghan Task Force, he knew firsthand that a well-executed covert operation could make a difference. But he also knew that it was a lot easier to drive a hated foreign occupier out of a country, as the Afghan Mujahideen had done with the Soviets, than it was to overthrow a sitting government, particularly one as ruthless as Saddam's. To understand that, all anyone had to do was look at the Iraqi Kurds—a pretty tough bunch of guys who had been trying for years to get rid of Saddam. In Anderson's mind, the only way to oust Saddam and his regime of thugs was to take over the country—in other words, with a U.S. military invasion.

Anderson went to his boss, the near-legendary Thomas A. Twetten, a thirty-year veteran of clandestine services who was now the CIA's deputy director for operations, the nation's top spy, and told him he thought the finding was bullshit—doomed to failure—and he wanted no part of it. But Twetten, in his characteristically soft-spoken Iowan manner, simply told Anderson, "If you want to be chief of NE [the Northeast Division], that goes with the job." In other words, providing political cover for the president and his war council was something he'd have to get used to. Twetten's words were both "true and wise," Anderson would later say. So Anderson saluted smartly and agreed to give the president what he wanted, the appearance of trying to overthrow Saddam in order to quell the rising chorus of mostly Democratic critics on Capitol Hill.

And with that illusion of a plan—the original sin that pervaded future U.S. policy toward Iraq—Ahmad Chalabi was on his way, the beneficiary of a $100 million covert action program born of policy failure and Washington's poisonous political culture. It would not be the last time Chalabi would ride that tiger.

He also profited from another Washington phenomenon—the rare instance when a policy that's supposed to wither on the vine actually blossoms into something real. Though Frank Anderson viewed the presidential finding with disdain, the team of agency officers tasked to flesh it out approached the assignment with all seriousness.

Their objective was to create a situation that would undermine Saddam, but only *gradually*, lest their actions trigger forces that might spin out of their control. The March 1991 uprisings had shown how susceptible the country was to fracturing along ethnic and sectarian lines as the Kurds in the north and the Shiites in the south rose up separately against Saddam's Sunni-led government. The revolts also showed how well positioned the Iranians were to impose their hegemony over southern Iraq, where much of the country's oil wealth lay; Iran supported Shia exile parties and an armed opposition group, which helped organize and spur the rebellions there. So the plan was to go slow and easy, sowing the seeds for Saddam's eventual ouster, but in a way that would allow the system in Iraq to remain in place, a system Whitley Bruner characterized as Arab, Sunni-led, and anti-Iranian.

"We had discussions about this," Bruner recalled. "How do you preserve the status quo in which 20 percent of the population [the Sunnis] is ruling 80 percent of the population [the Shiites and Kurds]? But that was the core of the policy—to get rid of the aggressive, unpredictable, and dangerous Saddam Hussein and bring in a kinder, gentler generation of generals."

By May 1991, however, anyone who might have helped the CIA carry out a coup was either dead or elsewhere in the region, not inside Iraq. That meant Frank Anderson's ITF had to build its own network of spies from the ground up, a network that could reach inside Iraq and get close to people who were close to Saddam—a tall order indeed. But the ITF was not without assets. One in particular provided a window into the inner sanctum of Saddam's regime so revealing that the ITF team thought it could be the basis for going forward. The inside look came courtesy of a most unlikely group of informants—the chefs, cleaning ladies, nannies, tea boys, and manservants of Saddam's closest military and political advisers. Many of the domestics were Kurds who for years had been supplying their brethren in the Kurdish intelligence services with information the Kurds were now passing on to their American protectors. One of the informants was the nanny employed by Qusay Hussein, Saddam's second son and his father's heir apparent, says John Maguire, an ITF operations officer who worked closely with the Kurds.

"We had great visibility into the family because of her," Maguire told me. "It wasn't operational. We couldn't task her to do something. But she could keep us abreast of where they were and what they were up to. For example, she gave us a report that Saddam's other son, Uday, had a series of Suburbans completely loaded with loot. He had paintings, gold, guns, ammunition, and giant silver tins—metal suitcases, really—stacked in the back of the vehicles, each tin filled with $1 million in cash. American dollars. We figured he was saving them for a rainy day should the regime fall and he had to go on the run."

What the maid and the other sources described inside Saddam's family, and the upper reaches of his regime, was a lifestyle of florid decadence and debauchery. "This was a group of people who were paranoid and impaired to the point of dysfunction," Maguire recalled. "Prolific drug use. Drugs to go to bed. Drugs to wake up. Heavy drinkers. And everybody's armed. There were incidents that had flared up and spiked and—boom!—three or four people ended up dead. Sometimes Saddam had to referee and smooth things out. Money was paid. But this is a society that believes in blood feuds. They don't forgive and forget."

This was a state of affairs the ITF thought it could exploit. "What we wanted to try and do," Maguire continued, "was pour as much gas on the situation as we could, to stress and weaken the inner circle, hoping to spark incidents, where the professional military corps—the staff officers who were just outside the inner circle—would ultimately make the calculation, 'This is really fucked up. They're gonna do somethin' that's gonna get us all killed. We gotta do something.' And then they decide to make a move."

But Maguire says it was Saddam Hussein himself who, they believed, would provide the ITF with its best chance of success. They figured all they had to do was provoke him and, because of his tendency to overreact when he was feeling threatened, Saddam would do the rest.

"We wanted to try to cast a perception of risk and threat for Saddam internally so that he would begin to kill his own guys," Maguire explained. "Saddam's view was, 'I will capture and execute seven hundred guys to get one guy who's plotting against me,' rather than not hurt the innocent guys and miss the one guy. And we knew that that calculus was something we could use for our advantage. If we could get him to kill his own guys, the likelihood of pushing a military officer toward us would increase."

From the same master list of exiles they had used to find Ahmad Chalabi, Maguire and the rest of the ITF team looked for Iraqis who had a brother, son, cousin, or friend still living in Iraq, people—in the words of Maguire—"who could set things on fire, shoot key officers, steal information that proved the existence of Saddam's nuclear program—anything to stress Saddam and his decision-making matrix."

A secondary source of stress would come from the political opposition front that Chalabi was recruited to help organize. Comprised of Iraq's main constituency groups—Sunnis, Shiites, Kurds, clerics, monarchists, and former military officers—the front would serve as both the main umbrella organization and the public face of an anti-Saddam political movement. It would publish newspapers that would be smuggled into Iraq and create radio stations that would beam their broadcasts in the direction of Baghdad.

The purpose, Maguire told me, was to let Iraqis on the inside know there were Iraqis on the outside who wanted to help them. The group would also be a conduit for information smuggled *out* of the country, information about the regime's atrocities. Eyewitness testimony, photographs, and other evidence would be funneled to the mainstream media in the West, which—the hope was—would then report it as news.

"This was supposed to be a global initiative," Maguire explained, "the strategic manipulation of politics and public opinion—a public perception-forming tool—to put a face on a movement that was against Saddam and that would convince people in the West how heinous Saddam truly was. To say, 'Look what he's doing: gassed Kurds, people hanged, people thrown into the meat grinder, people tortured.'" At the time, in May 1991, the image of Saddam Hussein lording it over a republic of fear had not yet settled in, Maguire noted, so it was necessary "to craft public opinion, primarily in Europe, where the people there would be forced not to look away and to support an anti-Saddam opposition movement and to pressure their governments into supporting sanctions against Iraq."

The hope was that by isolating Saddam internationally, the perception of his invincibility would fracture. "Saddam's primary tool for staying in power was casting that perception of invincibility," Maguire explained. "People were afraid to move against him because he seemed bulletproof. If we could crack that perception, we would put additional stress on him and he would feel like he had to address the crack, which we figured he'd respond to by killing more of his own guys. That would, in turn, convince some of the others either to flee and talk to us or work for us inside—or just shoot the guy."

Maguire says the ITF's plan envisioned a long-term horizon, one that would unfold over several years and in stages: "As you build this thing up, you expand and adjust. As the propaganda gets bigger, you'll get more intelligence. As your intelligence improves, your picture improves. You learn more, and then you can focus your covert action program at weaknesses more effectively. You gotta be patient, methodical, and relentless as you build a covert structure inside Iraq that could lead to an unexpected coup."

So the CIA's plan for ridding Bush of Saddam Hussein was a two-track approach that would employ a political opposition front in the service of a hoped-for coup d'état. Once Saddam was removed from power, the thinking went, the opposition party that Chalabi was asked to help build would then be shut down, along with its attendant propaganda apparatus. Power would flow to a new regime of army generals, one that would still be Sunni, Arab, and anti-Iranian.

The scheme, however, was rooted in several flawed assumptions, the CIA would later realize. One was that the country's Sunni minority would support the removal of Saddam from power. They had seen their own power wobble along with his during the March revolts. They feared that if the dictator were pushed over the edge, they would go right over with him. As Whitley Bruner would later observe, "They didn't like Saddam. But they had nowhere to go. If he fell and the Shiites took over, they'd be committing suicide, and we should've known that."

The other faulty assumption, Maguire now acknowledges, centered on Chalabi, whom the CIA saw as a means to an end who would eventually be shunted aside. "Once we got to where we needed to be for U.S. policy goals," Maguire said, "Chalabi would outlive his usefulness to us. The agency looked at him as a tool, [and] when we no longer needed the tool, we would throw it away. And that was the rub: Chalabi understood that."

In fact, he understood a great deal more than that. Even though the agency never told him about the coup side of its covert action program, Chalabi says he instinctively and immediately surmised where the CIA was headed: replacing Saddam with a new, more amenable generation of generals. "Saddam-lite," he would call it. But Chalabi had a different agenda in mind for the post-Saddam era, and it fundamentally conflicted with the CIA's in that he envisioned a leading role for both himself and Iraq's majority Shiites—and he was hell-bent on achieving nothing less.

That meant Chalabi would not be playing by the CIA's rules. Case officers, for example, are trained to maintain tight control over their agents. The Americans are the shot-callers, and the only interest that counts is the U.S. national interest. But as far as Ahmad Chalabi was concerned, those rules of engagement were exactly backward. He did not view his cause as subordinate to that of the United States, and he certainly didn't consider himself a CIA asset. To the contrary. "I saw *them* as an asset that I could use to promote my program," Chalabi would later say of the CIA. "This is the essential thing. It's like a man on a bicycle going up the hill. A train comes by. You catch the train. It takes you up and then when you want to go a different way, you let go of the train."

Thus, in May 1991, when Chalabi told Whitley Bruner over lunch that he was "in," the CIA was unwittingly taking on a host of troubles—a free agent with his own agenda and the moxie to push it forward.

While the agency spent the next several months sniffing out Chalabi and ramping up its overall covert action program, Chalabi ratcheted up his own plan of action. He did so in large part by systematically building and nurturing a separate network of influential supporters in Washington—both Democrats and Republicans alike. It would be a long-term effort, but he was patient and adept, a rising master at the art of wooing Washington's power elite. As he saw it, the best way to win their hearts was to appeal to their minds with the allure of ideas and the enchantment of inside information.

In the case of Richard Perle, Chalabi played on his hawkish policies toward the old Soviet Union. For example, in August 1991, just two months after the CIA approached Chalabi, the Soviet Union's first democratically elected president, Boris Yeltsin, stood down a coup attempt by those who were opposed to his policy of perestroika. Chalabi saw an opportunity to build on his introduction earlier that year to Perle, who was a leading cold warrior long before he became a leading neoconservative.

At the time of the failed Soviet coup, Chalabi was on vacation in Granada, Spain—the first holiday he can ever remember taking with his wife and four children together. Amid the twelfth-century Gothic cathedrals and Moorish designs of that ancient city, Chalabi managed to find a pay phone to call Perle.

"I was very conscious of Richard's role," Chalabi told me, "in driving the Soviet Union to bankruptcy by upping the ante in the arms race, which I thought was a very clever thing to do. I knew he was the driving force behind that. And I learned that he was also a driving force behind this program that let the Soviets steal American technology which had a time bomb planted in it—computer chips that would deteriorate after a certain period of time. I was very impressed with that. So I called Richard from a pay phone to congratulate him on the effectiveness of his vision and policy. Richard said, 'Nobody is going to remember that except you.'" Perle may have been right about that. But from Chalabi's point of view, that was precisely the point. It's the way thinking men seduce men of ideas, and it helped lure Perle squarely into Chalabi's camp.

Two months later, in October 1991, it was back to wooing members of Congress. Stephen Solarz, the New York Democrat who had celebrated Passover with Chalabi, arranged for his friend and tutor on all things Iraq to come to Capitol Hill to give a closed briefing to his colleagues on the powerful House Permanent Select Committee on Intelligence (HPSCI), the committee charged with overseeing the entire U.S. intelligence community, including the CIA. In those days, HPSCI met in a room next to the attic of the Capitol dome. To get there, Chalabi had to enter the rotunda of the Capitol building and walk down a flight of stairs to the "crypt," where he stepped into what HPSCI staffers like to call the James Bond elevator, a tiny, nondescript lift with two buttons, because it has only two destinations: the crypt and the attic four floors up. An armed guard is posted in front of the committee room, which is sealed with a huge metal door equipped with a combination lock and an alarm. The committee room itself was, in spy parlance, a secure compartmentalized information facility (SCIF)—a room with solid lead walls designed to block out any attempt at electronic eavesdropping on the committee's often highly classified deliberations.

Chalabi was neither awed nor impressed by the setting or the audience. It felt natural to him to circulate at the upper echelons of power as his father once had. When Chalabi entered the room, he sat down at a table and, in slightly accented but flawless English, seized command of the gathering, grabbing the attention of both the Democrats and the Republicans with his presentation. Shoulders squared, his eyes lit with confidence, Chalabi unveiled his plan for the liberation of Iraq: create a government-in-exile and plant it in northern Iraq—in Kurdistan—under the protection of the U.S. no-fly zone, and then use the sanctuary there as a base for overthrowing Saddam. Chalabi argued that the establishment of a provisional government would provide a rallying point for all the political forces opposed to Saddam. He also called for U.S. air strikes against Saddam's forces, something he said would encourage many of Saddam's army units to shift their allegiance to the provisional government. Once Saddam was gone, Chalabi continued, Iraq would be turned over to the government-in-exile, which would then usher in an era of democracy. That idea might have sounded Jeffersonian to those in the room, but to Chalabi it meant majority, or Shia, rule. It was a brilliant and elegant formulation that Chalabi had hit on by applying the transitive property of equality to the American policy debate over Iraq. If democracy equals majority rule, and if in the Iraqi context majority rule equals Shia empowerment, then Chalabi was all for democracy.

More to the point, Chalabi's proposal to HPSCI directly contravened the Saddam-lite approach the CIA had already set in motion at the behest of

America's commander in chief. But that didn't seem to bother the committee members, least of all its chairman, Representative Dave McCurdy—the hawkish Democrat from Oklahoma. McCurdy was so impressed by the briefing, Chalabi says, that afterward the congressman told him, "We need to take you to see the man who controls the money." At the time, that was Representative Jack Murtha, the powerful Democratic chairman of the House Appropriations Subcommittee on Defense with jurisdiction over the CIA's budget. Stephen Solarz set up the meeting.

"I introduced Ahmad to Jack, whose support would've been essential for getting money into the agency's budget for any effort to destabilize and hopefully bring down Saddam's regime," Solarz recalled with pride.

To see Murtha, Solarz and Chalabi boarded the open-air train that runs underground from the Capitol to the Rayburn House Office Building, where Murtha kept an office. Chalabi remembers the meeting as though it occurred yesterday. "Murtha met us outside his basement office in the capital. He's a big guy, a Marine. He took us into his cramped little office and said, 'I have a small office, but it's important,'" Chalabi recalled with a laugh. "He then took my hand and said, 'You want to overthrow that son of a bitch Saddam?' I said yes. He said, 'My friends say you are a good man. I believe them. I will give you a CIA budget of $700 million to get rid of Saddam.' So I said, 'Thank you very much, but we don't need that much money.'" Chalabi laughed again—this time at the incongruity of turning down money.

Then Murtha told Chalabi, "Here in this office is where the Afghan campaign to throw the Soviets out started. Here. And we can start the effort to overthrow Saddam from here. All my friends support you. And I will support you." And just like that, in an off-the-cuff meeting with no formal hearings or analyses, nor any input from either the CIA or the White House, Chalabi had won the backing of some of the most powerful Democrats on Capitol Hill—Democrats who wielded both the power of the purse and the authority of oversight when it came to the CIA.

Those Democrats communicated their support of Chalabi and his plan for overthrowing Saddam Hussein to Bush, which led to another meeting—this time with Richard N. Haass, who was a special assistant to Bush and the National Security Council's senior director for Near East and

South Asian Affairs. Haass was hostile right off the bat, Chalabi recalls, saying, "I'm meeting you only because you impressed some congressmen."

Over the next hour and a half, Chalabi made the same pitch to Haass that he had made to HPSCI, asking for U.S. backing of a government-in-exile that would spearhead a popular uprising against Saddam and his regime. Haass, for his part, found Chalabi to be a "clever, manipulative self-promoter" whose proposal failed the laugh test. Haass kept those feelings to himself. But he did tell the Iraqi exile the U.S. government would not extend any aid to him for the purpose of overthrowing Saddam; it would, however, support an umbrella organization of Iraqi opposition figures. In other words, Haass was telling Chalabi to stick to the CIA plan.

Chalabi, however, was a determined campaigner. And he was a lucky one. On November 13, 1991, he was back in Britain when the *Wall Street Journal* published an editorial he had written laying out the same ideas he had discussed with HPSCI, Murtha, and Haass. The piece prompted a phone call from Mohammed Bahr al-Ulloum, a leading political and religious figure in London's Shia community. Bahr al-Ulloum told Chalabi, "I am sitting here with a gentleman from the Iranian foreign ministry who read your article and he wants to meet you." Chalabi promptly invited the man to his home for tea.

At the time, Iran had no real coordinated policy toward Iraq except to support the Islamist parties it had created—the Supreme Council for the Islamic Revolution in Iraq (SCIRI) and its militia, the Badr Brigade—and provide some small-scale support for the Kurds. More important, Tehran had no operational capability to affect events inside Iraq. That's what stirred the Iranians' interest in the ideas Chalabi had written about—in particular, Chalabi recalled, "They wanted to follow up on the notion of using Kurdistan as a liberated area from which to launch a mass movement against Saddam."

As for the foreign ministry official with whom he met, Chalabi identified the man as Hussein Niknam, a senior diplomat who went by the honorific Seyed, which denotes that he was a descendant of the Prophet. Who exactly was this Seyed Niknam? His name has surfaced sporadically in the West. The first instance occurred in 1985 when he was identified as Iran's deputy chief of mission in Damascus, the embassy's number two official. While there, Niknam is said to have played an important role in the

Iran-Contra scandal, coordinating the release of American hostages held in Beirut in exchange for modified U.S. Hawk missiles that were airlifted to Tehran. In the late 1980s, Niknam's name appears again as the chargé d'affaires in Beirut, where he was reported to have overseen the activities of the Lebanese-based terrorist group Hezbollah and six of its top leaders, including the notorious Imad Mughniyah. Mughniyah is thought to have killed more Americans than any other Arab militant before the attacks of September 11, 2001—among them, the more than 350 who died in the Beirut barracks and the U.S. embassy bombings in Beirut in 1983. It is believed he masterminded both attacks. They, along with the kidnappings of Americans he is believed to have organized, all but eliminated the U.S. presence in Lebanon in the 1980s.

From his association with Mughniyah in Beirut, Niknam moved on to Western Europe, where, in 1989, he was reportedly spotted meeting numerous times with the leader of another terrorist organization, one that carried out anti-American and anti-Israeli operations on behalf of Iran, Syria, and Libya. Around the time of the Chalabi meeting, Niknam had been appointed head of the Iranian foreign ministry's Persian Gulf department in Tehran. His meeting with Chalabi signified a high level of interest by Iran early on in Chalabi and his ideas.

"Iranian intelligence doesn't meet with anyone," a former CIA case officer who tracked Iran during this period told me. "These are the guys who drove us out of Beirut and turned Lebanon into a proxy country. These are serious guys—deadly serious. And for Niknam to have met Chalabi means, one, that Tehran had green-lighted it and, two, that they took Chalabi seriously as a potential instrument of their policy, either witting or unwitting. It's a huge event."

During their encounter, over a cup of hot tea, Niknam asked Chalabi if he thought the Americans would seriously support the idea of using Kurdistan as a base to overthrow Saddam. Chalabi immediately responded yes. It was hardly the case, of course. But in Chalabi's mind, he wasn't really lying. He just wasn't telling the whole truth. As a matter of policy, the CIA, the State Department, and the White House categorically opposed Chalabi's scheme. But, as evidenced by Chalabi's briefing at HPSCI and his meetings with Solarz and Murtha, some influential Democrats in Congress thought it was such a good idea they were willing to fund it. That was just enough daylight for Chalabi, in his way of thinking, to straddle the fine line that separates embellishing a kernel of truth from telling an outright lie.

The real significance of the Niknam meeting, however, was that in a span of six months Ahmad Chalabi had sipped tea with house guests from both the CIA and its foremost enemy in the region, the Iranian government. On top of that, he had also established a nascent, yet independent, base of support in the U.S. Congress. No one realized it yet, but Ahmad Chalabi was developing his own covert action plan, the very one he had outlined in his head back when he was in college and that he had committed himself to in the wake of the Petra Bank scandal. All he needed to do now was set himself up in Kurdish-controlled northern Iraq. That would require a substantial refocusing of the CIA's covert operation.

As envisioned by Langley, the Iraqi opposition front was to be an umbrella organization that included Kurds, Shiites, Sunni Muslims, and former monarchists who were based in London, not northern Iraq, and Chalabi's role was to be decidedly middle-level and nonstrategic. The top three officials were to be Massoud Barzani, one of Iraq's leading Kurdish figures; Hassan al-Naqib, a Sunni who had been an Iraqi army general and ambassador; and Mohammed Bahr al-Ulloum, the London-based Shiite. Chalabi's function was to be that of a general manager, the behind-the-scenes, day-to-day administrator who basically would balance the books and help organize anti-Saddam public relations campaigns. Chalabi was not to be a political leader in his own right.

"But, of course," Whitley Bruner observed with the benefit of hindsight, "if you're as clever as Ahmad you set up the structure that you can manipulate to your own advantage, which is exactly what Chalabi did. He usurped the whole thing!"

For starters, he coined the group's name, the Iraqi National Congress (INC). His inspiration, he says, was the Indian National Congress, the political party in India that went by the same initials and that led that country's struggle for independence against British rule. "That was my model," Chalabi told me, saying that he identified with the party's leaders because they were "conscious of their culture and their role in confronting a colonial power that held the keys to their fate." The name had the added virtue of echoing Nelson Mandela's African National Congress, the anti-apartheid South African party that was widely popular in the West. This appealed to the public relations expert John Rendon, whose Washington, D.C.–based agency, the

Rendon Group, was being paid $326,000 a month by the CIA to oversee the creation and operation of what henceforth would be called the INC.

Next, when the CIA said that it wanted to stage a conference of the newly minted INC, it was Chalabi who seized the initiative. He selected the venue, Vienna, Austria, and had his good friend Tamara Daghistani—the woman who had helped him escape from Jordan after the collapse of Petra Bank—reconnoiter the hotels, procure the photocopy machines, and pick the location where the conference would be held.

In June 1992, nearly two hundred delegates from dozens of Iraqi opposition groups were flown into Vienna for what was truly a significant event, the first gathering of such a wide spectrum of Iraqi dissidents. With the exception of Chalabi and one or two others, none was aware of the CIA's involvement. That's the way the agency wanted it, and that suited Chalabi just fine, for it allowed him to cast himself in the most positive light possible. As far as any of the invited exiles could tell, it was Chalabi who set the conference in motion. He seemed to be the man with the money. According to a CIA official, everyone thought Chalabi paid for the conference with Petra Bank money, when in fact he was using secret CIA funds to cover everything from the cost of the conference hall to the delegates' airplane tickets, hotel rooms, and car rentals. And at the conference itself, it was Chalabi who assumed the air of host, welcoming and embracing delegates in a well-orchestrated masquerade.

At the conference, Chalabi studied his fellow exiles. Who were his most likely allies? Who could be useful? Who was a waste of time? Who represented a threat to his designs? He pulled some of the more promising delegates aside, engaging them in one-on-one conversations—the setting in which he is always the most beguiling. It was in the context of these meetings, however, that some of the CIA case officers got their first hint of a darker side to Chalabi. As the agency's John Maguire recalled, "He would sit down with one guy in a meeting and negotiate something, and then run off and talk to somebody else and tell him a completely different story of what he just said to the other guy. By the end of the conference, he had five or six people all pitted against one another, and when you're watching this as an observer you think, 'He's a fucking staff splitter. He drives a wedge between people and then makes himself the bridge that holds them together.' And as a case officer, you're thinking, 'Wrong guy. This will not work. This one's gonna be too hard to manage.' "

The ability to manage Chalabi had first arisen as a concern seven months earlier when, on December 22, 1991, Chalabi appeared on the CBS News program *60 Minutes*, attacking Jordan's King Hussein for allying himself with Saddam Hussein during the Gulf War in return for millions of dollars in Iraqi oil and cash. For Chalabi, the network news appearance was a carefully calculated hit job that had the virtue of being true. Its real purpose was to undermine the criminal charges against him in Jordan arising from the Petra Bank scandal.

"What was I going to do? Say that I'm innocent? That doesn't work," Chalabi explained. "So I attacked the person who was attacking me to show that he is unreliable."

For the CIA, the *60 Minutes* interview was an act of reckless insubordination and self-indulgence, one that threatened the rapprochement under way between the United States and Jordan. It rattled that process, infuriating King Hussein not only because the segment was broadcast on America's most-watched news program but also because it was carried on Israeli television, which meant that it was seen next door in Amman. The U.S. ambassador to Jordan was called in for an official protest, while in London Chalabi was called on the carpet by his purported CIA handlers.

"I'd been working with the CIA for six months by then," Chalabi recalled, "and they were very angry at me. They said, 'The Jordanians are fuming. They accused us of helping you. Why didn't you tell us about the *60 Minutes* story?' I said, 'You can't deal with U.S. media. You're prohibited by law.'" He had them there. The CIA generally is prohibited from placing information in the U.S. media. But that was hardly a satisfying answer. Chalabi's *60 Minutes* appearance triggered a heated debate at headquarters over whether or not to continue working with him.

Just as that brouhaha was subsiding, Chalabi put on his "staff-splitting" performance in Vienna. John Maguire and some of his colleagues now revived a push to sever Chalabi from the entire operation. But it was too late. By that time, Maguire said, Chalabi had acquired too much "voltage."

"He was known in academic circles," Maguire explained. "He had relationships with key members on Capitol Hill. He had cultivated relationships with people that had financial horsepower in the legislative branch of government—Congressman Jack Murtha, for example. I remember Murtha having a voice in it all, saying that money would be given to this process if Chalabi were involved. Chalabi had cultivated relationships with people who had access to the executive branch of the government. What's more, Chalabi knew that he had these various rat lines in and there was nothing anybody could do about it."

To be sure, Chalabi had his share of supporters inside the CIA—at least at that point he still did. Several senior officers were impressed by the organizational skills it took to pull together the Vienna conference and by Chalabi's ability to move large sums of money around the world without any of it getting traced back to Uncle Sam. The positives outweighed the negatives, they argued—and, in the end, that view carried the day. Chalabi survived—and pressed ahead.

Immediately following the Vienna conference, he urged the CIA to arrange a meeting between Secretary of State James Baker and a delegation from the INC. But the agency "couldn't deliver," Chalabi said, so he approached a senior Pentagon official he had met the year before, Paul Wolfowitz, who at the time was the principal staff assistant and adviser to Secretary of Defense Dick Cheney. Chalabi thought Wolfowitz might be helpful because he knew Wolfowitz was deeply anti-Saddam and had previously argued for an extension of the U.S. no-fly zone from northern Iraq to include the south, where Shiites predominated. "So I sent a message to Wolfowitz," Chalabi told me, and word came back that both Baker and National Security Adviser Brent Scowcroft would, indeed, host an INC delegation. At the meeting, on July 29, 1992, the secretary of state "assured the delegation that the United States will continue to stand firmly in support of the brave Iraqis who oppose Saddam's tyranny." For the Bush administration, the session amounted to mostly political posturing for the consumption of its domestic critics, and a bit of low-level statecraft aimed at tweaking Saddam. The White House and the CIA still viewed the INC as the disposable half of a two-pronged strategy to displace Saddam, and saw no harm in encouraging the exiles. But to Chalabi, the administration's public endorsement conferred on the INC an enormous amount of prestige among Iraqi exiles. "It catapulted the INC into prominence," was how Chalabi saw it. It also told him a lot about Paul Wolfowitz. "I knew that he was committed and that he had helped us," Chalabi said, "so I kept in touch with him."

At that same time, Chalabi began to plan for a second, larger conference to be held in the Kurdish-controlled city of Salahuddin in northern Iraq. The CIA was opposed to holding the conference there, feeling it was too dangerous a place to send Americans. And the State Department, which initially had asked U.S. ambassador David Mack to attend, ultimately thought better of it. "We thought Saddam might bomb the conference!" Mack explained to me. Northern Iraq may have been under the protection of U.S. warplanes, he said, "but we had no confidence that the Kurds themselves could keep out a truck bomb from Mosul or Baghdad."

The absence of Americans, however, was precisely the point, as far as Chalabi was concerned. It gave him the opportunity he needed to unravel his web. So, at a cost of $650,000 to American taxpayers, he organized the first ever meeting of Iraqi opposition figures on Iraqi soil.

"Imagine what it entailed," Chalabi recalled with pride, "to bring three hundred people from all corners of the world to northern Iraq in an area threatened by Saddam. They came through Turkey and Iran, and they were housed in a village which had had very little infrastructure until we got involved. This was not an easy task. It was very, very difficult."

Once in Salahuddin, he recalled with a sly grin, "I did something which cooked the influence of the CIA. I knew they would not be able to come to Iraq for a long time, so I drafted a new charter for the INC that said, first, the INC was to be headquartered on Iraqi territory. Second, we claimed the right to establish a provisional government. And, third, the charter treated the INC as a federal authority." The latter action gave the group immediate sway over parts of Iraq and granted it the future right to extend that authority over the entire country. The INC also called for the overthrow of Saddam Hussein's regime and the establishment of democracy in Iraq. The pièce de résistance concerned Chalabi's role: the delegates chose a twenty-five-member executive council, electing Chalabi as its chairman and president. In doing so, it elevated the CIA's would-be office manager into a bona fide political leader.

The CIA was furious. What Chalabi had engineered was, to say the least, a far more robust and expansive role for both himself and the INC than Langley had ever intended. "When I got back to London," Chalabi recalled, "the CIA wanted a meeting—immediately. They were very upset. One of them said, 'Who told you to be chairman and president of the executive council?' [I said,] 'I was elected.' They said, 'What do you mean, elected?' I said, 'Elected. People put their hands up and said we vote for him for the executive council, according to the charter.' 'Who told you to make a charter?' I said, 'The opposition. We want to overthrow Saddam; we have to have a charter.' 'We didn't tell you to do that.' 'Okay, what do you want to do? You don't want to cooperate? Okay. Goodbye.'"

It was at that moment that Chalabi began to turn the tables on the CIA. He wanted to be in Iraq. He wanted to make the Americans recognize and work with an Iraqi opposition from Iraqi territory. And he wanted to be a political leader in his own right. He marshaled what few assets he had and leveraged them to his maximum benefit. I asked him what made him so sure the CIA would blink.

"What else could they do?" Chalabi replied. "Abandon the policy when they had nothing else?"

It was a policy begun as a Washington ploy, to simply create the appearance of trying to overthrow Saddam Hussein and his regime. But now the CIA was the prisoner of its own ruse—and Ahmad Chalabi was about to make the most of it.

EIGHT

By late 1992, Chalabi had relocated from his posh residence in the exclusive Mayfair district of London to the rugged, mountainous surroundings of Kurdish-controlled Salahuddin in northern Iraq. He was physically separated from his wife and four children, and the mostly one-story homes of mud-brick and stone that predominated in Salahuddin, alongside the occasional sign that read, "Area Heavily Mined," stood in stark contrast to the privilege he knew.

Chalabi, however, moved into a spacious two-story, four-bedroom house overlooking a long, sloping canyon that itself was part of the dramatically majestic Zagros Mountains, which stretch across Kurdistan and into Iran, extending as far south as the Persian Gulf. The house was not ostentatious, but it was quintessential Chalabi, decorated with paintings and sculptures purchased from local artists and bedecked with furniture made of hardwood and walnut, crafted by a local carpenter using Frank Lloyd Wright designs supplied by Chalabi. And while few homes in Salahuddin had running water or electricity, Chalabi procured his own generator, a massive machine that rumbled like an army tank in full throttle. It powered everything from hot showers to the Mitsubishi stereo speakers, Kenwood amplifier, and Sony CD player that he also brought along so that he could listen to his favorite composers—Bach, Beethoven, Mozart, Vivaldi, and Brahms. Chalabi was willing to give up much for his quest—even his life, he says—but not his lifestyle. "Fighting Saddam does not mean you have to eat bad food or live in shabby surroundings," he declared as he lifted his right hand into the air and turned his index finger like a corkscrew. "Certainly not!"

Chalabi liked to read, especially mathematics and history books, so he had his servants lug boxloads of books to northern Iraq. Then there was the matter of sustenance. The stout, barrel-chested Chalabi liked to eat well—very well—and typically hosted late-evening feasts for as many as eight to a dozen guests. He hired a personal chef and, with the help of a small library of recipe books he brought along with him, educated his Kurdish cook on the cuisines of the world.

"There were ducks there, and we learned the technique of cooking Peking duck," Chalabi recalled with glee. "You have to inflate them so that the meat separates properly from the skin. We had various devices to do that."

No Che Guevara was this Ahmad Chalabi, who remained more Gucci than guerrilla even in the harsh and jagged terrain of northern Iraq. But for the first time in thirty-five years he was living on Iraqi soil again. Some 220 miles north of where he grew up in Baghdad, Salahuddin was still a long way from home. But he alone had masterminded his return to Iraq thus far, and he could not have been happier.

When he first arrived, he liked to go on archaeological hikes and picnic with visitors in the meadows and mountains of Kurdistan, a lush and luminous landscape packed with yellow-and-white daisies, purple vetch, dazzling red poppies, huge wild maroon hollyhocks, and other flowers. One of his favorite guilty pleasures from those days was watching all eleven episodes of *Brideshead Revisited*, the BBC serial based on the novel by Evelyn Waugh. Members of his security detail found that its absence of sex and violence made for an exceedingly boring viewing experience. But, as with the book, Chalabi was enthralled by the tale of a wealthy, aristocratic family and the passing of a more elegant and simple age when the English upper class—with their presumed intellect and training—was deemed the most fit to lead their nation. Chalabi certainly viewed himself in a similar way: as a member of the Iraqi elite, which was the most qualified group to lead the fight against Saddam. "I know about mobilizing people, and I know how things work in the West," he argued. "And I had thought about overthrowing Saddam for a long, long time."

In the years he contemplated the challenge of displacing Saddam, he says he turned to history and found a model and a kindred spirit in Charles de Gaulle, the leader of the Free French Forces during World War II. "De Gaulle had to rely on the British and the Americans to liberate his country, which was impossible without them," Chalabi noted. "At the same time, they looked with disdain on exiles. De Gaulle insisted, however, that he was not an exile, but rather that he represented France. And"—Chalabi's voice was now rising—"he stood up to the British and the Americans."

For de Gaulle, it was uniting the disparate resistance movements under his leadership that not only gained him leverage in his dealings with London and Washington but also formed the basis of his own legitimacy. Bringing together the collection of contentious elements that comprised the French Resistance—conservative Roman Catholics, Jews, liberals, anarchists, communists, refugees from German-occupied Vichy—and turning them into a coherent opposition loyal to him was no easy task. Among the key obstacles were the various resistance leaders themselves who fought against de Gaulle's leadership and jockeyed with him to represent France in Allied war councils and, ultimately, to serve as heirs to the French government. The fact that de Gaulle was a relatively low-ranking general without troops and a political figure without a mandate from the people of France—who yet prevailed—made his success all the more impressive to Chalabi. "He did all these things and he had nothing," Chalabi exclaimed. "But, you see, that's the point."

The point was personal. Chalabi similarly lacked clout and currency. He was a member of Iraq's lowest caste—the Shia Muslims—and belonged to no tribe, commanded no soldiers, and had no popular following inside the country on which to claim the mantle of leadership. And like the French Resistance, the Iraqi opposition was a fractious group—a bickering herd of alley cats who hated one another as much as they hated Saddam. The fact that de Gaulle had faced so many similar obstacles and was still able to catapult himself to the top of the political and military heap and, in the process, make himself a force that not even the Great Powers could ignore, resonated deeply with Chalabi.

De Gaulle had emerged victorious in large measure because of the success of his secret service, the Bureau Central de Renseignements et d'Action (BCRA). Knowing more about developments inside France than either the British or the Americans, or his rivals in the Resistance, was de Gaulle's most potent source of capital, and he leveraged it to make himself "the indispensable man."

"De Gaulle had a very good network of people in very high places," Chalabi noted. "And what I learned from him is that you have to be inside the country to develop those kinds of sources. You have to have links into the place, into the actual areas controlled by the dictator, and develop those contacts. That's why I put the INC into the north in Kurdistan."

The INC set up headquarters in a decrepit, bug-infested, fifty-two-room hotel notorious for its frighteningly wobbly ceiling fans. Using CIA funds, Chalabi began with a staff of forty. He hired broadcasters and propagandists and launched radio and television services that beamed reports to Iraqis and smuggled miniature news sheets into Baghdad. The operation was rudimentary, and its permeation of the Iraqi capital spotty at best, but it met the minimal requirements of the CIA, which—despite its initial opposition—came to realize the value of having the INC based in Kurdistan. The INC's mere presence on Iraqi territory was a powerful piece of propaganda in itself—an embarrassment to Saddam and a most useful thorn to stick in his side.

The CIA itself kept no permanent station in Kurdistan. Occasionally, a case officer would slip in to drop off equipment or cash. Beyond that, Chalabi was essentially left on his own—6,192 miles and eight time zones away from any meaningful oversight. For someone like Chalabi, a man with Gaullist aspirations and a nature Machiavellian to its core, that was tantamount to handing over the keys to the kingdom and rolling out the red carpet. Chalabi immediately set out to expand his authority and stretch the CIA operation far beyond the boundaries of its original mission.

His first foray in that direction was to let it be known among his fellow exiles that the INC was, in fact, a CIA-backed program. With the INC already established inside Iraq, he gambled that revealing the U.S. connection now would no longer be a stigma—the kiss of death, really—but rather would confer prestige and power. People in the Middle East respond to power, he reasoned, and there was no power greater than the United States. Being seen as having America's backing would be useful. It was a shrewd insight, defying both Arab politics and prejudices—so long as he could position himself to control access to the Americans and their largess. And to a great extent, that's exactly what he orchestrated, according to the CIA's Whitley Bruner.

"The INC was able to recommend that people travel, attend meetings, work with us Americans. And, basically, the INC *was* Chalabi," Bruner explained. "So he was the broker, the guy who would put in a good word with the Yanks, could make things happen. Or, conversely, he was the guy who could put in a bad word, freeze out an opposition politician—'He's too ambitious, too Ba'athist,' whatever—and deny him access to U.S.-financed efforts. The point was that Chalabi's self-defined role as the facilitator for the Americans made him the kingmaker. He could move his 'friends' ahead in the system. He could relegate his 'enemies' to Siberia."

Chalabi also held sway over the INC budget, which totaled $340,000 a month, or more than $4 million a year. He was not given direct control of the money because everyone knew about the Petra Bank story and, frankly, didn't trust him. But in addition to getting himself elected chairman and president of the INC's executive council, Chalabi also got himself made general manager, which meant that he was in charge of *disbursing* the INC funds—for legitimate expenses that were properly accounted for, of course. But receipts are difficult to come by in a war zone. While no one could prove it, the CIA's accountant at headquarters strongly suspected that Chalabi was padding the bills and using the skim not to fund a secret bank account for himself, but to finance a form of patronage—to promote his friends and purchase the support of anyone else who was open to such inducements. Chalabi denies it, insisting he used the pad, instead, to finance his own intelligence collection operation inside Iraq, like Charles de Gaulle. Either way, as the man in the middle through whom everything was funneled, Chalabi was able to outmaneuver and neutralize his competitors and nemeses within the opposition and, effectively, unite the INC under his leadership. "It was too easy," Bruner observed wryly, "and he is a master manipulator."

As Chalabi was settling into Kurdistan, back in Washington, D.C., a new president was just assuming office. Bill Clinton's interests were focused on issues closer to home—in particular, the U.S. economy and health care. His preference was to relegate Iraq to the back burner. But he recognized that for both domestic political and geostrategic reasons, Saddam Hussein could not be ignored. His administration immediately undertook a review of the Iraq policy it had inherited from George H. W. Bush. The State Department, the Joint Chiefs of Staff, the CIA, the National Security Council, and others weighed in. Their starting point was one bedrock fact of life: with 65 percent of the world's proven oil reserves, the region remained paramount to U.S. national security interests. The United States was committed to protecting the free flow of oil from the Middle East to the economies of Asia and the West. As for Saddam, though his army of 1.2 million had been all but decimated by the Gulf War, he had regained his equilibrium and consolidated his grip on power. The goal now was to prevent him from acquiring the kind of military prowess that would enable him to dictate the policies of his weaker oil-rich neighbors—Saudi Arabia, Kuwait, the United Arab Emirates, Bahrain, Qatar, and Oman.

The CIA's assessment was that, while it wouldn't happen quickly or easily, Saddam's regime would eventually collapse of its own weight if the U.S. could only keep the pressure on. The State Department's Iraq experts, however, voiced their strong concerns about an uprising by the Iraqi people. State feared the possible fragmentation of the country, a view that the other agencies shared. Martin Indyk, who was Clinton's Middle East adviser on the National Security Council, explained in his 2009 memoir the reasons for the apprehension:

> If the Iraqi people managed to topple the regime, Shi'ites and Kurds could well take their revenge on their Sunni oppressors. That, in turn, would leave southern Iraq wide open to the Iranians. If they gained control there either militarily or through an alliance with Iraqi Shi'ites, they could then threaten the oil fields of Kuwait and Saudi Arabia, thereby destabilizing the region and, arguably, the entire Western economy.

It was the same argument used before to oppose backing any uprising by the Iraqi people, Indyk noted. The Reagan administration had invoked it to justify supporting Saddam during the Iran-Iraq War, as had President Bush after the Gulf War in 1991 when he allowed Saddam loyalists to slaughter eighty thousand Iraqi Shiites and Kurds while American forces looked on. "When it came to choosing between supporting the human rights of the Iraqi people and preventing the spread of Iranian influence to the Arab side of the Gulf," Indyk wrote, "U.S. policy makers opted repeatedly for the latter, honoring a tradition of favoring stability over freedom."

Ahmad Chalabi hoped that Clinton would upend that practice and overturn the existing Middle Eastern order, rather than operate within its constraints. But Chalabi would have to wait for another president before that would happen. In February 1993, Clinton reauthorized the "findings" that his predecessor had signed directing the CIA to foment an officer-led palace coup, one that would leave the Sunni, anti-Iranian army in control of the country. That would be the covert side of the new Clinton policy. The overt face would be a policy of "aggressive containment": continuing the no-fly zones in northern and southern Iraq and pressing for the enforcement of all United Nations (UN) resolutions against Iraq. The Clinton team's assumption was that the combination of the UN's economic sanctions and covert operations would force the collapse of Saddam's regime in five years.

As part of its public campaign, the administration decided to provide political support for the INC. It would seek Saddam's indictment as a war criminal, as the INC had been urging. And in April 1993, Secretary of State Warren Christopher and Vice President Al Gore met with an INC delegation. Four months later, Gore wrote a letter addressed personally to Chalabi, pledging that he and Clinton would "not turn [their] backs on the Kurds or the other Iraqi communities subjected to the repression of Saddam Hussein's regime." The vice president also said it was U.S. policy to demand an end to Iraq's repression of its own people. There was only one way that would happen, Chalabi correctly reasoned—with the demise of Saddam's regime.

To the White House and the CIA, the meetings and the letter were merely tactical, aimed at complementing the CIA's subterranean plot to overthrow Saddam. But to Chalabi, they were imprimaturs of his and the INC's growing legitimacy, and, in the case of Gore's letter, promises to be kept.

Meanwhile, as far as the outside world could tell, the INC seemed to enjoy the full support of the Clinton administration. That translated into a growing profile for the INC and Chalabi, one that began to catch the attention of a number of actors inside Iraq, including Saddam Hussein. The INC posed no strategic threat to his regime, to be sure, but its occupation of sovereign Iraqi territory did prompt a number of attempted lethal attacks by Saddam's intelligence service, the Mukhabarat, including a handful of car bombings, some rocket attacks, and the poisoning of several INC men with thallium. Chalabi says that during this time some of his rivals in the opposition also began to cast a wary eye on him—in particular, those belonging to the INC's Iranian-backed counterpart, the Supreme Council for the Islamic Republic of Iraq (SCIRI).

Just as the INC was a creature of America's foreign intelligence service, SCIRI was a creation of Iran's. Founded in 1982 and based in Tehran, SCIRI united under one banner the various Iraqi Shia parties opposed to Saddam's rule, and aimed to establish a Shiite-led Islamic government in Baghdad. Its military wing, the Badr Brigade, consisted of several thousand Iraqi exiles, refugees, and defectors armed and trained by Iran. In February 1993, Chalabi says, SCIRI's leaders complained about him to Tehran. "They were attacking me for being a stooge of the Americans," Chalabi recounted.

In other words, he was being smeared as a stalking horse for the Great Satan, with SCIRI suggesting that the INC's base in northern Iraq would eventually be used to conduct operations against Iran. It was a serious charge, and Chalabi knew that if he allowed it to stick he was finished. Iran was a crucial piece in his scheme for overthrowing Saddam, and minimally he needed the mullahs in Tehran to remain neutral toward him and not oppose his efforts. Iran might not have been able to defeat Saddam on the battlefield, but it could easily undermine the INC in Salahuddin, which was only fifty-five miles from Iran's border. The SCIRI accusation represented a serious threat to Chalabi's continued viability in Kurdistan.

"So how do I counter this?" Chalabi thought to himself. His answer revealed that he understood how the Iranian system worked as well as he did that of the United States. "I go to an authority higher than even the Iranian government. The highest authority among the Shia are the *marja*." The *marja* are religious scholars, the most senior of whom are grand ayatollahs. They provide rulings and opinions, known as fatwas, to which laypeople and lesser religious scholars defer.

"A *marja* is like the pope and a division commander combined," Chalabi explained with a laugh. "But he doesn't have any soldiers. He has moral authority. I was not looking for any soldiers. I was looking for moral sanction to continue to work with the United States to overthrow Saddam. So I arranged meetings with the highest religious guides in Qom."

In the spring of 1993, Chalabi traveled from Kurdistan to the holy city of Qom in north-central Iran, some ninety-seven miles outside the capital. It was at the time the largest center for Shia scholarship in the world and the place where Ayatollah Ruhollah Khomeini returned in early 1979, from a fifteen-year exile, to institute a "reign of virtue" and proclaim an Islamic republic ruled by the clergy. Many of the *marja* there had spent time living and studying in Iraq and either knew Chalabi's father personally or knew of him. Chalabi arranged to meet two of them. One was as old as he was revered, Ayatollah Muhammad Raza Gulpaygani. He was ninety-four and regarded as a divine scholar and a pillar of the Islamic Revolution. Chalabi arrived at his residence in a suit and tie, and was escorted by the ayatollah's son into a private room where Gulpaygani was sitting alone on a bed with his legs crossed and his hands folded on his lap.

"He was not a frail old man at all," Chalabi recalled. "He had a very bright face, very distinguished. His hands were white, clean, and not too wrinkled. And he was conscious of what was going on. His son leaned over and whispered in his ear that I am the son of Abdul Hadi Chalabi. So the ayatollah nodded his head. He asked what do I want. I told him, 'Your Eminence, what I want is that you join us in fighting Saddam with the arrows of the night.'"

Among the Shia, "arrows of the night" are the prayers and execrations sent up to heaven by the oppressed and the innocent. The phrase is attributed to one of the twelve Shia imams, and it signifies both a believer's supplication to God and the power of the weak. "And what you ask God for at night, if you are a believer," Chalabi explained, "is that your prayers be answered and returned like arrows directed at your enemies."

Gulpaygani immediately understood the reference and smiled. He put his hands together, his palms turned upward, and raised them and his eyes toward heaven as he began to recite a prayer, which meant that he condoned what Chalabi was doing—fighting Saddam. Chalabi, however, kept from the ayatollah any mention of his alliance with the United States. It was unnecessary, Chalabi insisted, saying, "That's enough from this man."

The next meeting was scheduled for later that same day with a younger, more active *marja*. "I went there and he had about twenty Iraqi religious students and lesser religious authorities sitting around on the floor in his reception," Chalabi said. "I walked in there, and half a minute later he walked in. I greeted him and we sat down. He said to me, 'Your father was a strong man for Iraq. You be the same as him.' So I said to him, 'I've come to you because I'm working to overthrow Saddam, and I'm working with the United States to do so. And I'm getting attacked by the Iraqi religious parties.' He said, 'Why are they attacking you? Can they overthrow Saddam on their own? Don't respond to their criticism. You continue to work with the United States.'"

He asked Chalabi who in the U.S. government he was working with. Chalabi dodged. "I said, 'The State Department.' He said, 'They're no good to you.' Then I said, 'National Security Council.' He said, 'Yes, stick with them,'" Chalabi recalled with a grin. There was no mention of the CIA. But Chalabi got what he wanted: religious license to proceed with the Americans. "That was an important point," Chalabi remarked. "They can't attack me now," he said in reference to SCIRI's leaders. "Finished. That's it."

Well, not exactly. Following Chalabi's meeting with Gulpaygani, a representative from the Iranian government appeared out of the blue to tell Chalabi that he was wanted in Tehran for an audience with Agha Mohammadi, whom Chalabi knew to be the Iranian government official in charge of all relations with the Iraqi opposition. Chalabi was pleased by Mohammadi's interest. So, naturally, he refused, saying he had to return to Kurdistan immediately and would be unable to see Mohammadi. After some back and forth, however, Chalabi relented and made his way to Tehran.

"So I went to meet Mohammadi the next morning," Chalabi told me. "It was the first time I met him, and the first thing he said to me was, 'Had it not been for me yesterday, you would have been arrested by the minister of intelligence. Why do you go to Qom without telling us?' I looked at him and said, 'Mr. Mohammadi, it has always been the case that there is no barrier between a Shia Muslim and his *marja*. Now you are telling me in the Islamic Republic of Iran that we have to ask permission from the government to see the *marja*?'" Mohammadi smiled and then yelled playfully, "Sit down!" to Chalabi. "And then he asked me about the United States and what they intended to do in Iraq." Chalabi says they spoke for an hour. "He wrote copious notes."

His message to Mohammadi was that the United States and Iran shared a common goal: getting rid of Saddam. That's why the INC was in northern Iraq—not to help the CIA launch operations against Tehran, but to liberate Iraq. Chalabi wanted to make sure the Iranians in no way perceived the INC as a threat, lest they sabotage its operations.

While Mohammadi could immediately see that Chalabi was a serious person, it would take much more than one conversation to convince him that this Shiite could be trusted when he said that the CIA posed no threat. Iran would remain skeptical of Chalabi for some time, and cautious—even fearful—of his patron. But it was the beginning of what would become a complicated and controversial relationship between Chalabi and the Islamic Republic of Iran, one that would evolve, twist, and deepen over the years. For now, however, the Iranians followed up the encounter with a steady stream of meetings in Kurdistan between Chalabi and members of Iran's intelligence service and Revolutionary Guard. Chalabi even provided them with safe houses in Salahuddin, paid for by the CIA.

As his relationship with Iran ramped up, Chalabi went to school on the CIA, learning firsthand just how feckless the organization in general and the Iraq Task Force in particular had become. He constantly tested their mettle and discovered time and again just how docile and incompetent they truly were. For example, he was often "unavailable" when case officers in Langley or London attempted to reach him in Kurdistan. Other times, he was openly contemptuous of the agency's attempts to manage his operation from afar. Not only were his business receipts forever missing, but he shielded his communications from his overseers. He encrypted his e-mails using a code known only to him and his top lieutenant, Aras Habib Karim, an Iraqi Kurd. In another instance, he used the CIA's own equipment to keep his telephone conversations confidential from the CIA. That happened in 1993 when the agency issued a secure telephone unit (STU) to Chalabi and Karim. The device converts speech into digital signals that become indecipherable to anyone without the proper key, or decoder. The ostensible purpose for the STU was to enable Chalabi and Karim to secure their telephone conversations from Saddam's intelligence service. But, of course, Chalabi realized that since CIA technicians had programmed the STU, they could decode his conversations and eavesdrop on what he and Karim were discussing. He figured that was the CIA's purpose as much as anything for issuing the secured phones.

"But we did not want the CIA to know what we were saying," Chalabi recalled with a laugh. So he simply changed the code. The STU had sixteen codes—literally, buttons marked M-1 through M-16. The CIA had programmed it to use M-1. "But I read the manual [which came along with the unit, a Motorola] and figured out how to reprogram it," Chalabi gleefully told me. "We entered in a new sequence of numbers, which then became a different key to encrypt our messages back and forth. I remember configuring M-4, M-7, and M-11."

The CIA quickly realized what he had done and dispatched a case officer to Kurdistan to straighten things out. "You're not supposed to do that," the visiting case officer scolded. But Chalabi told the case officer that if his bosses didn't like what he had done with the STU, they could take it back. The case officer relented, allowing Chalabi to keep the equipment.

In his relationship with the CIA, Chalabi was able to operate with a remarkable degree of impunity—and the more he got away with, the more emboldened he grew. There is no more graphic illustration of that than the INC's ballooning presence in northern Iraq. After eighteen months on the ground, the initial staff of about forty had swelled to several thousand.

Included among the group's ranks now were administrators, translators, intelligence operatives, and soldiers, most of whom were deserters from the Iraqi army. Many moved into a second hotel that the INC had now completely taken over, while Chalabi's senior staff took up residence in nearby rented houses. In all, the INC now operated out of sixty-four locations across Salahuddin. Chalabi called his top aide, Aras Habib Karim, "the de facto mayor of Salahuddin." Meanwhile, the city's town hall—the INC's headquarters—had been transformed into a "beehive of activity," according to a visitor. "It bristled with state-of-the-art computer, communications, and spy equipment."

This wasn't mission creep; it was mission leap. The INC was supposed to be a narrowly drawn political and public relations operation—the throwaway half of a two-pronged U.S. strategy. But its presence in northern Iraq had now mutated into that of a ministate. And it all had happened without a discussion, a proposal, or even an argument. It was the job of the CIA's Iraq Task Force to oversee and manage Chalabi's operation. But by the time he moved to Kurdistan, the ITF had already degenerated into the feeble stepchild of the CIA's Near East Division. In 1993, it was renamed the Iraq Operations Group (IOG) and banished to an office space three floors down from where Frank Anderson, the division chief, sat—the bureaucratic equivalent of a demotion and a reflection of Anderson's continuing lack of interest in the whole enterprise. Moreover, with the Cold War recently concluded, the IOG was increasingly stocked with former Soviet-bloc officers who knew nothing about Iraq or the Middle East. They were "fish out of water," recalls Ambassador David Mack, who was the State Department's top official assigned to the INC account. He says many of the case officers were less than top-notch and, as a result, they'd meet Chalabi "and, lo and behold, pretty soon they're working for Ahmad, rather than vice versa."

And those were among the better case officers. When CIA official Robert Baer was assigned to the IOG in 1994 as its deputy director, he was told by the head of personnel, "You're gonna have your hands full. IOG is swarming with drunkards and whores." As Baer recalls, one case officer got caught having sex in the CIA's infirmary; another was found in the parking lot of the CIA passed out drunk behind the steering wheel of his car; a third, who was hand-carrying $200,000 in cash to northern Iraq, got arrested en route in Turkey after he flew into a drunken rage, busting up a hotel lobby and getting into a knife fight. Then there was the case of the outside contractor retained by the IOG. He was so old and frail, Baer recalls, that he often dozed off in the middle of meetings, even during National Security Council briefings at the White House. At one such gathering, Baer said, the contractor nodded off and actually fell face-first into the couch he was sitting on. "What do you do when something like that happens?" Baer asked. "You ignore it."

The point, however, is that Chalabi grew to understand just how "dispirited and defanged" the vaunted CIA had actually become, having lost its way after the Cold War and fallen into bureaucratic decay. "Look at the world through his eyes," Baer commented. "He realizes the CIA is wet spaghetti. He sees the people in IOG and recognizes the caliber of agents. You've got the walking wounded assigned to this operation, and it's just bleeding money for nothing. It was his education about how easy it would be to roll the CIA and the American government and drag us into a war. There is no other narrative."

It was a narrative in which Baer would soon find himself deeply entangled.

NINE

Robert Baer is a pleasant-looking middle-aged man with thinning brown hair and deep-set eyes that all but recede into his soft round face. He's quiet and unassuming, almost stoic in disposition. But to believe he is in any way ordinary or insubstantial would be, in the words of a close friend, "a grave error." For Baer is an unusual and endearing amalgamation of the serious and the roguish, a reserved and thoughtful daredevil who slides easily between the personae of Mad Max and Mr. Chips.

Baer grew up during the 1960s in California and Colorado, where, as a soft-spoken and somewhat shy teenager, he became a downhill ski racer. At Georgetown University he was famous for riding a Harley motorcycle right into a campus dining hall—and then the library. And after college in 1976, when most of his peers were smoking pot or railing against the post-Watergate government of President Gerald R. Ford, he signed up with the CIA's "DO," or Directorate of Operations, the clandestine service where spies were made. "The DO is the only arm of the federal government dedicated to breaking the law," Baer would later comment, "foreign law, but still the law."

At Camp Peary, the CIA's main training base near Williamsburg, Virginia—informally known as the Farm—he learned how to blow up cars, parachute out of airplanes, and fieldstrip just about every gun known to man. He was taught the finer points of tradecraft, from making dead drops to recruiting and running spies. And like the other plebes, he had pounded into his head the credo of a successful spook: "If you slavishly follow the rule book, you'll fail." In fact, Baer learned, there is no textbook for what you'll encounter in the field. You innovate.

Baer approached his apprenticeship in espionage like a Rhodes scholar. After graduating from the Farm, he became fluent in French, Farsi, and Arabic. And he read—literature, history, and most of all CIA cables. He came to work early and left late after poring through the CIA's database of top secret and secure compartmentalized information, becoming an expert on groups like Hezbollah, the Muslim Brotherhood, and the Islamic Jihad. For nearly fifteen years he would serve on the front lines of the CIA's war on terrorism—from the back alleys of Beirut to the mountain passes of ancient Sogdiana in Tajikistan.

In his undercover work, he liked to live on the edge—in ways that sometimes were unnerving to his bosses even during the relatively freewheeling days of the Reagan administration, when the agency's then director, William Casey, lifted many restrictions on covert operations and expanded their use and funding globally.

In 1984, as a case officer assigned to the CIA's Counterterrorist Center, Baer proposed to drive a wedge between Syria and Iran, the world's largest state sponsor of terrorism. Baer's plan was to have CIA teams attach explosives to Syrian diplomats' cars in Europe that would burn rather than explode on ignition. Baer cabled his superiors that, after the CIA had released a fake claim of responsibility by an Iranian-backed terrorist group, Syria would be bound to retaliate. The CIA's director of operations, Clair George, "screamed at the top of his lungs to forget it," Baer recalled. "He said it would be over his dead body that the CIA would set off bombs in Western Europe." The anecdote perfectly captures the duality of Bob Baer. He was considered one of the CIA's best on-the-ground field officers in the Middle East, but he also kept his superiors up late at night worrying in cold sweats about what they forgot to tell him *not* to do.

All of which made him an unlikely choice in 1994 for the number two position at the heretofore irrelevant, if not moribund, Iraq Operations Group (IOG). But a series of unrelated events converged, resulting in management's desire to "shake things up" at the IOG, where Frank Anderson—the Near East Division chief who regarded the IOG as a graveyard for burned-out and second-rate case officers—would soon be pushed out the door. The CIA was badly in need of a win after the Aldrich Ames fiasco. Ames was the CIA analyst who, in February 1994, was *finally* caught after compromising some of the nation's most closely held secrets. When news broke that the agency had failed to detect this mole in its midst for nine years—despite the fact that Ames had purchased a new house with

$540,000 in cash, started wearing tailored suits, and began driving to work in a $50,000 Jaguar (on a $60,000-a-year salary)—the CIA was subjected to a withering torrent of criticism and, worse, ridicule. From the committee rooms of Congress to the editorial pages of the nation's leading newspapers, the question was asked: With the Cold War over, why exactly is the CIA still necessary? The higher-ups at Langley understood they had to answer that question—or at least change the subject.

It was during this tumult that Baer was summoned to headquarters and told by a senior official, "Listen, we are so fucked after Aldrich Ames that we have to prove we're not irrelevant. Let's get something on the books that changes the story and makes us look capable." And Iraq seemed like just the ticket. There were rumors that Saddam Hussein was stockpiling chemical and biological weapons, and that he was close to acquiring a nuclear weapon. And now he was threatening to reinvade Kuwait. By October 8, 1994, he had lined up sixty-four thousand troops in southern Iraq and positioned an armored division just twelve miles from the Kuwaiti border. Under intense U.S. pressure, Saddam pulled back most of the units he had deployed to the south. But the near-crisis underscored a critical shortcoming of U.S. intelligence: for the better part of a year, it had been completely "deaf" in Iraq.

"You have to understand what 'deaf' means," Baer explained to me. "It means there are no electronic intercepts listening in on Saddam or his inner circle. It means there are no human sources inside Iraq who are reporting back on what the army is up to. There aren't any in the neighboring countries. There's nothing coming out of Amman. There's nothing coming out of Kuwait, Saudi Arabia, or Turkey. And there's nothing coming out of northern Iraq. There's nothing. Saddam could die in his bed and we wouldn't know."

Baer says he decided to take the assignment with one goal in mind: cracking the Iraqi sound barrier. Like Frank Anderson, he says he believed that the presidential finding calling for regime change in Iraq was a bunch of hokum designed to appease the anti-Saddam "crazies" on Capitol Hill. But getting ears on Iraq, he believed, was achievable.

His job was supposed to be a managerial position, pinning him to a desk in Washington. But he wanted to eyeball the CIA's operation in Salahuddin. So, in September 1994, he hitched a ride to northern Iraq with a delegation from the Senate Intelligence Committee. When he arrived, he met with the two main Kurdish leaders, Massoud Barzani and Jalal Talabani, and spoke at length with Chalabi, who Baer says immediately made him an offer he found irresistible: if the CIA established a permanent base in Kurdistan, Chalabi would, in effect, become America's new set of ears in Iraq, providing hard intelligence—codes, documents, informants—on the Iraqi army. He even promised to bring active-duty Iraqi officers across Kurdish lines and prove their bona fides. Baer was dubious, since no intelligence worth disseminating had ever come out of Chalabi during his two years in northern Iraq. But because the CIA had nothing else going, Baer decided to give it a shot, telling Chalabi exactly what he expected.

"We want someone inside the military who can answer one question: Will Saddam invade Kuwait again? We want an agent in place to tell us if the Iraq army is going on full alert again. I want to know if a commander has been told to gas up his tank and head for the Kuwaiti border. That's the kind of heads-up we want," Baer said. Chalabi vowed he could deliver. It was on that premise that Baer says he agreed to give up his desk job—he knew he wasn't cut out for management anyway—and return to northern Iraq three months later. There was no mention of regime change, he says, nor did it occur to him, since no one believed Chalabi had the connections to pull off anything like *that*—"not even the dreamers."

Besides, Clinton's national security adviser, Tony Lake, had made it clear that the CIA was forbidden to light that fuse without first coordinating with him. Lake did not want the president dragged into a Bay of Pigs–style fiasco. But, of course, that's exactly what would happen. In retrospect, it's easy to see why, given how broken the CIA was at the time and given the characters involved—Bob Baer, the edgy, derring-do spy, and Ahmad Chalabi, the single-minded master manipulator. What's remarkable, if anything, is how quickly it all occurred. Within eight weeks of Baer's moving to Salahuddin, the CIA and Ahmad Chalabi had the Clinton administration teetering on the brink of war.

Baer and his team of three fellow case officers arrived in northern Iraq on January 21, 1995. They spent two days getting there in the back of trucks only to discover that Chalabi had procured for them a house with no electricity, water, or heat. It was so cold the first night, Baer recalls, their canteens froze. The next day, Chalabi introduced the bedraggled Baer to an Iraqi major general who had defected and crossed into Kurdistan. The general, Wafiq al-Samarrai, was once Saddam's intelligence chief but had now joined Chalabi's Iraqi National Congress. Baer says that when he sat down with al-Samarrai he had no idea anyone was plotting to move against Saddam. But that's precisely what the general proposed. He told Baer that he was in communication with other disaffected commanders who controlled three Iraqi combat units and that they had a plan to move on Baghdad, which they believed would force Saddam to flee to a stronghold near his hometown of Tikrit. There a fourth unit, led by a colonel and a column of twelve tanks, would drive to Saddam's compound and capture him. It occurred to Baer that he had been played by Chalabi, lured into a coup plot with promises of hard intelligence on Saddam's army—a Chalabi bait and switch. But Baer says he was intrigued and decided to cable headquarters, informing his bosses of al-Samarrai's intentions. The reply from Langley: "This is not a plan."

In Baer's mind, that message left the door open for further discussions. "This is not a plan" is different from "This is not what we want" or "Close it down." So Baer continued to meet with the general, who supplied additional details, including the names of the four commanders and their unit designations. They all checked out in CIA databases. Al-Samarrai also sketched the family trees of the officers involved and showed Baer how everyone was related by blood—and therefore trustworthy. As for al-Samarrai, he wanted to know whether the United States would support a post-Saddam regime. Baer sent a second cable to CIA headquarters asking for their reaction. This time Baer got no answer. Over a three-week period, Baer says, he sent six comprehensive reports delineating the general's objectives. But headquarters never replied to a single one.

He was incredulous. Either Langley was more screwed up than even he realized, or he had really pissed off someone this time and was getting shut out. "Fuck it," he said to himself. And, in what can only be described as an epochal Mad Max moment, he decided to interpret Langley's absence of no as a yes; in not explicitly rejecting the general's plan, Baer reasoned, headquarters was approving it—more or less. Thus, when al-Samarrai asked him again about Washington's intentions, Baer—speaking in purposefully ambiguous Arabic—encouraged the general to proceed with his scheme, assuring him, "Washington wants Saddam out." Baer acknowledges he was operating on the edge of his orders, "out where the bright fires burn." But in his mind he kept falling back on U.S. policy: both Bush and Clinton had signed findings authorizing the overthrow of Saddam.

Chalabi knew that Baer was getting the runaround from his masters in

Langley and, though the stakes were high, he couldn't help but delight in the agency's dysfunction. Chalabi loved to see the CIA trip over its own feet and, in fact, had come to count on it. In this case, he saw an opportunity to roll his coup plan into Samarrai's. Chalabi had previously shopped his plan to the Clinton administration, but the administration had rejected it. Basically, it envisioned small-scale attacks along the northern lines of Saddam's army. Kurdish fighters belonging to Massoud Barzani and Jalal Talabani would lead the assault, with Chalabi's INC militia joining in. A simultaneous attack from the south would be launched as well. Chalabi predicted that because Iraq was fraying under the stress of UN sanctions, with frequent blackouts and widespread shortages of basic commodities, units in the armed forces would not fight to preserve Saddam's government and would join the revolt. While Barzani and Talabani hadn't even agreed to participate, Chalabi told Baer that once he threw down the gauntlet he believed they would. At Baer's suggestion, Chalabi picked a date to roll: March 4 at 10:00 p.m.

As for the southern front, Chalabi hoped to man it with fighters from the Badr Brigade, the army of Iraqi Shiites that had been supplied and trained by Iran and whose participation would require Tehran's assent. For that, Chalabi tapped into his growing network of Iranian contacts. Over the previous year and a half, Iranian intelligence and security officials had been engaging Chalabi at an ever higher level, sending officials from Iran to Kurdistan to see him. Within the Iranian security apparatus, however, there remained a profound uncertainty about him and the INC, he says. But Iran's degree of interest continued to arch upward. So in late 1994 and early 1995, Chalabi says, he was able to meet with officials "at the deepest levels."

During a series of encounters, Chalabi explained to the Iranians that he was getting ready to move against Saddam and wanted Tehran's support. Minimally, he told them, he wanted the Badr Brigade—or any of its members who were so inclined—to be able to leave Iran for Iraq and form the southern front of his planned insurrection. He predicted it would be a cakewalk. "I said, 'If you go in the south, Saddam will lose because his army is hungry, underpaid, and unwilling to fight,'" Chalabi told me.

The Iranians were highly skeptical of both Chalabi and his predictions. There was a faction within Iran's security establishment that still considered him a CIA lackey, and a secular one at that. Why help someone who was under the control of the United States? The far more serious concern had to do with the Iraqi opposition itself. The Iranians had little faith in its military capabilities, while they had great respect for Saddam's. To them, throwing Iran's weight behind a militarily doomed CIA-backed effort might tie up Saddam's forces for a while. But ultimately he would survive and Tehran's reputation would suffer.

"By going along with this effort," Chalabi said of the Iranians' concern, "it would undermine their own credibility in the region and in Iran that they were cooperating with the Great Satan. After all, Saddam continued to support the PLO [Yassir Arafat's Palestinian Liberation Organization] and had credibility with the Arab left."

If Iran were to get involved in any operation, its officials made clear to Chalabi, Saddam's removal had to be more or less assured. To them, that narrowed the options down to one. "They thought the only way to get rid of Saddam—since they couldn't do it themselves for eight years—was to get the United States to do it," Chalabi said of his contemporary discussions with Iranian intelligence and security officials. In other words, Chalabi said, the Iranians wanted the United States to invade Iraq—with boots on the ground. "They did not have serious expectations that the Iraqi opposition could overthrow Saddam," Chalabi said. "I believed that we could, but they thought the only way would be to get the U.S. to do it."

In 1995, however, a U.S. invasion was not in the cards. The Clinton administration wanted no part of that, and everyone knew it. An insurrection was the only play. But no one believed that Washington would throw its weight behind Chalabi's plan, either. And if it did, as unlikely as that was, then how could Iranian officials be sure the ensuing post-Saddam government would be no less hostile to Tehran? Their fear of U.S. designs had them tied up in knots, and Chalabi was getting nowhere.

It was at about this time that he says he met the equivalent of his Richard Perle in Iran, a man by the name of Mohammad Jafari. In the years ahead, Jafari would become the powerful deputy head of Iran's National Security Council and a senior commander of the Quds Force, the elite Iranian paramilitary organization the United States would later accuse of orchestrating attacks on U.S. troops in Iraq after the 2003 U.S. invasion. But in 1995 Jafari was only a field commander—albeit a rising star who, Chalabi judged, "could operate within the Iranian system in effective ways quietly."

Jafari believed Saddam was an enemy Iran could neither tolerate nor eradicate on its own. So, unlike most of his colleagues, he was in favor of the United States helping the Iraqi opposition get rid of him. It was a risk worth taking, and he thought Chalabi was just the person to get the Americans to do it. "He saw me as an energetic person who was on the front lines in Iraq with links in the United States," Chalabi explained. "He thought that I could harness the United States for the effort to bring down Saddam."

With Jafari's prodding, the Iranians signaled they would consider committing the resources of the Badr Brigade—but only if the United States also took part in the action. Chalabi insisted that the Americans would have no choice. "I told them that if we attack, the United States will have to make a choice—whether or not to let us be slaughtered. I told them the Americans wouldn't let us be slaughtered."

Chalabi has long denied that he hoped to stampede the Clinton administration into supporting his insurrection. But his representations to the Iranians seemed to suggest exactly that. Regardless, the Iranians wanted a rock-solid assurance. It was at about this juncture that Chalabi went for broke, according to Bob Baer. In early March 1995, just a few days before his planned insurrection was to begin, Chalabi met with two Iranian Ministry of Intelligence officials at his office in Salahuddin. The account of what happened next comes not from Chalabi, but from former CIA officials and what Baer says he was able to piece together from subsequent U.S. intelligence sources and investigators of this incident.

In this account, Chalabi told the Iranians that the United States had once and for all decided to get rid of Saddam—to assassinate him. The National Security Council (NSC) had dispatched a team to carry out the hit and had instructed Chalabi to ask the Iranian government for help. At one point during the meeting, Chalabi got up to take a phone call in another room, leaving the Iranians alone to read a letter left on top of his desk. It was written on NSC stationery and addressed to "Dr. Chalabi." It said that a "direct action" team, led by Robert Pope (a fictitious name), was en route to northern Iraq and had "the authorization to conduct lethal operations" to remove Saddam. "We need your full support, Dr. Chalabi," the letter concluded.

It was obviously a forgery, Baer says, one that Chalabi concocted to dupe Iran into throwing its support behind the coup plot. And the Iranian agents took the bait, hurriedly returning to their safe house in Kurdistan and sending an encrypted message to Tehran about the supposed assassination plot, a message that a former U.S. intelligence official confirms was intercepted by the National Security Agency (NSA), the Pentagon's global eavesdropping facility. "We just saw this letter," the Iranian cable began.

Baer says he unwittingly lent credibility to what he calls the Chalabi charade: Chalabi knew that Baer was prohibited from holding any private meetings with Iranian officials, but there was nothing to stop him from being *seen* by them. So he asked Baer if he would be willing to walk across the parking lot in front of his office in Salahuddin just prior to Chalabi's meeting with the Iranians and in plain view of them. The idea, Chalabi told him, was to telegraph CIA support for his planned coup. There was no such support, but Baer readily agreed to mislead the Iranians. He figured if Iran fell for it, that was their problem, not his. So, at the appointed time and completely unaware of the allegedly forged letter that Chalabi was about to show the Iranians, Baer appeared outside the INC office building and—with unshaven stubble, combat boots, and a blue vest with an AK-47 slung over his shoulder—he walked right into Chalabi's con.

Baer, however, immediately proceeded to perpetrate a con of his own. Just as Chalabi was meeting with the Iranians, Baer met with representatives of the Badr Brigade, knowing full well that whatever he told them would be reported to their Iranian benefactors. "I told them any plan to get rid of Saddam, we support," Baer says. "Then they asked me, 'Do you support *this* plan?'"—referring to Chalabi's insurrection operation. "Any plan," Baer replied. "We can't live with this fucker anymore."

If Baer had come to Iraq only to collect intelligence, as he asserts, he was now doing everything he could—wittingly and otherwise—to start a war against Saddam, including making representations that far exceeded his orders. "There are no good guys in this story," Baer conceded.

Chalabi denies that he ever fabricated a written communication from the NSC or any part of the U.S. government. "I have no idea what NSC stationery even looks like," he asserted to me. But he acknowledged that he did meet the Iranian intelligence officers, seeking their support for his planned insurrection. And with Baer's cameo appearance in the parking lot, he says, the pieces were falling into place.

But then on March 2, 1995, just forty-eight hours before the scheduled launch of the insurrection, the NSA in Washington intercepted a second transmission, revealing that Saddam had gotten wind of the pending coup attempt. He had put his army on full alert, canceled all leaves, and sent elite Republican Guard units thundering toward northern Iraq. U.S. intelligence also picked up activity by the Iranians. Their intelligence and security personnel were flowing into northern Iraq, while Iranian armor was dispatched to the Iraqi border in the south to support the Badr Brigade forces that Chalabi had requested. In addition, Turkish armed forces were preparing to move into Kurdistan. The three largest armies in the Middle East were on a collision course, mobilized for a coup attempt that they all believed the United States was behind. Ahmad Chalabi had really outdone himself this time. In an effort to orchestrate a joint Iranian-U.S. operation against Saddam, he had the entire region girding for war.

The White House was caught completely unawares. Until Clinton's national security team was briefed that morning on the intercept, no one at the National Security Council, the Joint Chiefs of Staff, or the State Department had ever heard of Wafiq al-Samarrai, the Iraqi major general who broke ranks from Saddam's army. Nor had they a whiff of Chalabi's scheduled insurrection. As it turned out, not only had CIA headquarters in Langley failed to respond to any of Baer's six cables outlining the operation, or to a seventh specifying the precise date and time that Chalabi intended to roll, but the CIA's chief of the Near East Division, Steven Richter, had never bothered to pass any of the cables on to the NSC—even though he had made himself the sole channel of communication with the NSC. As a result, the Clinton administration found itself perched precariously on the edge of war.

In the early hours of March 2, 1995, the president's national security team convened an emergency meeting in the basement offices of the West Wing, where the Situation Room is located. Among those present were National Security Adviser Tony Lake; NSC adviser Martin Indyk; the NSC's senior director for intelligence, George Tenet; three members of the Joint Chiefs of Staff via secure videoconference; and the twenty-nine-year-old NSC director for Persian Gulf Affairs, Kenneth Pollack. Pollack says a palpable sense of anger and fear hung over the room as the team grappled with the unfolding crisis.

"There was intense anger at the people who blindsided us because there had been explicit instructions that this was not supposed to happen," Pollack recalled. "This is exactly what Tony Lake and the principals were afraid of—that the opposition would go off half-cocked, try an operation that they weren't prepared to handle themselves, and the United States would find itself in a position of either having to go in and rescue them, which would mean a massive American military intervention, which we were not interested in and not ready for, or else allow them to be slaughtered in a second Bay of Pigs, which was the absolute last thing that anyone wanted. At the same time, there was tremendous fear, because it seemed clear that this thing was going ahead, and the Iraqis knew about it. And so there was a real, profound sense that perhaps we were already on the horns of that dilemma."

As those present sifted through their options, they realized just how badly they had been painted into a corner. Pollack recounted, "If you start thinking about, 'Okay, how do you prevent these guys from getting slaughtered?,' then you realize how screwed you are. The airpower was certainly inadequate. If you've only got a wing of aircraft up in Turkey, which is all that we had, they're not going to be able to stop three or four Iraqi divisions all by themselves. So what do you do? Do you start flying aircraft from the United States—B1s and B2s? Would we have to intervene with ground forces to prevent their slaughter? Do you send in a brigade of the 82nd Airborne, para-drop them in the hopes that this is gonna stop the Iraqis? This was the United States' worst nightmare, to be dragged into a war completely unprepared, especially since we had made an explicit decision that we didn't want to fight a war."

And now, Chalabi—through Bob Baer—was conveying a message to the Americans from the Iranians, who wanted to know whether the United States would attack their forces if they participated in the insurrection. Tony Lake, the president's national security adviser, was furious. Using a secure line, he got the acting CIA director, Admiral William Studeman, on the phone and demanded a full and complete briefing. He also made it clear that he wanted this thing turned off—now. Lake then took the unusual step of personally sending a very clear and curt cable to Bob Baer from the White House. He instructed Baer to deliver the following message immediately to the Iraqi and Kurdish leaders in the north: "The action you have planned for this weekend has been totally compromised. We believe there is a high risk of failure. Any decision to proceed will be on your own."

When Baer read the cable to Chalabi, it was less than thirty-six hours before the planned coup was timed to go down. Chalabi had hoped to hustle the United States into supporting the insurrection—indeed, echoing the Bay of Pigs. He had been assuring al-Samarrai and the Kurds that the U.S. government would provide close air support. But he now knew American involvement was dead in the water. Gone, too, was the hope of reeling in the

Iranians and their Badr Brigade of Iraqi Shiites. Without the United States, Iran would lend no support to the operation. One of the two Kurdish leaders, Massoud Barzani, also pulled out, taking with him his guerrilla force of approximately fifteen thousand.

"What will you do?" Baer asked Chalabi.

"I'll let you know in due course," Chalabi responded, upon which he went to see Jalal Talabani, the other Kurdish leader (who would later become the first president of post-Saddam Iraq).

"I said to Jalal," Chalabi recalled, "'We have an opportunity to fight Saddam. Are we going to squander that?' Jalal thought not. He was very happy."

Chalabi joined his militia of three thousand with Talabani's fifteen thousand Peshmerga guerrillas, and they proceeded to engage Saddam's army on the battlefield some fifty miles south of Erbil, the capital of Iraqi Kurdistan, acquitting themselves well. Baer witnessed the battle from the rooftop of his house, peering through a pair of binoculars. The hybrid INC-Kurdish forces annihilated two Iraqi infantry brigades and captured a battery of disaffected Iraqi soldiers, including the brigade commander. Talabani's fighters also turned back an Iraqi Republican Guard force bringing in reinforcements, destroying an armored personnel carrier and several troop transports. But with no U.S. or Iranian support, and dwindling ammunition and other supplies, the assault soon petered out. Saddam rounded up al-Samarrai's accomplices and sent in elite Republican Guard units to roll back the Kurdish advances. Chalabi himself was forced to retreat to his sanctuary in the no-fly zone. But he, too, was a happy man.

"Think about it," he said to me. "I started our operations in the north in 1993 with nothing. Two years later, we were fighting Saddam in a military campaign."

The fact that his promised insurrection of Iraqi army units never materialized was beside the point, he says: "I always knew it would be only a battle. You have to understand, I was not motivated by the prospect of immediate success. I was motivated by the fact that we must demonstrate to the world that we are prepared to fight Saddam and that we are prepared to die in the process. We may not have the resources now to win. But it showed we had the courage to do it. We were finally doing something that Saddam and the people of Iraq could understand. That was the critical issue for me at the time. This fact is never understood."

Equally important, he says, the March 1995 operation "enormously" enhanced his credibility with the Iranians. It showed them that, rather than being an American stooge, he was in fact his own man, someone who had disputes with Washington and who was willing to go his own way. That was key, he said, in his campaign to win Tehran's future trust and backing.

As for his American patrons and protectors, Chalabi felt little obligation toward them despite the fact that they were paying the INC's bills and that their patrolling of the skies ensured his safe haven in northern Iraq. "So what?" Chalabi snapped. "They didn't do it for me. They did it for their own purposes."

Baer was ordered back to Washington, where the Justice Department launched a criminal investigation of him for conspiracy to violate the federal murder-for-hire statutes. If convicted, Baer could have faced the death penalty or life imprisonment for the supposed assassination attempt of Saddam. Nonetheless, Baer was half amused: he was under investigation for the attempted murder of a man who had prompted two presidents to sign lethal findings authorizing his overthrow.

After more than a year of digging through Baer's life and records, the government cleared him of all charges; the CIA even awarded him a merit unit citation for his work in Iraq. But his career at the agency never fully recovered, and in 1997, after twenty-one years as a field officer, he quit.

In retrospect, Baer now believes that the Wafiq al-Samarrai affair was in all likelihood an elaborate Chalabi swindle. Chalabi realized the Americans wanted a Sunni general to take over from Saddam; that was the brass ring. So he got his own general, al-Samarrai. In fact, Baer says, when Chalabi moved to northern Iraq in January 1995, he had already more than inferred Washington's desires. He had learned about something known as Silver Bullet, a plot the CIA was then directing out of its Amman, Jordan, station. It was the second and most important track of the CIA's two-pronged strategy toward Saddam, one organized under the auspices of another Iraqi exile, Ayad Allawi, a former Ba'athist who had survived a gruesome assassination attempt by Saddam's henchmen.

Baer says Chalabi knew all of the plot's operational details, correctly identifying the key conspirators in the scheme—everyone from the military officers involved to the couriers who were passing secret messages between them and the CIA station in Amman. Baer distinctly remembers the conversation in which Chalabi spilled what he knew. "He was almost gleeful," Baer recalled of Chalabi's demeanor.

Chalabi warned that if he knew about Silver Bullet, then so did Saddam. Chalabi was right about that, and about the consequences for its participants. But, as Baer recalls, the subtext of Chalabi's admonition was to make an entirely different point. "The implication was clear," Baer recalled. "Ahmad was saying, 'Stick with me. You want a Sunni general? Yours is compromised. Here, I have one.'"

Baer now believes there was much less to al-Samarrai than he had initially thought. The general never delivered a single shred of intelligence about the Iraqi military, Baer says, nor did he ever provide independent corroboration that he was communicating with any of his purported accomplices. "We couldn't even get them to take a piss on the side of their tanks at a certain time so we could take a picture from the satellite," Baer declared. Chalabi knew that the CIA was deaf in Iraq and was therefore unable to check out al-Samarrai or any of his claims.

"I wanted to believe this thing would work," Baer now says. "I was hoping with time I would be able to verify if al-Samarrai was for real or not. But it all happened too fast." He adds that on the day of Chalabi's insurrection, al-Samarrai donned his general's uniform and paced back and forth with nowhere to go. He looked preposterous, Baer recalls, a corpulent, mustachioed pretender straight out of central casting's department for tin-pot dictators.

"It was all a big ponzi scheme," Baer says, "like going into business with Bernie Madoff. You go in with the capital and he goes in with the experience. When it's over, he leaves with the capital and you've got the experience. Chalabi pulled a giant con on us."

I asked Baer if he harbored any personal animosity toward Chalabi after the murder-for-hire investigation and the premature end to his career.

"I'm not mad at him," Baer answered, "because I would have done exactly the same thing. You don't think if I had a chance to get rid of Saddam I would have sacrificed Chalabi himself? In a heartbeat, I would have. I mean, that's the way the game's played."

TEN

Despite the March 1995 debacle in northern Iraq, the game between Chalabi and the CIA changed remarkably little. Langley did not sever ties with its man in Kurdistan, nor did it even trim the Iraqi National Congress's budget of $340,000 a month. But headquarters did send Chalabi a cable. "This cannot happen again if we are to work together," admonished the missive, adding meekly, "The task now is to regroup around our common objective"—the isolation of Saddam.

Toward that end, Langley dispatched a new base chief to northern Iraq, Warren Marik, a Chalabi enthusiast who had spent most of his twenty years in the agency fighting the old Soviet Union. Marik admired Chalabi for his energy and intellect, and credited him with having helped keep the pressure on Saddam's regime for the previous three years. But Marik was among a shrinking and increasingly marginalized cadre of Chalabi supporters within the agency. The more common view, especially among senior officials, was one of wariness over his coziness with Iran. A growing number of case officers found him to be personally untrustworthy. An on-site audit of Chalabi's operations in northern Iraq later in 1995 reinforced their suspicions.

The audit was conducted by John Maguire, the case officer who had observed Chalabi at the INC's 1992 Vienna conference and took a dislike to his "staff-splitting." Even without that encounter, Maguire and Chalabi were never destined for an easy relationship. For one thing, Maguire was impervious to Chalabi's usual powers of charm. Chalabi typically beguiled his CIA interlocutors with his vast knowledge of history, impressing them during their downtime with stories of eleventh-century Iran or discourses on how the differences between Platonic and Aristotelian thought mirrored the sectarian divisions in the Middle East. But that kind of conversation had little impact on Maguire, the antithesis of Chalabi in almost every way. Whereas Chalabi was the well-educated scion of privilege, Maguire had grown up on the streets of Baltimore, the son of a Teamster. He helped pay his way through college with a job repossessing cars in some of the city's toughest neighborhoods. And when he finished his studies, he became a cop with the local police department. He was a bomb expert with its SWAT team when the CIA recruited him in 1982. Maguire could talk for hours about hot-wiring speedboats in Beirut or the "brisance" (the CIA's term of art for explosive power) of Semtex and C-4. But he could not care less about ancient Iran or Chalabi's intellectual prowess.

At six foot three, with broad shoulders and a thick, bushy Fu Manchu mustache, Maguire may not have had a PhD attached to his name, but from the moment he arrived in Kurdistan, he was clear-eyed about whom he worked for—and it wasn't Ahmad Chalabi. So when the CIA tasked him to conduct a routine audit of the INC to see how the CIA's money was being spent, he figured he owed Chalabi no heads-up. And, rather than limit his review to the INC's books, he decided to personally inspect its propaganda operation—the television and radio stations, as well as the building where its newspaper was supposed to be printed. Propaganda, after all, was one of the INC's main directives, accounting for much of its $4-million-a-year budget.

Chalabi in the past had effectively discouraged Americans from visiting the facilities, citing security concerns. But since the CIA was paying the bills, Maguire decided to ignore that tradition and, donning local garb and a three-day-old stubble to blend in, made a series of surprise visits. What he found, he told me, amounted to a Potemkin village: "a radio broadcast that was not broadcasting, and a newspaper printing operation that was not printing a newspaper." When he went to the newspaper facility, Maguire recalled, "there was only one employee and he told me he hadn't been paid in a year and it had been eight months since the last newspaper was printed. I sent people into Baghdad to see if they could find a newspaper. The INC was supposed to produce five thousand copies every second day. They couldn't find a single one."

Chalabi had been tasked to collect intelligence in October 1994. But Maguire says the INC never produced any intelligence of value and offered up a string of mostly low-level defectors who were "puffed up"—coached—to make it seem like they knew more than they actually did.

"Chalabi was in constant search of the flavor of the month," it seemed to Maguire. "What are the Americans looking for today? If it was weapons of mass destruction guys, he'd find us one and puff him up into something important." It was all designed to make Chalabi the CIA's "indispensable man," Maguire believed. Chalabi denies it, but Maguire says the procurement of dubious deserters would prove to be a case of "what's past is prologue," a harbinger of Chalabi's coming controversy with Iraqi defectors.

Maguire also pored through the INC's books and found that Chalabi was "moving money all around as he saw fit. He'd spend it on one thing, but account for it in another way. It was like two sets of books." Was Chalabi—the convicted bank embezzler—lining his pockets? the case officer wondered. After an exhaustive audit, however, the conclusion Maguire reached was an unequivocal no. For one thing, it made no sense. There were a lot easier and safer ways to embezzle money than by sitting in a war zone, taking on Saddam's army. Moreover, Chalabi never took a salary from the CIA and even spent some of his own fortune and that of his wife to help finance the INC's operations in northern Iraq, according to a former CIA official who worked closely with the Iraqi opposition in those days.

So, what *was* Chalabi doing with the CIA's money? The answer had been hiding in plain sight: he was spending it on his own agenda—on a security force, for example, that was curiously large and very much like his own private militia, and on trying to cultivate his own intelligence network inside Iraq, the INC equivalent of Charles de Gaulle's Free French Forces. Chalabi never made much headway with that, CIA officials say, but to Maguire, that was neither here nor there. The bottom line was this: the CIA had enlisted Chalabi to promote the *United States'* foreign policy goals, but instead Chalabi was using the CIA's money to promote *his personal* goals and ambitions. To Maguire, that was a misappropriation of CIA funds, plain and simple. (In his interviews with me, Chalabi acknowledged—indeed, boasted—that he was using the CIA for his own purposes. But he insisted, "They got more than their money's worth from me.")

Maguire confronted Chalabi, telling him, "Look, Ahmad, we've got a serious problem. I went around and looked at these places and discovered you're billing us for a radio station that's not on the air. I'm paying for a newspaper facility that's not printing newspapers. I'm not paying for that anymore."

Chalabi became enraged, Maguire says, barking, "You don't understand our work. It's expensive. You've got to be able to cultivate sources of information."

Maguire disagreed, and slashed the INC's budget. He also wrote up a report detailing his findings. The response: a flood of recriminations from Capitol Hill, with Representative Jack Murtha and other members of Congress accusing the agency of trying to sabotage the INC and demanding a full accounting of Maguire's conclusions.

"He had such a wide-ranging network on Capitol Hill," Maguire recalled with amazement, "that he could pull all sorts of levers and press any number of buttons. Before we knew what hit us, we were being blitzed and then tied up in knots answering Congress's questions."

It was another indication of things to come, Maguire noted drily. But at the time, Maguire recalls, he felt mystified as to why the White House never came to the agency's defense. After all, no one was more furious at Chalabi than Bill Clinton's national security adviser, Tony Lake.

"I think the White House felt really vulnerable," Maguire surmised. "Publicly, it professed to want the regime in Baghdad overthrown. But when Chalabi engineered the opportunity to do something about it, the administration backed away. If that was exposed, it would create a political firestorm for Democrats. They would be accused of letting Saddam off the hook. I know there was a furious exchange of ass-covering memos about this between the White House and the CIA. I think in the end the calculated decision was made just to quash everything. The last thing the CIA or the Clinton White House wanted was for this story to leak to the press."

The story, however, eventually did leak to the press—by Chalabi's hand. But before it did, Saddam would have his revenge, beginning in 1996 when key elements of U.S. policy began to unravel. The first of those elements to go was the CIA operation to overthrow Saddam. Maguire, after his stint in northern Iraq, was assigned to the CIA station in Amman to head up the team that was overseeing the covert action from Jordan. As he tells it, by the summer of 1996 the agency had spent millions of dollars developing well-placed contacts inside the Iraqi military and security apparatus to carry out the plot known as Silver Bullet. That moniker, though, was actually a misnomer, Maguire says, as it incorrectly suggested that the CIA was cultivating a straightforward solution to the vexing problem of Saddam Hussein—putting a bullet through his head. In fact, the actual plan—part of an overall strategy code-named Achilles—was much more elaborate and improvisational than its informal name would suggest, focusing on what the agency regarded as Saddam's most deadly weakness: his perception of invincibility.

"Iraq was like a shark tank," explained Maguire. "If it looked like Saddam was weakened, he'd be vulnerable. The only thing that kept him in power was the perception of complete authority. The plan was to rupture that perception of complete authority."

To do that, the agency had recruited some twenty Iraqi officers—mostly colonels and brigadier generals—in the army, the air force, the Republican Guard, even the Special Republican Guard. In all, the mutinous officers had several hundred men loyal to them, including many from armored units that were prepared to drive into Baghdad and fire on Saddam's palace. The number of conspirators was too few to oust Saddam in one fell swoop, the agency realized, but enough to start a hell of a fistfight in Baghdad. Maguire figured that if he and his co-conspirators could get that far, they had a chance of winning over more and more defectors, and perhaps even getting a loyalist from Saddam's inner circle to turn on him.

"These guys in the inner circle were wired tight," Maguire said of his reasoning. "They used drugs. A lot of them were on antidepressants. They were murderers. They were greedy. And they were conspiratorial. Our view was, 'Let's stress the shit out of 'em. Light 'em up. Make their life suck so bad that they'd be afraid to close their eyes because they didn't know who to trust. Shrink their circle of trust. Tighten it, squeeze it, and shrink the circle of those that are on the life raft with Saddam—those that are really bloody, and those that have to hold on to Saddam because they had no other way out. And, as you squeeze, you'll force other officers away from that circle, because those who don't have bloodied hands will have to make a choice: Do I want to align myself with these guys who look like they might not make it, or do I want to sit on the fence, or do I want to join up and say, 'Fuck it, I'm going to go for broke and see if I can come out on the winning side'?" Even if Saddam eventually put down the mutiny, Maguire figured, it would still be a lose-lose situation for the dictator, because the plot's very existence would serve to undermine Saddam's perception of total control.

But when Chalabi got wind of the supposedly top-secret operation, he tried to persuade the CIA to shut it down, asking Richard Perle to arrange a meeting for him with CIA director John Deutch. That meeting occurred in March 1996 in a hotel suite on the thirteenth floor of the Ritz Carlton in Pentagon City. Chalabi arrived with a gift, a book by Hanna Batatu about the social and political history of modern Iraq. Batatu's book is a veritable tome: 1,283 pages long, written in tiny print with scores of appendixes, maps, and illustrations. There is one index for families, one for tribes, and another for personal names that alone runs twenty pages long. And there are numerous tables detailing, among other things, the old central committees of the Iraq Communist Party, the Free Officers, and the first and second Ba'ath Parties. As Chalabi handed the magnum opus to Deutch, he told the CIA director, "Iraq is complicated. Read this." He just as easily could have been referring to himself.

Both men laughed and then engaged in some friendly banter about their alma mater, MIT, and their respective majors: mathematics and, for Deutch, chemistry. Finally, Chalabi turned to the business of the CIA's coup plot, telling Deutch, "I came here to see you for one reason: to warn you. You are a superpower and you do whatever you want. But it is my duty to tell you that you are weaving a conspiracy in Baghdad that is known to Iraqi intelligence. We have information on this, so watch out." Chalabi says the CIA director was stunned. His aide, Steven Richter, turned yellow. "The blood drained from his face," Chalabi says. After what seemed like thirty seconds of silence, Chalabi finally spoke up: "Thank you very much. That's what I wanted to tell you." And then he stood up and left.

CIA officials remember the conversation differently, recalling that the focus of Chalabi's comments was on Chalabi. He made a pitch that he was the CIA's go-to exile, and that whatever the agency might be planning against Saddam, it could not possibly succeed without him.

Both accounts of the meeting seem plausible, and they are not mutually exclusive. Regardless, headquarters pushed forward with the planned coup, even predicting that Saddam would be gone no later than July. But, as Chalabi had warned, Saddam's Mukhabarat had gotten wind of the plot and, after stringing it along for a while to uncover its full extent, sprang its trap in June 1996, arresting two hundred army officers and executing eighty. To add insult to injury, Iraqi intelligence officers made contact with the CIA using captured communications equipment the CIA had smuggled into Baghdad. Their message was directed to the Iraqi general who had been orchestrating the planned coup from the CIA station in Amman. "We've got your three sons," they told the general, Mohammed Abdullah al-Shahwani. "We're standing next to one of them. We know what's going on. We know what you've done." They wanted al-Shahwani to return to Baghdad. "We'll release your sons if you trade yourself for them." But al-Shahwani and the CIA knew the release would never happen, so al-Shahwani stayed in Amman, remaining stoic despite knowing full well the fate that awaited his sons. Indeed, after several weeks of brutal torture—all of which was tape-recorded and filed away until the tapes were discovered following the 2003 invasion of Iraq—al-Shahwani's three sons died at the hands of Saddam's henchmen.

For the CIA, the spectacular and ruthless decimation of its covert operation was an unmitigated disaster, a black day in the history of the agency. But Saddam wasn't done yet. Two months later, in late August 1996, he capitalized on a shooting war that had broken out between the two main, perennially feuding Kurdish factions, forging a temporary alliance with one of the Kurdish leaders, Massoud Barzani. Saddam then took aim at Chalabi and the INC, dispatching thirty thousand troops to Erbil, the northern Iraqi city where Chalabi's INC was now headquartered after Chalabi's own falling-out with Barzani. Two Republican Guard divisions and three regular Iraqi army divisions rolled into Erbil and overran the city in a matter of hours. Chalabi was in London at the time, meeting with the CIA about the situation in northern Iraq. He was sitting in the basement of the U.S. embassy when he learned that more than two hundred of his men had been lined up and shot dead.

"It was a tragedy for us," Chalabi recalled with a subdued heaviness in his voice. "'Twas a devastating blow."

Saddam's troops also seized the INC's computers and identified everyone who belonged to the group. Their lives were now in jeopardy. Chalabi and the CIA temporarily set aside their growing animosity and worked feverishly together to get the INC's remaining six thousand members airlifted from Turkey to safety in Guam. But the damage had been done: during one hot, bloody summer, Saddam had eviscerated everything the CIA had spent years and millions of dollars building. Saddam emerged stronger from the episode, while the Kurds were crippled and both the Iraqi opposition and all U.S. intelligence personnel were driven from Kurdistan.

Frank Anderson, the agency's division chief who had never liked the presidential finding on regime change in the first place, turned out to be right. The CIA could not do covertly what George H. W. Bush did not do in 1991 with 700,000 U.S. and coalition forces sitting on Saddam's doorstep. The Iraqi dictator was just too smart and ruthless for anything the CIA could cook up.

For Chalabi, losing his foothold in northern Iraq was a huge setback. For the Central Intelligence Agency, it was the end of its Iraqi National Congress experiment. By the end of 1996, the agency had decided it would cut off the group's funding and sever all ties with Chalabi. "There was a breakdown in trust," the CIA's then deputy director, George Tenet, would later explain, "and we never wanted to have anything to do with him anymore."

Top CIA officials blamed Chalabi for betraying the failed coup, believing he had sabotaged it lest the country wind up in the hands of a Sunni general. "Everyone at the CIA believed that," a former intelligence official familiar with the failed plot told me. "And it certainly was in keeping with Ahmad's modus operandi: the ends justify the means, in this case the end being Ahmad Chalabi in charge of Iraq. That's the key. Everything I've seen about Ahmad is not about creating a wonderful, democratic Iraq. He's about creating an Iraq in which he is in charge."

Chalabi denied any role in exposing the CIA plot. In fact, since the 2003 invasion of Iraq the CIA has learned that one of its own couriers, an Egyptian smuggler—and not Chalabi—was the real culprit. But in the latter part of 1996 it wouldn't have mattered anyway. By then, the agency's mistrust and anger toward Chalabi already ran too deep. Headquarters not only intended to shut down the INC but also issued a "burn notice" against Chalabi personally. CIA personnel were directed to have no further contact whatsoever with him and to disregard any intelligence he might offer in the future. As far as the CIA was concerned, Ahmad Chalabi was dead to them.

Six years earlier, the agency had plucked Chalabi out of obscurity. Now, they figured, without U.S. backing he would just fade away—return to his home in Mayfair and take up the life of a parlor exile. But, once again, the CIA underestimated Ahmad Chalabi. They understood little of his mettle or his motives, and even less of his capacity for righteous indignation. To Chalabi, killing off the INC in the wake of Saddam's attack was a monstrous injustice—a betrayal—and it left him bitter and vengeful.

"I was angry, very angry," he said, the malice still resonant in his voice more than a decade later. "In true fashion, the CIA was like the umbrella and the insurance company. They're around when the sun is shining. But as soon as it rains, they take the umbrella away and cancel the policy."

Chalabi still had a country to reclaim. On that, he says, he never wavered. But first the CIA would have to pay for its perfidy. Anger, to paraphrase *King Lear*, has its privilege.

ELEVEN

Driven out of northern Iraq by Saddam's forces and cut off in Washington by the CIA, Ahmad Chalabi was once again living in England full-time with his wife and four children. He hadn't seen much of them during the four years he was based in Kurdistan, an absence that weighed heavily on his family, especially the children, who were haunted by the fear that something bad might happen to their father. They were elated to have him home. But, as always, Chalabi's mind lay elsewhere. Alone in the spacious sitting room of his Mayfair flat, he looked out at the overcast skies above the chilly streets of London in the winter of 1996–1997 and contemplated his next move—against the CIA.

"I made a determination," Chalabi recalled, "that since the CIA was our adversary we should deal with them in the place where they are weakest, which is in the United States." And they were weakest, he believed, in Congress and in the media. "Anywhere outside of the United States," he thought, "they can carry out covert actions with very few restrictions. But they can't do anything in the United States. So go to the United States."

Chalabi wanted to level the battlefield. He understood that beyond exacting retribution, he was also in a fight for survival—first, the survival of the political opposition movement he had jumbled together under the auspices of the CIA. He was also in a fight for the survival of his idea—that Saddam should be overthrown not by another Sunni strongman, but by a Chalabi-led insurrection that would usher in an era of Shiite ascendancy.

It was time to return to his original conception, the one to which he had committed himself eight years earlier after the demise of Petra Bank and before the CIA had ever come knocking on his door: to get the United States to remove Saddam Hussein from power. He would do this by making Iraq a domestic political issue in the United States, just as American Jews had done with Israel. That would require a public campaign, something he would wage not in the shadows of a covert operation where the CIA enjoyed all of the advantages, but out in the open, under the spotlight afforded by Congress and the press. He would make the CIA his foil.

"The CIA itself was not a loved organization in America," Chalabi explained. "Its past—the Church Committee . . . ," he said, his voice trailing off. He was referring to the little-remembered but culturally enduring congressional committee led by Senator Frank Church of Idaho in the mid-1970s. The committee carried out an investigation of the CIA and its operations, detailing a long list of abuses, including assassination attempts against foreign leaders and efforts to subvert democratically elected foreign governments—even working with the Mafia to kill Fidel Castro of Cuba. Chalabi then rattled off a list of CIA betrayals, from the Bay of Pigs to "how the CIA let down its allies in Vietnam. The CIA had a record of this."

Chalabi thought he could position himself in the pantheon of freedom fighters who had been deceived and then discarded by the agency. "I wanted to tell the story of how the U.S. had betrayed the Iraqi opposition," he related before sketching out the rest of the narrative, "selling out these poor guys to Saddam, the monster." He says he was very conscious of framing the story in this light, understanding it would resonate with both liberal Democrats, who were naturally antagonistic to the CIA, and with Reagan Republicans, who subscribed to what Thomas Jefferson once called the "Empire of Liberty"—America's duty to spread freedom across the globe.

The tale, of course, was far more complicated. The CIA *was*, in fact, trying to oust Saddam—just not with Chalabi at the center of the effort. But Chalabi believed in his version of the story—that he was the victim—and, equally important, in the value of a plot line that appealed to both the left and right of American politics. It was a story that would play well in the harshest terrain possible for the CIA—in the committee rooms of Congress and in the newspapers and on the television screens. As a matter of law and policy, the CIA would never publicly discuss a classified covert action program, even to defend itself—and Chalabi fully understood that. Eight years earlier, in the wreckage of Petra Bank, he had reacted with serenity and purpose, calmly analyzing the options before him and setting a course for his redemption. Now, in 1997, Chalabi was once again plotting with icy calm an equally improbable comeback.

When he arrived in Washington that spring, the odds against him could not have been steeper. The second Clinton administration was just taking office and, while Madeleine Albright—a hawk on Iraq—had taken over as secretary of state from the dovish Warren Christopher, the more influential national security adviser, Samuel R. "Sandy" Berger, was a pragmatist. He was sympathetic to the hard-liners' arguments for cracking down on Saddam, but he worried that an aggressive Iraq policy would interfere with the administration's other foreign policy objectives. More to the point, the president for whom he worked was determined not to make Saddam the focal point of his foreign policy.

As for Chalabi, he had virtually no leverage to speak of. There was no ministate or private militia at his beck and call. There was just himself and a coterie of four young loyalists. He and these lieutenants, all in their thirties, were now effectively what remained of the Iraqi National Congress. First among them was Aras Habib Karim, the Iraqi Kurd who had been Chalabi's chief of intelligence in Erbil. The year before, when Saddam's forces overran the INC, Karim had barely escaped with his life. As members of the Iraqi army burst into the room where he was hiding, he slid behind the door and pressed a revolver into the base of his chin, prepared to blow off his head rather than be taken captive. Then there was Nabeel Musawi, who fled Baghdad in 1981 at age nineteen, two years after Saddam came to power and shortly after his father was taken away by agents of the regime for his support of a local opposition network. Musawi, who would learn years later that his father was tortured and killed while in custody, was running a pizzeria outside London when he joined the INC in 1991. Zaab Sethna was the U.S.-educated son of a Pakistani diplomat. He also met Chalabi in 1991 when he went to work for the Rendon Group, the public relations firm the CIA had hired to oversee the INC's anti-Saddam propaganda in London. And, finally, there was Francis Brooke, a red-haired, freckle-faced native son of Virginia who had worked in Georgia state politics before joining the Rendon Group himself. A devout Christian with a seemingly insatiable thirst for beer—indeed, he had once served as a beer industry lobbyist—Brooke was a political animal with an abrasive personality who came to devote himself to Chalabi and his cause. Together, Chalabi and these four young stalwarts, three with unusual sounding names and Middle Eastern miens, went to Washington to wage a most unlikely assault on a sitting president and the CIA.

"Once we made the decision we're gonna fight," Brooke recalled, "the question became, 'How are we gonna do it?' Ahmad didn't have a plan. I didn't know for sure how it would work. And so we asked a lot of smart people, 'How the hell do we do this?'"

One of the first people they asked was Francis Brooke's old boss and mentor from Georgia, Hamilton Jordan, President Jimmy Carter's former chief of staff. As Brooke well knew, Jordan had masterminded the election of the little-known peanut farmer, born-again Christian, and one-term governor to the highest office in the land. What impressed the group most was Jordan's role in getting the controversial Panama Canal Treaties passed by Congress. He had tipped the balance by organizing a series of White House briefings for influential people in key senators' districts. Brooke figured that the old master just might have something to teach Chalabi, and asked him to fly up from Atlanta to Washington for a meeting.

Over lunch and, later, in Chalabi's Georgetown townhouse, Jordan explained to the exiled Iraqi and his loyalists how Washington works: where the power centers lay, who actually made things happen. And he reaffirmed to them where to focus their energy—Congress and the press—given the White House's opposition to Chalabi's policy goals and the CIA's special animosity toward him personally. "He didn't think we had very good prospects," Brooke said, "and I have to admit, I thought he was right."

Even more blunt about their prospects was Robert Satloff, a neoconservative and early supporter of Chalabi. As the executive director of the Washington Institute for Near East Policy (WINEP), then the leading think tank devoted to U.S. Middle East policy, Satloff was (and remains) highly influential and well respected in Washington policy circles. As Chalabi recalls, Satloff took him aside and said, "Look, Ahmad, you've got a president who has a 62 percent approval rating. You're gonna cross him over an issue like Iraq and the Kurds and the INC? Nobody has heard of the INC in the U.S. Come on!"

Satloff's advice was basically the same as Hamilton Jordan's: Chalabi should take his lumps and lie low, and eventually the administration would come back his way. But Chalabi didn't believe it. He figured his only chance was to make a fight of it, so he pressed on. His perseverance was rewarded, ironically enough, by an old CIA hand, Linda Flohr. Six years earlier, she had played an integral role in helping launch the INC. After she retired from the agency in 1994, she decided to help him, taking up his cause. She knew that, with the cut-off of CIA funding, he was badly in need of money to get the INC up and running in northern Iraq again, so she turned to someone she thought might be able to help—Duane "Dewey" Clarridge, a cigar-chomping, action-craving ex–career officer who ran the CIA's secret war against Nicaragua's Sandinista government in the 1980s. When Clarridge ordered the mining of Nicaragua's harbors in 1984, Congress outlawed all financial assistance to the CIA's army of Contra rebels. That's when someone working with Clarridge, Lieutenant Colonel Oliver L. North, stepped in and famously secured secret funding from third countries to keep the Contras afloat. Clarridge had been out of the spy business for a decade, but Flohr knew he had some thunder left in him and so she asked her old colleague to hear Chalabi out. Clarridge traveled across the country from his home near San Diego to meet with Flohr and Chalabi over dinner at Morton's Steakhouse in Georgetown. "It was literally a dark and rainy night," Clarridge recalled.

Clarridge was impressed—actually, blown away—by Chalabi's intellect and charm "and by his dedication to wanting to get on with it in Iraq." They followed up that meeting with a second one. This time, Clarridge received Chalabi at his comfortable Spanish-style home in Escondido, California, where remnants of a hearty risk-taker's career in espionage decorated the walls: miniature spy cameras, an AK-47 mounted on a plaque that read "1983—We Kicked Ass in Grenada. Nicaragua Next," a signed photograph from President Reagan and then CIA director William Casey, a photograph of Clarridge in the Oval Office with President George H. W. Bush, and Clarridge's most prized possession—his Christmas Eve 1992 presidential pardon for his role in the Contra part of the Iran-Contra scandal of the mid-1980s.

By the end of the second meeting with Chalabi, Clarridge was in. He was thrilled. "The juices were flowing again. It's in your blood," he said of the excitement that was now bubbling up inside of him. "It's what I do best. I'm good at it, and I've done schemes before. That's why people come to me. Plus, I don't know what's happened to the CIA. But these things need to be done, and they weren't being done." If the U.S. government wouldn't fund Chalabi and the INC, Clarridge thought to himself, then he'd find someone else who would. He immediately tapped into the old Contra network. "I called Ollie North," Clarridge told me, "since he was the only person I knew who had ever raised money for something like this. Ollie said I should get ahold of Bill Clark."

William P. Clark was Ronald Reagan's longtime friend and fellow rancher, the man who coined the expression "Let Reagan be Reagan." From 1982 to 1983, he served as the president's national security adviser. A 1983 *Time* magazine cover story called him "The Man with the President's Ear," while official Reagan biographer Edmund Morris dubbed him "the most important and influential person in the first administration." When he retired from government service in 1985, the remarkably unflamboyant Clark retreated to the privacy of his thousand-acre ranch near Paso Robles, in the heart of California's central coast wine country. He was there in 1997 when Oliver North phoned him on behalf of Clarridge.

As it turned out, no introduction was necessary. Clark remembered Clarridge well, as the two men had worked closely together during the Contra war. "I was in the Situation Room with him a lot in those days," Clarridge recalled fondly. In "those days," Clark was the president's "chief instrument" for implementing the so-called Reagan Doctrine, a new hard-line approach for dealing with the old Soviet Union. Throughout the Cold War, U.S. foreign policy had been rooted in the principle of containment, a strategy for limiting the spread of communism around the world. Under Reagan, the policy became much more muscular, as the administration sought less to contain, and more to roll back Soviet influence.

And it was Clark who presided over this controversial shift in policy, where military assistance was funneled to a host of anticommunist guerrilla movements in such Soviet-supported countries as Afghanistan, Angola, Cambodia, and, most notably, Nicaragua. If anyone was philosophically attuned to supporting someone like Chalabi and the INC, it was William P. Clark. He readily consented to see his old confederate Clarridge, agreeing to fly down to San Diego in one of the planes from his private collection of vintage aircraft: a fixed-wing Cessna Bird Dog that had been used during the Korean War as an artillery spotter. The single-engine two-seater still had the U.S. Air Force markings on it, and he piloted it himself.

It had been nearly fifteen years since the two old cold warriors had tried to overthrow a government together. But as they dined at an outdoor restaurant in Del Mar, the upscale beach town along the Pacific coast, it was like old times. Clarridge briefed Clark on the situation—both in Iraq and about Chalabi—and the former implementer of the Reagan Doctrine immediately began thinking about how he could help. They agreed to meet again—next time with Chalabi.

About a month later, in the summer of 1997, Clark hosted a gathering at his son's law office in Paso Robles. Among those present were Chalabi, Clarridge, Flohr, and an oilman from Texas by the name of Doug Courville. The agenda was basically twofold. The first item was how to raise money from private donors so that the INC could reconstitute itself in northern Iraq. That's why the Texan was present: not to contribute money, but to provide expertise in oil, Iraq's only asset of value. His brief was to tell those assembled how much oil there was in Iraq, independent of Saddam's estimates, and what he thought it was worth. The idea was to lure would-be bankrollers with the promise of preferential access to Iraqi oil and oil leases in a post-Saddam government.

The second item on the agenda was how to pressure the Clinton administration into supporting a Chalabi-led insurrection against Saddam. This was a challenge, to say the least, since President Clinton's former national security adviser, Tony Lake, had shut down that very same operation two years earlier. If nothing else, Chalabi was relentless—and a man convinced of his own strategy. He told the group Saddam's army was so dispirited and disaffected that it was ripe for mass defections. Chalabi maintained that a reassembled INC militia could march across the country and—city by city, town by town—pry away one Iraqi army unit after another all the way down to Baghdad. All that was necessary, Chalabi asserted, was for the U.S. military to enforce a no-fly, no-drive zone in the north and south of Iraq, keeping Saddam's helicopter gunships out of the air and his tanks and other armored vehicles off the roads. "Chalabi didn't want American boots on the ground," a participant at the meeting recalled. "He wanted American planes in the air."

Everyone there liked the plan. "Unlike Tony Lake," the participant told me, "they weren't afraid of it because they had done it before. They had all been involved in guerrilla movements in the past," from Vietnam (where Flohr was one of the last Americans in 1973 to leave the U.S. embassy in Saigon, just hours before the final helicopter airlifted off the roof) to Grenada,

Panama, and Angola, all in the 1980s. But it was the secret war in Nicaragua that was the most binding experience. In one capacity or another, they had all been deeply involved in the Contra conflict. And when Congress cut off aid to the Contras in 1984, it was Ollie North from his basement office in the White House who kept the rebel movement alive by circumventing Congress and raising funds from private sources.

Ultimately, the U.S.-backed Contra army failed to roll back the Sandinistas' communist regime in Nicaragua. But from that experience—and the other proxy wars in Angola, Afghanistan, and elsewhere—those at the Clark meeting believed they had learned what it would take for a resistance movement like the INC to triumph. They each had a checklist for success in their own minds: Is there an organized opposition group? Do you have a charismatic political leader? Are the rebels motivated enough to risk their lives? Are you trying to change a government that really needs to be changed? When it came to the last question, there was no doubt in anybody's mind that Saddam had to go. By that point in 1997, he had already raped, tortured, and gassed tens of thousands of his own people—and invaded two countries, Kuwait and Iran. They believed he was working toward building a nuclear weapon (which, in fact, he was, having launched a "crash program" to develop a nuclear weapon after the August 1990 invasion of Kuwait) and, besides, they all thought Saddam was just plain nuts. So, yes, in their collective minds, Iraq met the criteria for a "good" war.

The only real concern was Chalabi himself. They all agreed: he had serious credibility problems. What worried them the most was not the bank fraud conviction in Jordan or even his falling-out with the CIA. It was that he had no connections to the Iraqi military. They believed that Iraqi soldiers would defect in droves rather than die defending Saddam's thuggish regime. But how could Chalabi convince anyone else of that? "Usually, you look for a general who's already defected to give you that kind of assessment," one of the meeting's participants explained. "Instead, here you have a guy with a PhD in mathematics who never served a day in his life in the Iraqi army, telling you how to wage a coup. That was the problem."

It would be a problem for Chalabi in both Iraq and Washington. "In Iraq," the participant observed, "he'd have to convince military leaders that if they follow him they weren't walking straight into their own demise. And in Washington, he had to convince policy makers that this brilliant man who was good at mathematics but had no military experience had a viable plan and that he could make it happen. So it was a hard sell for him on both sides of the fence."

Washington would be a *really* hard sell. He would have to win over the White House, Congress, the Defense Department, and to some degree the State Department. "If you could get the first three," they figured, "you'll get State. But everybody pretty much had to be on that train."

And so, at this most unlikely of conclaves, in the heart of California wine country, a plan for Chalabi's comeback began to take shape. It started with a strategy to overcome Chalabi's credibility deficit: market him like a politician running for office.

"It's like selling a product," the participant explained. "Once you put it on the market, you have to draw attention to it. People have to know it's out there and it's an option to buy." It was not unlike the strategy portrayed in *The Selling of the President*, Joe McGinniss's 1968 best seller about the marketing of Richard Nixon and *his* comeback. In Chalabi's case, the objective was simply to get people in Washington to meet Chalabi, "because, with him, he was his own best advertisement if you can get him in the room with somebody. He's very Westernized and very smart, and therefore persuasive. But you needed people to validate him before anyone would agree to meet him."

That's where "the boys" would come in, as the participant in the meeting referred to Richard Perle, Paul Wolfowitz, Stephen Solarz, and a handful of other Chalabi enthusiasts who were well regarded in most Washington policy circles. They were all already supportive of Chalabi and the goal of ousting Saddam from power. When Perle and Wolfowitz were advisers to Republican presidential nominee Robert Dole during the 1996 campaign, they argued for a policy of regime change. But with Dole's trouncing at the polls and Chalabi's split from the CIA, a regrouping was necessary. Up to that point, their support of Chalabi was informal and ad hoc. If they were serious about making him the centerpiece of U.S. policy toward Iraq, their approach would have to become much more focused now.

"You can sit around and sip tea and drink scotch and talk about it all day long," the participant said. "But if you don't do anything, then it's just hot air. So this campaign would organize and give direction to what was already happening."

The plan was to get Perle, Wolfowitz, and the others to take a more active, systematic approach to promoting Chalabi—in particular, opening up the think tanks of Washington and the doors of Congress to him and his ideas. Once in, Chalabi would have to be the one to close the deal.

Meanwhile, Clark and Clarridge would pursue the financial track. They figured that, in addition to the approximately $150,000 a month Chalabi and his wife were kicking in from their personal fortunes, it would take millions more to keep the INC going. Clarridge flew to Israel twice to see if he could dig up some money there. He says that on both trips he met with Uri Lubrani, a senior Israeli Defense Ministry official and close personal friend of Bernard Lewis, the Princeton University Middle East scholar who had become a strong supporter of Chalabi.

Clark pursued a different path, telling Clarridge he thought the government of Taiwan was the best place to go. Not only was Clark chairman of the U.S.-Taiwan Business Council at the time, but Taipei had a track record of helping out in such a situation. Back in the 1980s, Ollie North got Taiwan to pony up $2 million for the Contras. As the country's foreign ministry acknowledged during the Iran-Contra hearings in 1987, Taipei raised the cash from private business interests and then funneled the money to the Contras through a secret Swiss bank account supplied by North. Why not again for the Iraqi INC?

Clark set up a meeting at the Georgetown Club with Taiwan's top diplomat in Washington, Stephen S. F. Chen. Clark didn't attend, but he sent his personal representative, David Laux, a former senior analyst at the CIA and Clark's director of Asian Affairs on the National Security Council in 1982 and 1983. Clarridge also attended, as did Chalabi. When it came time to discuss money, Clarridge did all the talking—in his usual direct way.

"I said, 'Would the government of Taiwan put up money for the INC in return for economic preferences?'" Clarridge recalled. He further specified that Taiwan could expect special consideration "for things like construction projects and oil sales" in a post-Saddam government. The Taiwanese diplomat seemed receptive, Clarridge went on, but said he'd have to check with Taipei.

The answer came back a few days later: It was a qualified yes. "Yes, the Taiwanese government would fund the INC," the diplomat reported, "but only if the U.S. government will give us a nod that this should be done." He said it didn't have to be spelled out in an official letter or communiqué. It could be done strictly off the books, Clarridge said, telling me, "There are ways to do this, you know."

ARROWS *of the* NIGHT   127

Or so he hoped. But, as it turned out, getting the money on the down-low—from Israel or Taiwan—proved far more difficult than doing it on the up-and-up. All Chalabi and his circle of supporters had to do was get the Republican majority in Congress behind them and then shove Chalabi down President Clinton's throat. That proved to be easier than any of them imagined possible.

TWELVE

Talking to reporters was anathema to the studiously low-profile Bill Clark and his CIA cohorts Dewey Clarridge and Linda Flohr. But to Ahmad Chalabi, it was a vital component of the campaign he was about to wage. The press would be his launching pad for his intricately conceived march through Washington.

"Look, I went about this systematically," Chalabi confided. "I knew I had no constituency at all in America. We had no Iraqis who were influential in America. The Arab states (all of which are Sunni-led) were against us. The CIA was against us. The State Department was against us. The Clinton White House was against us. What I needed to do was make a strong effort in the United States to get Americans who are significant in the American political constellation to support what I'm doing and make it an issue of American politics. So first we had to publicize the cause."

He had no illusions that Americans—significant or otherwise—would flock to his cause. But he believed that enough of them would flock to their own. "It was my job," he explained, "to bring out those aspects of American political culture that would get groups to support a certain cause because it was in consonance with their own cause."

For Reagan Republicans, it was the moral imperative of spreading democracy across the globe. For conservatives, it was national security—the idea that by not confronting Saddam more aggressively, the Clinton administration was putting America's security at risk. For liberals—they were to be courted, too—and for the rest of America, the principle to be trumpeted was betrayal, in particular, the CIA's purported betrayal of Chalabi and his fellow Iraqi freedom fighters in the mountains of Kurdistan in 1995. "Always," Chalabi emphasized, "we are the underdog."

It all started with the press. Months before the 1997 Bill Clark meeting even convened, Chalabi had already dispatched his American aide, Francis Brooke, to put out the INC's story. In late 1996, Brooke had reached out to an old childhood friend, Mark Atkinson, who was now a producer at ABC News. "Mark, I got a hulluva story for you," he proclaimed with all the vim and vehemence of Hildy Johnson, the flamboyant reporter in *The Front Page*. "I mean, this is really gonna make tremendous TV."

And Brooke knew exactly what he was talking about. He had never worked a day in his life as a journalist, but he had been well schooled in what makes one tick. From 1992 to 1996, he worked for the Rendon Group, the public relations firm hired by the CIA to run the Iraqi National Congress's anti-Saddam propaganda operation. During that time, he ate, slept, and breathed the news business, reading hundreds of stories each morning about Iraq written by every journalist working for every significant newspaper or television program in the world. "There was not a word in the world written on Iraq that we didn't follow," Brooke says. "We were right on top of it." In those years, he had set out to raise the INC's profile. "And we were wildly successful," he says. "When we started out, the Iraqi National Congress didn't exist. Four years later, virtually every article written about Iraq mentioned us."

Brooke had first learned about American journalism in 1986 when he was hired as a campaign aide for Hamilton Jordan's run for the U.S. Senate in Georgia. "He essentially ran a national media campaign, trying to get elected senator in Georgia," Brooke told me. "Now it didn't work. But what was good for me is, I got to see somebody at the top of his game, working with the very top people."

Jody Powell, President Jimmy Carter's former press secretary, pitched in. With Brooke observing, they worked the likes of David Broder, Al Hunt, Mark Shields, and just about every other national news reporter worth his or her salt. "And what I learned was, this wasn't magic," Brooke recalled. "They were just like reporters from down the road—no different. They need a story. Their business is putting stuff in the press. And if you have a story, then you're a great asset for them. The trick is to have a story."

And the stories that appealed most to reporters, he learned, featured conflict and controversy. "Flamboyant characters are good, too," Brooke added, "someone who jumps off the newspaper or television screen and commands your attention. And Ahmad is just a tremendous character. He is nothing but colorful. If you can't get a story after a twenty-minute conversation with him, you're just a moron." Brooke laughed at his bluntness. "But, seriously, you are."

With all that in his background, Brooke proceeded to pitch Mark Atkinson, his old pal at ABC News: Ahmad Chalabi would tell the story of how he and other Iraqis were fighting the tyranny of Saddam from inside Iraq—only to be abandoned by the CIA and the Clinton administration in their hour of need.

Atkinson loved it. He poked around and verified enough of it to warrant flying Brooke and Chalabi up to ABC News' headquarters in New York City to meet with Peter Jennings, the anchorman, and Tom Yellin, the executive producer of a program called *Peter Jennings Reporting*. The broadcast was an hour-long, prime-time series of specials that each focused on a single subject. It was a prestigious show, one that enjoyed critical success and the luxury of time to tell complicated stories such as the CIA's efforts to overthrow Saddam Hussein. But *Peter Jennings Reporting* was broadcast only a few times a year, so Brooke had to beat out the other stories vying for the program's limited airtime.

Brooke knew he had to offer up something special, but first he laid the groundwork. "I showed them the cast of characters: there's the CIA and its complicated relationship with us. There's the whole romantic Kurdish stuff in the north—living and fighting Saddam in the mountains of northern Iraq. There's the whole backstory of the CIA's secret efforts to overthrow Saddam." It was all very enticing. And then Brooke delivered the pièce de résistance: "I promised them I could take an ABC camera crew into northern Iraq, which no one had ever done before at that time. That place was off-limits. Nobody went there. There wasn't even a U.S. diplomat there. And there were no journalists there at all. Zip." Brooke knew that was the kind of element that would be very alluring. "That's the kind of show it is," Brooke understood. "It needs unique access and unique video."

Indeed, Atkinson says, the prospect of getting into northern Iraq was a huge draw for ABC. "At the time, that was a part of the country that had largely been sealed off from the media," he explained. "That's where one of the worst atrocities of our time, Saddam's Anfal campaign of genocide against the Kurds, had occurred. And so we would be going to a place where very few people had had a chance to do any original reporting on. It was fascinating."

For Peter Jennings, the most fascinating aspect of the story was Chalabi himself. "Peter was very impressed by Chalabi's breadth of knowledge, his contacts in the Middle East and his contacts in Washington—Richard Perle, Paul Wolfowitz, and so forth," Atkinson recalled. "And Chalabi is just a *good* storyteller. Peter found him compelling."

The story was a go. Now all Brooke had to do was deliver on his promise to get a camera crew into northern Iraq. No easy feat, especially since Saddam's army just the year before had overrun the INC and driven its members out of the country.

Undeterred, Chalabi directed Aras Habib Karim, the Iraqi Kurd who had been his chief of intelligence in Kurdistan, to slip back into northern Iraq in anticipation of ABC's arrival. Joining him was another Kurd, Kamran Ahmed. Together they reconnoitered the INC's old stomping grounds in Erbil and Suleimaniah and confirmed that, indeed, the camera crew could slide in and out of northern Iraq without Saddam ever knowing about it.

Next was to get the camera crew there—another tall order. Brooke, Atkinson, a cameraman, and a sound technician all traveled to Tehran and attempted to make their way to the Iraqi border. But they quickly ran up against the Islamic Revolutionary Guards Corps (IRGC), the elite branch of Iran's army charged with keeping internal security. It seems nobody had cleared the trip with the IRGC, and its commanders were none too happy about a U.S. news team traipsing through their country. The IRGC threw people in jail for far less than that. For the next week, Brooke and the ABC crew sat grounded in Iran until Chalabi could fly to Tehran and meet with Agha Mohammadi, the Iranian government's point man for the Iraqi opposition and the man Chalabi first met four years earlier after his trip to Qom. Chalabi and Mohammadi were nearly old friends themselves by this point.

"I told him I need these people to go into northern Iraq because we need to tell the story," Chalabi recalled. Mohammadi immediately acquiesced, arranging safe passage for Brooke and the news crew. "It was the only time I know of during the Saddam period that the Iranians let an American TV crew cross the border from Iran into Iraq," Chalabi told me with pride. "They did it for me."

By this time, the CIA had already gotten wind of the trip and the story that was in the works. Langley was concerned, to say the least. One of its case officers, Regis Matlock, tried to get Chalabi to cancel it, warning him through an intermediary that the CIA could not guarantee the group's safety in Iraq. Chalabi erupted. "I don't need their support," he yelled. "It's not their country. It's my country, and I'm going in."

Once Chalabi got in, it was Langley's turn to erupt. "They just really panicked now," Brooke recalled. "Fucking ABC News is in Iraq, and the CIA's not. I mean, it made them look really bad, and they knew it." Brooke decided to rub it in, sending a fax to Tony Lake, the national security adviser who had pulled the plug on the March 1995 operation that Chalabi and ABC News had now come to document. "The INC has reestablished itself in northern Iraq," the fax to Lake proclaimed. "Free Iraq lives!"

To this day, Brooke still cannot get over the audacity of his fax. "That was hilarious: We were back!" Indeed, they were—not in great numbers, but enough to tape a news segment.

For the CIA, the only thing worse than having an ABC News crew in northern Iraq was watching the story itself. Titled "Unfinished Business: The CIA and Saddam Hussein," it was broadcast nationally on June 26, 1997.

"In northern Iraq today," Peter Jennings began, "there is still a campaign going on to get rid of Saddam Hussein. It has been going on since the end of the Gulf War. The people who persist in this struggle do so in the name of democracy, but they are fighting alone today. And this is the story of how they were abandoned."

For Atkinson, it was a story that had much to do with U.S. government hypocrisy, with the Clinton administration "talking about supporting freedom and human rights abroad and at key moments when we could have made a difference not doing anything about it. If you believed Chalabi's thesis, and not the administration's—which was that Chalabi was going to drag us into a war that we didn't want; and, in retrospect, they were right about that. But at the time, Ahmad's argument that the Iraqi people would've greeted the overthrowing of Saddam with roses was very compelling."

Either way, the story brought into sharp focus the conflict that lay (and still lies) at the heart of U.S. foreign policy in the Middle East, the conflict between American values and American interests—between those who supported democracy for Iraqis and those who placed a higher priority on securing the free flow of oil for the West.

Much of the broadcast's on-camera testimony and criticism came from

Chalabi himself, which only further infuriated the agency. "This was beating the CIA up in public and they don't take that well," a former case officer said of Chalabi's appearance on ABC News. "It was the ultimate act of betrayal."

But for Chalabi, it was a case of sweet revenge. He had been given an extensive platform by ABC News, while no one from either the agency or the Clinton administration agreed to participate in the broadcast—just as he had anticipated. If, indeed, revenge is a dish best served cold, Chalabi had just rolled his out on a bed of ice. "In the teeth of CIA opposition," Chalabi beamed thirteen years later, "we managed to get the Peter Jennings report broadcast. And it made a big splash!"

In terms of audience size, it was no *60 Minutes*. But the broadcast was complemented by a story that ran the same day in the *Washington Post*, "How CIA's Secret War on Saddam Collapsed." Written by Jim Hoagland, Chalabi's friend who was by now one of America's most influential journalists, it ran 2,820 words long and was spread out over three pages, telling essentially the same story as ABC: that the U.S. government had callously abandoned a small but valiant army of freedom fighters on the battlefield, preferring instead a palace coup by Saddam's generals. But that coup never materialized, because the plot was penetrated by Saddam's intelligence service, the Mukhabarat.

For Chalabi, the story in Washington's newspaper of record on top of an hour on prime-time network television was the journalistic equivalent of blackjack: being dealt a face card while holding the ace of spades. In a single day, Chalabi had made his case to both the educated lay public and to America's small foreign policy elite. As Francis Brooke saw it, their story was now part of the intangible Washington alchemy that made the worlds of policy and politics go around. "If journalists write about something, politicians will see it," he explained to me. "They're attracted to high-visibility issues, things that people are talking about. And if politicians speak about it, think-tank people will convene and start talking about it. It's a circle. They all work on their own, but they feed off of each other."

And now Chalabi and his cause were firmly planted in the mix. It was only a start, but the selling of Ahmad Chalabi was officially under way. Next stop: Capitol Hill.

THIRTEEN

For Ahmad Chalabi, Capitol Hill was the crucial battleground. With the executive branch firmly opposed to both him and his approach to regime change, Chalabi's only chance was to win over a different branch of government, one with the power—and, he hoped, the inclination—to bend a president to its will. To almost anyone else, he recognized, the notion of enlisting Congress in a call to arms on behalf of a foreigner would seem like a pipe dream. But, as the summer of 1997 drew to a close and Congress returned to session, Chalabi moved forward bristling with energy and an abiding belief in his ability—indeed, his right—to shape U.S. foreign policy according to his goals and ambitions.

He didn't know how his assault on Capitol Hill would play out. It was just important to get started and to know where he wanted to end up: with U.S. backing for an Iraqi opposition army and an Iraqi provisional government based in northern Iraq. Along the way, he'd seize opportunities as they presented themselves. But, bottom line, he realized that to succeed he needed both the Senate and the House of Representatives solidly behind him; one chamber or the other was insufficient given the magnitude of his objective.

He already had entrée to a number of influential members of Congress, including Senator John McCain, the Arizona Republican; Senator Bob Kerrey, the Democrat from Nebraska; and House stalwarts like Stephen Solarz and Jack Murtha, both Democrats. That was a start. But the one American who would do the most to propel Chalabi's cause and to insert him at the center of the debate over U.S. policy toward Iraq was not a legislator but

Richard Perle, the former Reagan administration official Chalabi had met six years earlier, in 1991. Perle, Chalabi says, was decisive. "Richard was the person to get things going and to get things done," Chalabi told me. "He had this rare quality that combined intelligence on an intellectual level with the ability to mobilize and organize people."

Perle was a true foreign policy intellectual and a skilled Washington apparatchik who could navigate the vortex where the currents of theory met the practice of foreign policy. For thirty years he had been converting many of his conservative ideas into policy and his often controversial causes into concrete action, always under the suspicion that his main motive was protecting Israel. He had employed such sophistication in his mastery of Washington's byzantine bureaucracies that his enthusiasts called him by the same ominous names as his many detractors, albeit with affection: Prince of Darkness, Darth Vader, and Evil Genius.

Throughout the fall of 1997 and into 1998, Chalabi and Perle spent more and more time together talking, strategizing, and organizing. That Chalabi would welcome Perle's advice and assistance is self-evident. But why did Perle embrace this controversial Iraqi exile and his aspirations? The answer, Perle says, lies in the movement he has come to embody: neoconservatism, one of the most controversial yet consequential political philosophies of modern times. Over a quarter-century, Perle's path would become inextricably entwined with the evolution and ascendancy of that philosophy. Eventually, a core group of its leading adherents, with Perle at the center, would coalesce around Chalabi and his single-minded pursuit of returning home to Baghdad. There is a history in all men's lives, Shakespeare wrote. But in Richard Perle's, there was history itself.

Perle's story began with a most unlikely introduction into the world of foreign policy, one that came early in his life and totally by happenstance. While a student at Hollywood High School in Los Angeles, where he earned mediocre grades, he had the good fortune to sit next to an attractive young girl in his Spanish class named Joan. He failed the course but found a girlfriend. And one afternoon, while lounging around her swimming pool high in the Hollywood Hills, he met her dad, who happened to be Albert Wohlstetter, one of the nation's leading experts on the theory and strategy of nuclear war.

Wohlstetter's concerns about a surprise nuclear attack by the Soviet Union would eventually lead to the second-strike and fail-safe concepts of nuclear war—and would help inspire the film *Dr. Strangelove*. It was this notion of American vulnerability to a surprise nuclear attack that Wohlstetter spoke of to his daughter's young friend as they sat around the shimmering pale-blue water of the swimming pool. By the end of their conversation, Wohlstetter had given Perle an article to read, a pioneering paper Wohlstetter had written in 1959, "The Delicate Balance of Terror."

"I was blown away by it," Perle recalled. "It was so beautifully argued and so concise I was really impressed."

The chance meeting changed his life, Perle says. He went on to earn a degree in international relations at the University of Southern California, and then to study at the London School of Economics and Princeton University, where he earned a master's degree in political science in 1967. He and Wohlstetter's daughter went their separate ways, but Perle became a lifelong acolyte of her father, his admiration for Wohlstetter undiminished to this day. "The word 'brilliant' doesn't do justice to him," Perle says of his mentor.

In 1969, Wohlstetter arranged a summer internship in Washington, D.C., for Perle and one of his other young disciples, a graduate student he taught at the University of Chicago—Paul Wolfowitz. The two student interns hit it off immediately. "We had one big thing in common in that we were both protégés of Wohlstetter," Perle said. "We were also interested in the same things. And we saw the world in pretty much the same way."

Their worldview differed sharply from that of most of their contemporaries. While students across the country were protesting the war in Vietnam and the malevolence of U.S. military force abroad, Perle and Wolfowitz went to work for two of the most hawkish hard-liners in America, Dean Acheson and Paul Nitze, both elder statesmen of the U.S. defense community and architects of the Cold War. At Wohlstetter's urging, Acheson and Nitze agreed to hire his two young apprentices for their clunky-sounding Committee to Maintain a Prudent Defense Policy. Perle and Wolfowitz's job was to help them lobby the Senate to approve funding for an antiballistic missile (ABM) defense system. "The committee had no staff at all, and the principals were all doing other things," Perle recalled. "So we were it."

It was Perle and Wolfowitz's initiation into the politics of Congress and the art of coalition building. The two young graduate students organized testimony, wrote research papers, and whipped out fact sheets debunking their opponents' arguments. "That was sort of our specialty," Perle recalled in an interview. "We would get out a short paper refuting an argument within hours. This was all before e-mail, so we had copies Xeroxed, hand-carried to dozens of offices on the Hill, and then you'd see it effected in debate the next day; that is, a senator on our side would deploy the argument we had developed in response. So one of the lessons we learned was, arguments make a difference and if you had a good argument you could have substantial influence."

But the key person to influence, he learned, was not the senator or congressman. It was his or her staffer—the faceless, decidedly unglamorous functionary who more often than not told the boss how to think about an issue. "A lot of people don't understand that," Perle explained to me. "I know people who would kill for twenty minutes with a senator and wouldn't bother to take a plane to Washington to have an hour with the staff. That's a big mistake, because senators and congressmen are extraordinarily busy; they have tremendous demands on their time. So if you want to move something forward, it's really important to have the staff on board." That's a lesson Perle would employ to perfection many years later on Chalabi's behalf. But in 1969 the issue was missile defense, and Richard Perle and Paul Wolfowitz were still learning their way.

Their efforts paid off on August 6, 1969, when the Senate voted to approve the ABM defense system—by a single tie-breaking vote, 51 to 50. "It came down to the wire, but it had a big impact," Perle remarked. "It established the concept of defending ourselves from a nuclear attack rather than hoping to deter one with the threat of massive retaliation." The vote was a significant victory for hawks, one that laid the groundwork for decades of clashes over arms control and the development of weapons systems, including what Senator Edward "Ted" Kennedy (D-Massachusetts) derisively called "Star Wars," President Reagan's controversial Strategic Defense Initiative.

After the Committee to Maintain a Prudent Defense Policy disbanded, Perle was set to return to Princeton to complete his PhD in political science. But one of the senators he met in the course of the ABM debate, Henry M. "Scoop" Jackson, a Democrat from Washington state, offered him a job. "Scoop said to me, 'Here you are studying in an academic way how Congress works. You'll never really understand unless you have direct experience. Come work for me.' It was supposed to be for one year. I wound up staying for eleven."

Perle also wound up finding a new mentor—and a movement—upon joining Jackson. In the 1970s, the Democratic senator was a favorite among those belonging to the still-nascent neoconservative movement. Like Jackson, these neoconservatives were Democrats who found themselves adrift from the increasingly liberal George McGovern wing of the party. But, even as they moved toward a more conservative point of view, they rejected some important aspects of the Republican Party's traditional conservatism. In the 1970s, they repudiated the policy of détente toward the Soviet Union, specifically in the area of arms control. Scoop Jackson believed that evil should be confronted with power, and he felt that President Richard Nixon's policy of easing relations with Moscow amounted to accommodation, if not appeasement. "We wanted to fight the Soviets," Perle explained, "not find areas of cooperation with them."

Fighting the Soviets would become official U.S. policy with the election of Ronald Reagan in 1981 and his administration's adoption of the rollback strategy. In the meantime, Perle did everything he could to undermine the easing of American policy toward Moscow, emerging as the driving force behind congressional opposition to arms control with the Soviet Union. In 1975, for example, he used damaging documents leaked to him by Donald Rumsfeld, then the youngest secretary of defense in history, to kneecap President Gerald Ford's push for détente. And before that, Perle pushed through legislation, the Jackson-Vanik Amendment, that targeted the Soviet Union's restrictions on the emigration of Jews and other dissidents by limiting trade to the West. That legislation became a thorn in U.S.-Soviet relations and "drew a red line around the more ambitious lines of détente that Nixon and [National Security Adviser] Henry Kissinger were pursuing," Perle told me. In getting the amendment adopted, Perle succeeded in outmaneuvering a sitting president, forcing Nixon to sign legislation he opposed. Kissinger would later write in his memoirs that Perle "proved as steadfast as he was ingenious in pursuing his larger aim: to stymie the administration's arms control policies."

Seeing himself as a champion of Western security, Perle recruited new talent to the cause. In 1975, he enlisted Douglas J. Feith, a Harvard Law School graduate, getting him his first job in Washington working for Scoop Jackson. And after hearing a speech by Professor Bernard Lewis, the Princeton University Middle East scholar, he introduced Lewis to Jackson. From that point on, Perle says, "Lewis became Jackson's guru, more or less." As for Perle's good friend Paul Wolfowitz, he, too, became an enthusiast of

Scoop Jackson, calling himself "a Jackson Democrat" until 1981, when Wolfowitz switched parties and began calling himself "a Jackson Republican."

Twenty-five years later, these four men—Perle, Feith, Lewis, and Wolfowitz—were the leading figures of the neoconservative movement and seminal figures in the campaign for Iraqi regime change. The fact that they all met through Jackson and became his devotees once prompted George Packer of the *New Yorker* to half jokingly suggest to Perle that the Iraq War began in Scoop Jackson's office. "There's an element of that," Perle replied.

But there was another, equally significant element, Perle says: the continuing influence of Albert Wohlstetter. In the 1970s, the old nuclear theorist began to broaden his focus beyond the Soviet Union to include potential threats emanating from the third world. The one Wohlstetter homed in on, Perle recalls, was Iraq and its new revolutionary government, the Ba'ath Party. Wohlstetter's concern, Perle says, was soon reflected in both his own thinking and Wolfowitz's, although Wolfowitz told me that it was he who put Wohlstetter onto the issue of Iraq and not the other way around. "If Albert were still around, he would probably forget that he got the idea from me," Wolfowitz said, chuckling. "But I do think it started with me."

Their focus on Iraq emerged in 1977 when Wolfowitz was a young midlevel analyst at the Pentagon and was asked to write a study for the secretary of defense analyzing potential military threats to the United States lying outside of the superpowers' central battleground, Europe. Wolfowitz zeroed in on the oil reserves of the Persian Gulf.

"The importance of Persian Gulf oil cannot easily be exaggerated," Wolfowitz wrote in his limited contingency study. If the Soviet Union were to move southward to control Persian Gulf oil, he went on, the impact would "probably destroy NATO and the U.S.-Japanese alliance without recourse to war by the Soviets." Wolfowitz then took his analysis further, postulating that a country from within the region—independent of the Soviet Union—could also impose its hegemony on the flow of Middle East oil and thereby present an equally dangerous threat to U.S. interests. Other analysts pointed to the risk posed by Iran, then in the throes of an Islamic—and deeply anti-American—revolution. But Wolfowitz thought the main threat emanated from another country.

"Iraq," he wrote in 1977, "has become militarily pre-eminent in the Persian Gulf, a worrisome development because of Iraq's radical-Arab stance, its anti-Western stance . . . and its willingness to foment trouble in other local nations." Wolfowitz went on to warn that "Iraq may in the future use her military forces against such states as Kuwait or Saudi Arabia."

Wolfowitz's limited contingency study represented the Pentagon's first detailed analysis of the need to protect the Persian Gulf. The intelligence community, however, dismissed his analysis. "They said Iraq would never threaten its neighbors because one Arab country won't invade another," he recalled, shaking his head in disbelief. But he was right, anticipating by more than a decade Saddam's invasion of Kuwait. Iraq would remain a central concern for Wolfowitz, one to which he would return over and over again.

Richard Perle first sounded the alarm about Iraq in the 1980s when he was an assistant secretary of defense in the Reagan administration. After Saddam invaded not Kuwait, but Iran, Reagan sided with Baghdad, publicly declaring that the United States "could not afford to allow Iraq to lose the war to Iran," and that his administration "would do whatever was necessary to prevent Iraq from losing the war with Iran." The United States supplied Saddam with battlefield intelligence and economic aid, sending Donald Rumsfeld to Baghdad in 1983 for a meeting with the dictator. Perle strongly disagreed with the administration's policy, arguing that it was Saddam, not the ayatollah in Tehran, who posed the greater threat to U.S. national interests.

When Perle left the Defense Department in 1987, with the Iran-Iraq War still raging, he went public with an editorial in *U.S. News & World Report*, writing that while he was no fan of the Islamists in Tehran, it was a huge mistake for the Reagan administration to continue supporting the aggressor in that conflict:

> There is no doubt that it is Iraq that started the war with Iran. It is Iraq that began attacking commercial shipping, and it is Iraq that initiated the use of chemical weapons and the bombing of civilian targets. Indeed, as objectionable as Iranian fanaticism is with its disregard for diplomatic convention, support for terrorism, hostage taking and fundamentalist zealotry, Saddam Hussein's Iraq is ruled by one of the most brutally repressive regimes in the world. Saddam Hussein's approach to dissent at home is to murder dissenters. And as we protect Iraq, it is well to remember that Iraq has protected terrorists Abu Nidal [a Palestinian political leader who was widely regarded as

the world's most dangerous terrorist in the 1970s and 1980s] and Abu Abbas [another terrorist leader whose organization in 1985 hijacked the Italian cruise ship the *Achille Lauro* and murdered American Leon Klinghoffer].

Perle's editorial contained many of the themes neoconservatives would marshal in later years in support of Iraqi regime change: overthrowing tyranny, promoting democracy, and confronting the threat posed by Saddam's alliance with terrorists. But at the time, Perle—a leading Cold War hawk—saw the issue through the prism of U.S.-Soviet competition. He feared that removing what he called the "last vestiges of American neutrality" in the Iran-Iraq War would play into the hands of the Soviet Union by driving Tehran into the arms of Moscow.

Perle's concerns about Iraq grew exponentially with Saddam's invasion of Kuwait on August 2, 1990. Iraq's occupation of its tiny neighbor to the south—with the world's fifth-largest proven oil reserves—put Saddam on the doorstep of Saudi Arabia, the world leader in proven oil reserves. If Saddam had rolled on to Riyadh, he would have controlled nearly 40 percent of the world's oil supply. "And then Saddam would have had his boot on our throat," Perle told me. "One of the great mysteries," he added, "is why Saddam just didn't press right on to Riyadh. Even if in the end he had agreed to leave Saudi territory—which he could easily have taken—he could have insisted on Kuwait as the price for doing that. In which case he would have wound up with Kuwait. So the idea of a dominating power in the region that was orientated as Saddam was—Ba'athist, totalitarian, and perfectly happy to work with the Soviets—that was a huge threat to U.S. national security. Remember, it was the end of the Cold War. But it was still the Cold War."

The end of the Cold War, however, did not diminish Perle's apprehensions about Iraq. He says he strongly disagreed with President George H. W. Bush's decision to leave Saddam in power after the Gulf War concluded on February 28, 1991. "My view in '91 was that Bush should have finished off Saddam," Perle said. "I don't think you had to go all the way to Baghdad to do that. If we had disarmed the Republican Guard [Saddam's elite troops], which we had surrounded in the desert, that would have been fatal to the regime."

So Perle—who had rejected détente in favor of destroying the old Soviet Union—was not content to leave Saddam sitting tall in Baghdad. Neither were his fellow neoconservatives. They believed that Reagan's rollback strategy was more than a strategy for security; it was a moral imperative: evil must be confronted. Any regime that rapes, tortures, and murders its own citizens as a strategy to ensure its authority is a threat to all, they said. It could not be trusted to honor any code or commitment—including those between states—and therefore it posed a danger to international stability.

But there was not much Perle and his fellow neoconservatives could do about Iraq after Bush signed the cease-fire agreement with Saddam. And their frustration mounted during the next administration, as President Clinton merely sought to tame Saddam through UN sanctions and weapons inspections.

Perle had always believed that arguments and ideas matter—and that those of the neoconservatives were on the right side of history with regard to Iraq. But after Clinton was reelected in 1996, even Perle began to wonder: After nearly seven years of repeated exhortations—in newspaper columns, think-tank dissertations, and congressional appearances—would all their effort amount to a futile exercise in fist-shaking? At that moment of frustration, Perle says, Ahmad Chalabi arrived on the scene. "When Chalabi showed up," Perle related, "those of us who wanted to see Saddam's regime brought down regarded him as a very important find. If you're going to make the case it should be American policy to bring about a change in Iraq in which Saddam's regime is driven from power, you have to answer the question, 'What would replace it?'" Now, Perle says, they had the answer.

Better still, in Chalabi they had an Iraqi who could make an articulate, intelligent, and credible case for regime change. "Otherwise," Perle explained, "it would have been just a bunch of American policy wonks. Most senators, congressmen, even journalists at that time had little knowledge about Saddam's regime, and they had even less contact with it. Having an Iraqi speak about it was crucial."

As for Chalabi, it was the consummation of his systematic courtship of those in Washington with the power to exert influence over U.S. policy in the Middle East. Over the coming summer and fall of 1997, he would cement his alliance with the neoconservatives, becoming both their point man for Iraqi regime change and their principal means for achieving it.

FOURTEEN

Ahmad Chalabi did not create the debate over Iraq policy, nor did he invent Washington's indelicate and often poisonous game of partisan politics. But he understood America well, including its weaknesses, and he was able to capitalize on the confluence of policy and politics to an extent that astonished even him. What made his success possible was, from his perspective, a fortuitous overlapping of events: In November 1994, the Republican Party seized control of the House of Representatives for the first time since 1954, and of the Senate for the first time since 1986—and many in the GOP were prepared to exploit the foreign policy dispute over Iraq for domestic political gain just as the Democrats had done earlier when a Republican, George H. W. Bush, sat in the Oval Office. To Chalabi's added fortune, the Republicans maintained their majority in the 1996 congressional elections while Saddam Hussein escalated his defiance of United Nations weapons inspectors, giving his neoconservative enemies in Washington an abundance of ammunition to press their case for regime change.

We now know that by this time, the late 1990s, Saddam's weapons of mass destruction (WMD) had been dismantled either by UN weapons inspectors or by Iraq itself. But to keep his regional enemies at bay—in particular, Iran—Saddam acted as if he were hiding something. Since the end of the Gulf War in 1991, the United Nations had extended a near-full trade embargo on Iraq and created an inspection regime to ensure that Saddam had destroyed his WMD and was not producing any more. Saddam's game was to insist publicly that Iraq no longer possessed WMD, but to block surprise inspections and hinder routine ones. He also moved equipment that many believed could be used to manufacture biological or chemical weapons out of the range of video cameras that had been installed by UN inspectors. And he threatened to shoot down American U-2 surveillance aircraft flying over Iraq in support of the inspections, as well as to evict Americans from the UN weapons inspections teams. It was all a grand deception, Saddam would confide to his debriefer at the Federal Bureau of Investigation (FBI) after his capture by American forces in December 2003. But throughout the second Clinton administration (and beyond), Saddam had fooled everyone from the mullahs in Tehran to the UN inspection team, the CIA, and other intelligence agencies in the West.

The fear was that Iraq had a stockpile of biological and chemical weapons and perhaps a dozen long-range ballistic missiles. It was widely assumed as well that Iraq could be as little as a year away from producing a crude nuclear device. Still, the Clinton administration thought it could keep Saddam in his box with the weapons inspections and trade sanctions. The president's national security adviser, Sandy Berger, said at the time that while it would be "aesthetically pleasing" to get rid of the dictator, it was "strategically sufficient" to contain him.

The neoconservatives disagreed. They argued that, given Saddam's presumed cache of weapons and a growing weariness on the UN Security Council for both sanctions and weapons inspections, U.S. policy toward Iraq should aim at removing the dictator and his regime from power. Some neoconservatives argued that only a full-scale invasion of Iraq would guarantee the removal of Saddam and his regime. But they were in the minority at the time, and Richard Perle was not among them. He regarded the threat from Baghdad as insufficiently imminent to warrant a second ground war in less than a decade. Moreover, he thought the idea of American boots on the ground would never fly. "Politically, it was a nonstarter," he told me.

That was another reason why he found Chalabi so appealing. "The idea that all Ahmad was asking for was support short of U.S. military intervention made it pretty easy to say, 'Sure, why not?'" Perle explained. "If Ahmad had said, 'You've got to send the marines,' he wouldn't have gotten very far in my view. But the demands were modest."

What Chalabi wanted was what he had always been seeking: U.S. air support that would keep the skies clear of Saddam's helicopter gunships and the roads free of his tanks while a force of free Iraqis made its way south from Kurdistan down to Baghdad, picking up defectors from the Iraqi army along the way. His plan hinged on the belief that what made Saddam strong also made him weak—and ripe for a popular uprising. The dictator was so hated by the Iraqi people and the army's rank and file, Chalabi argued, that the place was ready to blow. All that was needed, he said, was a match to light up the insurrection—and that's where Chalabi said he and the Iraqi opposition came in.

In the mid-1990s, the U.S. Department of Defense had war-gamed Chalabi's assumptions and scenario, and concluded that he had no chance of succeeding—none whatsoever—because, among other reasons, Chalabi had no following inside Iraq. Neither the country's soldiers nor its people would risk their lives to line up behind him or his INC banner, the Pentagon believed. At Langley, most of the CIA's senior leadership thought that Chalabi's plan was merely a ruse to drag the United States, one step at a time, into another war with Saddam. The State Department saw it that way as well. But Perle says he was "drawn" to Chalabi's concept. To him, it seemed plausible—even the notion that Iraq's Sunni minority and Shiite majority could overcome centuries of mutual enmity to unite against the authoritarian rule of Saddam. If Chalabi's plan worked, Perle thought, then Saddam's regime would fall into the hands of Iraqis—"and there would be no issue of the legitimacy of the subsequent government." And if it failed, well, it "entailed virtually no risk for the United States."

On that basis, Chalabi and his cause became the central focus of Perle's vision for Iraq, and that of Paul Wolfowitz, Doug Feith, and others among the core group of leading neoconservatives. There was never a moment when they all sat down and said to one another that they were allies, but they shared a common purpose and a joint vision. The alliance between them was unspoken, but well understood. Moreover, they all serendipitously agreed on how best to move forward. The idea was to get Congress to support the Iraqi opposition and then to pressure the Clinton administration into embracing that policy. For Perle, this was a tried-and-true formula for success. "If the executive branch is unresponsive," Perle explained, "you go to Congress. There are instances in which Congress seizes an issue and takes over. Most commonly, you can get some compromise from the White House."

The group set out to win the political war in Congress by first creating what Perle called "a climate of opinion and a set of perceptions about Saddam" that would prepare the ground for congressional action—and ultimately lead to a policy of replacing Saddam's Ba'athists with Chalabi's INC. "Arguments and ideas matter," Perle said, "and you have to be patient. Sometimes you can't get something going for a lot of reasons, and then all of a sudden it becomes possible."

It's the "perfect storm" school of politics, he said, cloud-seeding a debate with your ideas and arguments in the steadfast belief that eventually the circumstances of history will combine to produce the outcome of your choosing. The important thing, he added, was to use whatever resources were available now and catch up to events as they unfolded. Initially, Perle said, the neoconservatives' strategy involved no more than mobilizing people to make the argument in as many places as possible—in meetings at think tanks, in letter-writing campaigns, in television and newspaper interviews, and in the committee rooms of Congress—building momentum until the time was ripe to focus their efforts on organizing a coalition to enact legislation. In some instances, he said, the neoconservatives coordinated their actions, while in others they acted independently as self-starting intellectuals and ideological insurgents.

The first salvo in their battle of ideas was fired in the December 1, 1997, issue of *The Weekly Standard* magazine, the neoconservatives' bible. In huge black type emblazoned over a bright yellow cover, the magazine headlined its issue with the bold directive "Saddam Must Go: A How-To Guide." It contained five articles, including a lead one by Paul Wolfowitz and Zalmay Khalilzad, both of whom would later assume prominent positions in the administration of President George W. Bush, with Khalilzad becoming the White House's special envoy to the Iraqi opposition.

"If we are serious about dismantling Saddam's weapons of mass destruction, and preventing him from building more," Wolfowitz and Khalilzad wrote, "we will have to confront him sooner or later—and sooner would be better." They called for a "new strategy" that set as its goal "not merely the containment of Saddam but the liberation of Iraq from his tyranny." They also pushed for a revival of the Iraqi opposition, including support for a provisional government that would be given control of the $1.6 billion in Iraqi government assets then frozen in the United States. Wolfowitz and Khalilzad asserted that "we should arm and train opposition forces" and "we should be prepared to provide military protection for Iraqi units defecting from Saddam to the resistance movement." It was straight out of Chalabi's playbook.

Around the time that article was published, UN weapons inspectors in Iraq initiated a series of aggressive inspections targeting presidential palaces and other sites previously restricted by the government there. This prompted Saddam Hussein on January 17, 1998, to issue an ultimatum: either the UN lifted its economic sanctions by May 20, or Iraq would cease all cooperation with weapons inspectors. The ultimatum ignited another crisis between Washington, the UN Security Council, and Baghdad—and furnished the neoconservatives with a fresh round of ammunition to make their case.

Like everyone else at the time, Charles A. Duelfer, then the deputy head of the UN inspections team, says he assumed Saddam was hiding WMD. But now, having studied the FBI's interviews of Saddam—and after having conducted his own talks with members of Saddam's inner circle—he realizes Saddam was, quite simply, fed up. "By 1997, the Iraqis knew that they'd given up just about everything," Duelfer explained. "We didn't know that. But they knew that. So, from their mind-set, they were saying, 'Enough is enough.'"

The Clinton administration responded to Saddam's provocation with a buildup of U.S. forces in the region. The purpose was for a possible military strike against Baghdad—not to finish off the regime, but only to bomb Iraq's suspected weapons sites. It was a classic containment strategy—and it prompted the neoconservatives to swing into action. On January 26, 1998, their newly formed pressure group, the Project for the New American Century (PNAC), released an open petition calling on Clinton to adopt a new strategy of regime change in Iraq. "PNAC was little more than a post office box," Perle told me. But its membership included many of the nation's leading foreign policy conservatives. Eighteen of them signed the petition, including not only Perle, Wolfowitz, and Khalilzad but also Richard Armitage (a former assistant secretary of defense) and Donald Rumsfeld.

They warned that should the president fail to act, the consequences would be dire, with Saddam "almost certain" to acquire the capability to deliver weapons of mass destruction. "The safety of American troops in the region, of our friends and allies like Israel and the moderate Arab states, and a significant portion of the world's supply of oil will all be put at hazard," the signatories warned. Perle's drive to create a "climate of opinion" and "perception of Saddam" conducive to regime change was now at full throttle.

On the heels of the PNAC letter, Perle penned a two-thousand-word opinion piece for the Sunday *Washington Post*'s Outlook section entitled "No More Halfway Measures." Perle presented his case for Iraqi regime change, in part advocating "open support for the Iraqi National Congress [because] support we have given them in the past has been hopelessly inadequate." He took on the CIA directly, deploring "the breathtaking incompetence of the U.S. government team responsible for Iraq policy, especially the CIA," and blaming it for Chalabi's reversals:

> [T]he agency has never been enthusiastic about supporting the democratic opposition, maliciously undermining the Iraqi National Congress, squandering substantial sums on consultants and public relations firms instead of supporting those Iraqis who are fighting to free themselves from [Saddam's] terror. The team responsible for dealing with Iraq, with the CIA leading the way, should go peacefully. But it may be harder to remove than Saddam Hussein. Baghdad first, then Langley.

Reaction to Perle's article was instantaneous and pervasive. It was discussed all over major print and television media sources, including the *New York Times*, the Associated Press, and CNN, in large part because the Republican foreign policy leadership was ready to back Perle up. As the *Washington Times* reported, Perle had pushed hard "to persuade Republican leaders on Capitol Hill to embrace [the INC] as an alternative government for Iraq." Republican senator Chuck Hagel of Nebraska made a strongly supportive statement on the Senate floor the day after Perle's article, saying, "I believe Secretary Perle's analysis and general recommendations should be taken seriously." Senator John McCain echoed Perle's proposals at a press conference, advocating expanded propaganda broadcasts into Iraq, expansion of the no-fly and no-drive zones, and logistical support to dissident Iraqi groups. "The time for talk may be over," he said. "And we should be prepared to act alone if necessary."

Perle pressed on. Appearing that week on a *Nightline* segment titled "Could an Attack on Iraq Do More Harm Than Good?" Perle emphasized that "[t]here is a democratic opposition. It broadly represents all the people of Iraq. With a bit of support from us and some of [our] very skillful air power to protect the territory from which they operate in northern Iraq, I think we can bring Saddam down. But that means a political as well as a military strategy."

A few days later, Perle traveled with McCain and Senator Joseph Lieberman, then a Democrat from Connecticut, to a security conference in Munich. He used the plane ride and the conference to buttonhole the senators about the INC, Perle said. Then, along with several other leading neoconservatives, Perle went to the White House and pressed the case in a meeting with Sandy Berger, Clinton's national security adviser. Years later, Berger spoke about the encounter during an event at the Council on Foreign Relations, recalling, "The neocons came to visit me in '98—Rumsfeld and Wolfowitz and Perle and Bill Kristol and others—and they said, 'We want you to create a free Iraq; we want you to basically provide a no-fly zone in southern Iraq, protected by American air power, fly back Chalabi and all the Iraqi exiles; give them guns and let them go and they'll get rid of Saddam Hussein. And I listened to that and I said: 'I've seen this movie before. It's called the Bay of Pigs.'"

When asked in a February 1998 town hall meeting in Dayton, Ohio, why the United States didn't support Iraqi opposition groups militarily and unfreeze assets to help them, Berger said, "[W]e have had experiences in this country in the Bay of Pigs, in Hungary in 1956, and in Iraq in 1991, where perhaps our rhetoric has gone ahead of what we are prepared to do. And we have been very careful not to let that happen again."

In other words, the White House wasn't budging from its policy of containment. And so Perle and his coterie bore down. On February 19, 1998, they issued another open letter to Clinton, this one specifically urging the administration to replace Saddam's regime with Chalabi's Iraqi National Congress. That same day, Perle moderated a panel discussion about Iraq at the American Enterprise Institute (AEI), the conservative Washington think tank where Perle, Wolfowitz, and most of the other leading neoconservatives reside today as scholars and fellows. The discussion, held at the AEI's Albert Wohlstetter Conference Center, featured Paul Wolfowitz, Stephen Solarz (who had left Congress by then), and Ahmad Chalabi. They spoke before a packed audience. "The people who come to these events are influential," Perle said matter-of-factly.

Immediately following the AEI briefing, Chalabi headed to Capitol Hill, where Perle had arranged for him to address the House Republican Policy Committee, the GOP's principal incubator for legislative initiatives. The committee's chair—at the time Chris Cox of California—is the fifth-most-senior member of the House Republican leadership, and its meetings are attended by both the representatives and their staff, those anonymous but decisive players. On this day, it was Chalabi providing the ideas: that Saddam's regime was brutal, dangerous, and at the same time vulnerable. Masses of Iraqis were eager to see the end of his tyranny, Chalabi told them, and the INC had been doing something about it from its base in northern Iraq until the Clinton administration pulled the plug on their operation. He argued that the approach of the CIA and two successive administrations to depose Saddam through a palace coup was doomed to failure. "Saddam is coup-proof," he maintained.

Among those listening to Chalabi that afternoon was Stephen Rademaker, at the time chief counsel to the House International Relations Committee and its staffer in charge of drafting legislation. Outwardly, Rademaker was so slight and soft-spoken as to appear utterly innocuous. But deep inside him burned the heart of a partisan activist and a Reagan Doctrine diehard who had long before eschewed containment in favor of rollback. During the 1980s, he was the State Department lawyer who advised the Nicaraguan Contras, and as he listened to Chalabi's story, his old fervor began to well up. "For me, personally, this was like Nicaragua," he recounted to me. "Chalabi came in and told the story of how he was pursuing regime change in Iraq until the Clinton administration got cold feet. They could easily go back to doing it, but—just as in Nicaragua—they needed a secure base to mount an insurgency." To Rademaker, it all made sense and, given what the Iraqi exile was prepared to do, "it sounded like it was right for the application of the Reagan Doctrine."

Immediately after the presentation, Rademaker introduced Chalabi to his wife, Danielle Pletka, who was the senior Middle East adviser to Senator Jesse Helms, chairman of the Senate Foreign Relations Committee. She, in turn, introduced Chalabi to Randy Scheunemann, the foreign policy adviser to Trent Lott, a Mississippi Republican and Senate majority leader. By the end of that afternoon, February 19, 1998, Chalabi had picked up three new dedicated recruits, all shrewd legislative operators who enjoyed the confidence of their bosses: the powerful chairmen of the House and Senate committees on foreign affairs and the Senate's boss of bosses.

That night, Rademaker went home, sat on his living room couch, and typed on his laptop a bill that would come to be known as the Iraq Liberation Act. It was meant to be a congressional statement of policy, one that would make it the policy of the U.S. government to support Chalabi and the democratic opposition in their effort to depose Saddam's regime. "I wouldn't have written it," Rademaker told me, "if I hadn't first heard the presentation from Chalabi and the light going off that 'Hey, there's a context in which this would actually work.' And it was Chalabi who first made me aware of that."

The next day, Rademaker showed the bill to Chalabi. But they agreed the time wasn't yet right to introduce the bill in Congress. More groundwork still had to be laid. So Rademaker put it in his top drawer and waited for Saddam to make another mistake.

FIFTEEN

Chalabi was on a roll. His march through Washington, however, was not without its share of difficulties and detours. For one, he was hurting financially. The attempt by Dewey Clarridge, the ex-CIA man, to raise money from Israel fizzled, while the Clinton administration put the kibosh on Bill Clark's overture to Taiwan. The State Department's third-ranking official, Thomas Pickering, told Taipei's representative to Washington there would be no wink or a nod sanctioning off-the-books financing of the Iraqi National Congress. Instead, Pickering advised that Taiwan should steer clear of Chalabi and his friends. For Chalabi, that meant there would be no bridge money, so to speak, to tide him over until he ran out his string on Capitol Hill. His staff, though tiny, was forced to work without salaries while Chalabi had to pay all INC expenses out of his own pocket. In those days, he maintained an INC office in the United Kingdom and flew between London and Washington about once a month. No matter what it cost, however, he flew first-class only. That was the Chalabi way: work hard, live well.

While wooing the neoconservatives, Chalabi and his Kurdish aide-de-camp, Aras Habib Karim, pursued a second track, approaching Clarridge with a plan that had a whiff of Operation Valkyrie, the German resistance's 1944 plot to kill Adolf Hitler. Neither Perle nor any of the other neoconservatives had anything to do with *this* scheme: a plan to assassinate Saddam. It was strictly limited to Chalabi, Karim, and Clarridge.

Chalabi and Karim told Clarridge they had recruited the chief of security of a building in Baghdad where Saddam sometimes attended high-level meetings. The building's security chief gave them a sketch of the cabinet room Saddam supposedly visited. It showed the desk Saddam used, next to a large air-conditioning unit and a row of tall windows. Chalabi and Karim said it wouldn't be easy, but they believed it was possible to smuggle a bomb into the room and hide it inside the air unit next to Saddam's desk. They showed Clarridge the spot where they more or less wanted to plant the bomb.

"How much money do you think we'll need to pull this off?" Clarridge asked.

"Two hundred and fifty thousand dollars," Karim answered. The money, he said, would be used to purchase secured communications, rent safe houses in Iraq, and relocate the conspirators' families outside the country.

Clarridge was no expert in explosives, but he knew enough to worry about the windows in the room. If the bomb wasn't situated just so, the force of the blast would escape through the windows and not get the job done. So Clarridge showed the diagram to an old friend who *was* an expert in explosives. That friend showed Clarridge precisely where to place the bomb for maximum effect.

Clarridge then flew off to Geneva, Switzerland, to meet with the only people he knew who might finance something like this off the books. "Unfortunately," he told Chalabi and Karim after he returned from the trip, "all I can raise from them is $50,000. I don't know where else to go."

Clarridge arranged to have the money wired to INC coffers anyway—to help defray Chalabi's other expenses. But the shortfall in funding ended the INC's venture into the world of assassination plots. Chalabi now says he was always against the idea, telling me he found it "abhorrent." But Clarridge would long lament the missed chance to kill Saddam. "It's really a goddamn shame," he said years later. "It could've all ended there."

Instead Chalabi pressed forward with Plan A, working with the neoconservatives in Washington to stoke the calls for regime change in Iraq. By the end of February 1998, their focus would become passage of the Iraq Liberation Act, but along the way Chalabi continued to encounter setbacks, political and otherwise.

The first was news that UN Secretary General Kofi Annan had flown to Baghdad to negotiate a new agreement with Saddam to end the January standoff. Annan promised that UN personnel, including weapons inspectors, would "respect the legitimate concerns of Iraq relating to national security, sovereignty and dignity." Annan also consented to new restrictions on the inspections of eight huge "presidential" sites where UN weapons inspectors believed Iraq was concealing material used in Saddam's WMD program.

It was bad enough, Chalabi thought, that the Clinton administration had countenanced Annan's concessions, but now Washington might be trying to end its Saddam headache by inching toward a full rapprochement with the dictator—eventually removing sanctions and then normalizing relations with Iraq. For the first time, Chalabi felt apprehensive that his American gambit might actually fail.

On the same day he heard about the Kofi Annan–Saddam entente, Chalabi learned that his brother in London, Rushdi, who had long been ill, had taken a turn for the worse. The eldest of the Chalabi brothers, Rushdi had become a father figure to Ahmad and the person who most embodied the family's aspirations and determination to return home to Baghdad. At a breakfast meeting in Washington, a senior State Department official—aware of Rushdi's condition—told Chalabi, "Go home to London. This phase of confronting Saddam is over. It's time now for you to take care of your family."

Rushdi died one hour before his brother's plane touched down at London's Heathrow airport. "On the one hand," Chalabi explained, "here are the Americans making a deal with Saddam, killing the hope of the Iraqi people of getting rid of him. And, on the other hand"—his voice now cracked with emotion—"my brother, who was for me a symbol of confronting Saddam and who was talking all the time about wanting to return to Iraq, died and I wasn't there."

Chalabi's pain was made worse by the fact that he had to bury his brother in London. "For me," Chalabi said, his hushed voice now rising in anger, "it was a terrible crisis when anybody in my family died in exile: my father, my mother. It didn't matter. I just hated for somebody from my family to die and we couldn't bring them back to be buried in Iraq. It was devastating."

Just as he had done when he buried his father, Chalabi performed the Islamic ritual of purification, washing Rushdi's face, arms, head, and feet. Chalabi wrapped the corpse in a plain cloth, set aside his anguish, and returned to Washington.

There, the formidable and hard-charging aide to Senator Jesse Helms, Danielle Pletka, had organized a Senate hearing for March 2 called "Can Saddam Be Overthrown?" The lead witness was Ahmad Chalabi, who was at his subversive best during his testimony that day: intellectual and indignant, charismatic and self-confident, but most of all utterly audacious as he skipped over a series of inconvenient facts to argue against Clinton's policy of containment and for regime change led by the INC.

"I am here as an elected representative of the Iraqi people," Chalabi began, slyly alluding to his election six years earlier as the chairman and president of the INC's now-all-but-defunct executive council. He failed to mention that just three hundred Iraqi exiles had participated in that vote, and that the only INC members still living inside Iraq, all Kurds, were more often than not engaged in a civil war, shooting live rounds at one another and not Saddam. He continued his testimony with a denunciation of Kofi Annan, calling the UN secretary general "craven" and characterizing his deal with Saddam as nothing more than "appeasement."

What then followed was a masterpiece of propaganda and popularization, as he denounced the evils of Saddam and trumpeted the virtues of the INC, which he claimed could, with just a little help from Washington, deliver a pro-U.S. ally endowed "with lakes and lakes of oil." He spoke graphically of Saddam's (then nonexistent) "chemical and biological warfare industry," saying it "enslaves tens of thousands of Iraqis who are virtually unprotected from their poisonous productions."

He attacked the CIA and its support for a palace coup. "It is not up to the CIA to determine Iraq's leadership," he asserted, his voice brimming with resentment. "It is up to the Iraqi people." And he confronted head-on the U.S. government's contention that he had no following inside the country, insisting that through INC "networks" and diplomacy the group "is well-known inside Iraq and has a large but unorganized following."

All that was needed, he said, was "not a U.S. army of occupation, but an Iraqi army of liberation." He asked for help setting up INC safe havens in northern Iraq, to be protected by U.S. air support. And then, he assured the senators, Iraq's people would desert the regime en masse—and so would its army. "Saddam's divisions, even his Republican Guards, will come over to us," he predicted, adding that Saddam's regime would collapse "within a matter of months."

Senator Sam Brownback, the Republican from Kansas who chaired the hearing that day, declared Chalabi's statement "powerful" and then proceeded to call two additional pro-Chalabi speakers to testify. It was left to the final witness, Richard Haass—who had been a member of George H. W. Bush's National Security Council during the Gulf War—to inject a dose of skepticism into the day's proceedings. In arguing against regime change, Haass warned that ousting Saddam would likely lead to a "scenario where Iraqis are at one another's throats along ethnic lines, geographic lines, and political lines." Another danger, he said, was that the United States could get hopelessly bogged down in Iraq: "I just think it would be terribly, terribly complicated and expensive, by every measure of the word 'expensive,' to pull off." While Haas said he sympathized with the plight of the Iraqi people, and agreed that they'd be better off without Saddam, that was "not the same as saying that his overthrow ought to dominate American foreign policy."

Of course, that's exactly what Chalabi wanted in the long term. But for the moment he was just hoping to insert himself into the discussion, and in that he succeeded wildly. His testimony propelled the Iraqi opposition into the national debate. For the first time a group of senators—led by Brownback, the Kansas Republican, and including John McCain and crucially Trent Lott, the majority leader—was suggesting that the best way to deal with the threat of Saddam's WMD was to replace his regime with a democratic opposition. "We need an open program which recognizes an Iraqi government in exile," Brownback said following the hearing, "and we need to do what is necessary to make this a strong, viable alternative to Saddam."

Some of the senators took up Chalabi's years-old campaign to have Saddam declared a war criminal and tried by an international tribunal. They spoke of funneling tens of millions of dollars to a reactivated Iraqi opposition. And Lott organized closed-door briefings by Perle, Wolfowitz, and Wayne A. Downing, a retired four-star general who had served as the commander of special operations during the Gulf War and had been recruited to the cause by Dewey Clarridge.

"When you have military and civilian experts like them telling you that this serves U.S. interests and that this is a viable option, that's very powerful," said Randy Scheunemann, the foreign policy adviser to Lott. "Chalabi took his vision and gave it credibility."

A year and a month earlier, the CIA had cut Chalabi off and left him for dead. Now Chalabi had pumped new life into his dreams and ambitions, with the help of politicians mainly in the Republican Party. Perle had pointed him to the realm of partisan politics, and Chalabi had succeeded in making Iraq a domestic political issue while expanding his appeal from the principled few to the GOP's many. For the many, supporting Chalabi had less to do with finishing off Saddam and his regime than with hammering Clinton and his administration.

Jim Hoagland, the *Washington Post* columnist and longtime friend of Chalabi, took early note of that instinct in a March 5, 1998, column, writing, "The GOP will be tempted to use Chalabi and his organization, the Iraqi National Congress, as a club to swing at Clinton."

Richard Perle wasted no time jumping into the partisan fray, telling reporters on the day of Chalabi's testimony, "They in the Clinton-Gore administration face the prospect of having to go into the next election with a monumental failure to defend"—their Iraq policy.

And Francis Brooke, the American aide who represented Chalabi on Capitol Hill, said he found the vein of raw politics so rich it was easy to mine. "All that was required on my part," Brooke recounted, "was to make a credible argument that some congressman can stand up and repeat because all he wants to do is go out and beat up President Clinton. I mean, that's what we were doing. We got a Republican majority, they want to make the case that President Clinton is irresponsible on foreign policy. Okay. So we're prepared to help you. And I can teach you how to make that case, and I can offer you another way to deal with Saddam that sounds good to America. We love freedom fighters." It was that simple. And, he says, that cynical: "Yep. That's right. It's the adversarial system. And so we were glad to help 'em." Brooke says he helped members of Congress and their staffs in everything from writing policy papers attacking the administration's Iraq policy to preparing witnesses for congressional testimony.

There were a handful of hawkish Democrats who also supported Chalabi—among them, Senators Bob Kerrey of Nebraska and Joe Lieberman of Connecticut—but they were the exceptions. In the late 1990s, it was the Republican Party that championed Chalabi and capitalized on his cause. And he was only too happy to accommodate them as he took center stage in the increasingly incendiary debate over Iraq.

In the summer of 1998, Chalabi threw gasoline on the fire in both Washington and Baghdad. It started with a phone call from Scott Ritter, a chief UN weapons inspector in Iraq who felt the Clinton administration was insufficiently supportive of inspections. Ritter told Chalabi he was holding a sensitive document in his hands that summarized the most recent findings of UN weapons inspectors, findings that seemed to prove Saddam had put deadly VX nerve gas into Al Hussein (Scud) missile warheads before the

Gulf War. If true, it would have contradicted claims by the Iraqi government that it was unable to make a ballistic missile using the nerve agent. It also would have meant the Iraqis were concealing the extent of their WMD capability, which had particularly lethal implications since just a few drops of VX could kill a human being in minutes.

Chalabi immediately brought Ritter to Washington and put him up in his Georgetown townhouse. Chalabi then made a copy of the report—a laboratory analysis of Iraqi ballistic missile warhead parts—and called Lott's adviser Randy Scheunemann, who in turn organized a meeting of Republican congressional leaders for that weekend. After Ritter briefed them, the GOP leadership drafted a pointed letter to Clinton demanding to know if the administration would back up UN weapons inspectors in a confrontation with Baghdad. Trent Lott signed the letter, as did Jesse Helms, the chairman of the Senate's Foreign Affairs Committee, and their House counterparts, Speaker Newt Gingrich and Ben Gilman, chairman of the House Foreign Affairs Committee. "Can't get better than that," Chalabi beamed.

Actually, it did, when Chalabi leaked a copy of the VX report to Hoagland at the *Washington Post*. On June 23, the story broke on the front page.

"This is a smoking gun," Chalabi was quoted as saying in the article. Hoagland disclosed that he had obtained the VX report from Chalabi's Iraqi National Congress, and made this observation about its larger ramifications:

> The new indications of Iraqi deception also are likely to reverberate in U.S. politics, where conservative Republicans are increasingly critical of what they see as a failure by the Clinton administration to support strongly either aggressive [UN] inspections for Iraqi weapons of mass destruction or efforts to overthrow Iraqi leader Saddam Hussein.

Chalabi said he shared the report with Hoagland to "make the issue open and make the policy of Clinton dealing with Saddam repugnant and also to give the impression—I mean, confirm the fact that Saddam was fooling the United Nations."

As it turned out, Saddam wasn't fooling the United Nations. Iraq had not "weaponized" VX in ballistic missile warheads as UN weapons inspectors had suspected. "That conclusion we drew was wrong," Charles A. Duelfer now says. Duelfer was the number two official overseeing the UN weapons inspections team at the time. Later, after the 2003 invasion of Iraq, he headed up the Iraq Survey Group, the U.S.-led team of inspectors that scoured the country in search of Saddam's purported cache of WMD. Duelfer says that after looking for more than a year, and after debriefing all of Saddam's top chemical weapons personnel, "no evidence could be found that Iraq had weaponized VX in missile warheads." The findings cited in the *Washington Post* article, he says, were only preliminary and therefore never intended to be made public. "We weren't sure of the conclusion," Duelfer explained, "and we hadn't yet had a full dialogue with the Iraqis about it."

The *Washington Post* story, however, pushed the Iraqis over the edge, as Duelfer learned during his interviews with Tariq Aziz, Saddam Hussein's close adviser, after Aziz surrendered to American forces in 2003. "That was the straw that broke the camel's back for the Iraqis," Duelfer told me. "It caused them internally to conclude, 'The Americans are gonna make shit up just to keep the economic sanctions on.' And this is a quote from Tariq Aziz, 'We decided we can have sanctions with weapons inspectors or we can have sanctions without inspectors. Thank you very much, we'll have 'em without the inspectors.'" And so, Duelfer says, throughout 1998 Saddam kept ratcheting down the weapons inspectors' access to suspected WMD sites, while Chalabi and his Republican allies in Congress kept ratcheting up the pressure on President Clinton to do something about it.

It was during this time, Chalabi says, that Stephen Rademaker approached him about introducing one of two pieces of legislation: either Rademaker's bill that called for the arming and training of Iraqi opposition forces to overthrow Saddam, or a resolution declaring Saddam in "material breach" of his international obligations—and calling on Clinton to "take appropriate action."

"I said to Rademaker, go with 'material breach,'" Chalabi told me. "I thought it was still too early to ask Congress to arm and train Iraqis. Congress is slow. It has to be moved gradually. And the advantage of the 'material breach' resolution was to show that Saddam was in violation of UN weapons resolutions and, at the same time, to provoke Saddam into further clamping down on the weapons inspectors." Their best ally, Chalabi knew, was always Saddam: "We could really get his goat."

And right on cue the Iraqi dictator triggered a new crisis. After the House and Senate passed the material breach resolution, Saddam demanded that the UN Special Commission (UNSCOM), the group specially formed to oversee weapons inspections in Iraq, declare that Iraq had completely dismantled its stockpiles of WMD. Since UNSCOM officials (mistakenly) believed just the opposite, they refused to accede to Saddam's demands. In response, Iraq's parliament of figureheads "voted" on August 4 to end cooperation with the weapons inspections. Saddam then ordered all weapons inspections suspended and demanded changes in the leadership and personnel of UNSCOM to reduce the American and British roles in the commission.

The standoff between Iraq and the weapons inspectors fueled the pressure in Washington to do something about Saddam. That's when the three key staffers—Steve Rademaker, Danielle Pletka, and Randy Scheunemann—decided the time had arrived to introduce the bill Rademaker had written to make support of regime change in Iraq the policy of the United States government. Rademaker's bill authorized the president to provide $97 million worth of lethal and nonlethal aid to Iraqi opposition forces, everything from beans to bullets, from desktop computers and radio broadcasters to combat boots, helmets, field kits, and rifles. "We were giving the president tools," Rademaker explained. "Because of the separation of powers, we couldn't tell the president how to use the tools. But we gave him the authority, and it was real."

The Clinton administration strongly opposed the bill, especially since it was tailored to most benefit Chalabi and his Iraqi National Congress. But at that time the politics of Saddam were so white-hot the administration had no chance of stopping the legislation. When Trent Lott introduced the bill in the Senate, he was expecting a landslide, saying the vote would represent a "strong demonstration of congressional support for a new policy toward Iraq, a policy that overtly seeks the replacement of Saddam Hussein's regime through military and political support for the Iraqi opposition." Jesse Helms noted that the president would have to designate an Iraqi opposition group, or groups, to receive the military assistance called for in the bill. "The president need not look far," Helms advised. "The Iraqi National Congress once flourished as an umbrella organization for Kurds, Shiites, and Sunni Muslims. It should flourish again, but it needs our help."

And so on October 7, in defiance of Clinton, the Senate voted to adopt the Iraq Liberation Act of 1998 by unanimous consent. Not a single Democrat spoke out against the bill. In the House, the vote in favor of the bill was an overwhelming 360–38. Clinton had no choice. Later that month, on

Halloween, he held his nose and signed the legislation into law, making the overthrow of Saddam Hussein official U.S. policy.

Chalabi had come back from the dead. In less than two years, he had engineered a masterful reversal of fortune—from that of a pariah with a CIA "burn notice" to Congress's point man, a shrewd political operator with both a plan and the resources to back it up. It was the latest example of his epic ability to rise from the ashes—through guile and perseverance and his almost herculean drive to return home to Iraq in glory. There was no letting up now.

SIXTEEN

Congress can't make a commander in chief go to war, and signing the Iraq Liberation Act into law didn't legally bind President Bill Clinton into organizing an Iraqi opposition army to overthrow Saddam Hussein. But Ahmad Chalabi and his supporters expected nothing less, and would use "the will of Congress" as a cudgel against anyone, including the president, who got in their way.

Senate Majority Leader Trent Lott hailed the new law as "a major step forward in the final conclusion of the Persian Gulf war," saying he expected the administration to move from containing Saddam Hussein to "a policy of 'rollback.'" Meanwhile, Richard Perle and Paul Wolfowitz, who was by now dean of the Johns Hopkins School of Advanced International Studies, pronounced the Iraqi opposition ready to fight.

As for Chalabi, the usually dispassionate mathematician allowed what was for him a rare bout of exuberance. "We were very excited," he said of America's new law of the land. He thought for sure Saddam Hussein was "cooked"—that, finally, the despot's days were numbered, while his own long journey home was at last truly on course. American commitment to the overthrow of Saddam had long been the cornerstone of his vision, and now it had been codified into law—with the signature of the president of the United States of America.

Chalabi was so buoyant he let himself view the Iraq Liberation Act as the modern-day equivalent of Lend-Lease, the World War II program in which the United States supplied England and other Allied nations with vast amounts of materiel prior to formally entering the global conflict. "I knew all about Harriman living in the Dorchester Hotel and working with Churchill," Chalabi said of W. Averell Harriman, the United States' special representative for Lend-Lease. Supporters of the program saw it as a way to fund the British war against Germany without America having to become a combatant itself. "When there were problems with the United States actually going to war," Chalabi told me, "the Americans did something short of war that helped their allies and maddened their enemies." No matter that Lend-Lease aid totaled more than $50 billion (about $700 billion at 1998 prices) compared with the Iraq Liberation Act's $97 million. For Chalabi—who often thought in historical, and grandiose, terms—it was a beginning.

Now he wanted to take the next step: to arm and train his still-nonexistent army of Iraqi exiles. But first it was time to reconstitute the Iraqi National Congress, the source of both his leverage and his legitimacy. In April 1999, he geared up for what would be the Iraqi opposition's first conference in seven years. It was to be held near London in Windsor, a location that also carried great historical resonance for him. It was there at the thirty-five-acre Oakley Court country house overlooking the river Thames that Charles de Gaulle brought together the French Resistance during World War II. Chalabi was energized by the impending conference and its connection to one of his heroes. But just as the Windsor conference was getting under way, he was confronted with a series of new obstacles.

The first involved the top U.S. military commander in the Persian Gulf, four-star U.S. Marine Corps general Anthony Zinni, who thought the Iraq Liberation Act was plain crazy—and wanted no part of it. "It was the siren song of the nineties," Zinni said years later. "The idea that we can end Saddam's regime. No blood. We can do it on the cheap. All I have to do is take this guy Chalabi, give him 97 million bucks in military support and he can turn Iraq into a democracy, and then democracy will begin to spread in the Middle East. I mean, this wasn't even a viable movie plot, let alone reality."

For one, Zinni said, the idea of providing air cover for a Chalabi-led insurgency was a nonstarter. "You couldn't get one country in the region to sign up to provide the bases to operate from, to support this scheme, to give any credibility to or recognize Chalabi. I can tell you; I know. I'd been out there. I had asked that question."

Moreover, Zinni thought the notion of putting U.S. Central Command forces at Chalabi's disposal was the most absurd idea of all. "The U.S. military is gonna be run by the planning of Chalabi, given his character?" Zinni said sarcastically, referring to Chalabi's bank fraud conviction in Jordan. "Why should Ahmad Chalabi control the military piece of this? This is your military. You will be seen as dropping the bombs. What if he said, 'Put a bomb on that building.' It might be a Sunni he doesn't like, as opposed to the enemy."

As far as Zinni was concerned, containment—while messy—was working. "Nobody was afraid of Saddam Hussein anymore. He had a shell of a military that we knew we could pop and crack in a heartbeat," he said, snapping his fingers.

But regime change, he went on, risked unleashing all sorts of unpredictable and uncontrollable forces in Iraq. "This place was full of rats inside and outside. And when you kill the King Rat, these other rats are gonna come swarming all over. And you would release all these problems. Why do I want to inherit that damn place? I can contain it."

When Zinni tried to explain his concerns to members of Congress, they just rolled their eyes, he said. "The idea that you present complexity to a politician in the United States who wants simplicity," Zinni said, interrupting himself in exasperation and rolling his own eyes. "This is the way it goes," he added. "They want sound bites, not understanding that all around are the roots of complexity and complications that have no bet-the-ranch answers."

Zinni believed then, and still does, that Chalabi understood that most members of Congress lacked any analytical rigor—or even the predisposition to scratch beneath the surface—when it came to the issue of Iraq. In fact, Zinni believes Chalabi banked on it, telling the politicians exactly what they wanted to hear, without fear of a probing cross-examination. As far as Zinni was concerned, America's elected representatives were easy marks for this Iraqi interloper. "This was a con man's dream: 'I can actually con the greatest power on earth and everybody else into actually getting me a country. It's not just getting money or power. I could actually get a country out of this,'" Zinni said. "I think this was the master stroke."

To a large degree, Frank Ricciardone, the senior State Department official designated by the Clinton administration as its point man for the Iraq Liberation Act, agreed. "We in the State Department are used to silver-tongued Middle Easterners who tell us what we want to hear," Ricciardone told me.

A career foreign service officer, Ricciardone is fluent in Arabic and served extensively in the region, including a tour at the U.S. embassy in Baghdad before the Gulf War. He says that he admired Chalabi's energy and intellect, and especially respected him for not having retreated to the life of a country gentleman after the CIA cut him off in early 1997, but that the Iraqi was so hell-bent on realizing his ambitions that he didn't trust him—at all. "After spending time with Ahmad, I'd pat my pockets to see if he picked them," Ricciardone told me. "I saw Ahmad a lot in the 1990s. And I enjoyed seeing him. But I'd tell him, 'You want to go to war against Saddam. And you want to drag the U.S. into a war behind you. This president will not go to war!'"

And, in fact, for the first six years of his presidency, that's precisely what Clinton's policy was: to contain Saddam but not to engage him on the battlefield. For a brief window of time, however—beginning in December 1998—the president's national security team began to rethink its approach toward Iraq. That month, after repeated crises with Saddam, American and British forces launched Operation Desert Fox, a four-day campaign of air and cruise missile strikes targeting Saddam's sources of command and control, including Republican Guard barracks and internal security facilities. Then, in early 1999, the administration turned its attention to developing realistic options for overthrowing Saddam's regime. The uniformed military thought the only viable option was a full-scale invasion. "Don't dribble in," Zinni explained. "If you're gonna go to Baghdad, then go to Baghdad. Go with 400,000 troops. Take it down. Reshape it the way you want to."

But no one in the administration thought the public would support an invasion. So, Kenneth Pollack, Bruce Riedel, and others at the National Security Council began to meet and discuss other avenues short of invasion for taking down Saddam and his regime. As envisioned, Chalabi would have a role to play—his drive and organizational skills were such that even those wary of him agreed they needed him. But he and the Iraqi opposition would play only a minor, supporting role. "We didn't want U.S. policy to support Ahmad Chalabi," Ricciardone explained. "We wanted Ahmad Chalabi to support U.S. policy."

He said as much to Chalabi when he saw him at the Windsor conference in April: "I told him, 'Ahmad, I am not here to resurrect the INC and put you in charge.'" Ricciardone also made clear that the "Iraqi diaspora," as he put it, was not entitled to impose or constitute a new government for

Iraq. That would be left to those Iraqis living inside Iraq, whether it was a general who succeeded Saddam or some semblance of a civilian authority. But it wouldn't be the INC. The opposition, however, could help with propaganda, Ricciardone told Chalabi, and perhaps draft a blueprint for maintaining government services the morning after Saddam fell—how to keep the hospitals and schools running, the courts functioning, and the electricity flowing.

Chalabi was alarmed. "He wanted an armed opposition," Ricciardone observed. "He wanted to re-create what he had done in northern Iraq in the early 1990s, the same rolling coup strategy that had already failed."

Iraqi exile leaders from Europe, the Middle East, and elsewhere attended the two-day Windsor conference, as did many American and British diplomats and politicians. When it came time to address the delegates, Chalabi gave what was described as an emotional discourse, invoking Henry V's St. Crispin's Day Speech. "We in it shall be remembered," Chalabi intoned. "We band of brothers."

Ricciardone had to laugh. "The guy's great. You gotta give it to him."

As Chalabi continued to speak, however, he grew visibly upset, his face flushed, tears welling up in his eyes and rolling down his cheeks.

"I think he was being heartfelt," Ricciardone later recalled. "He was baring his soul as he was getting close to the point where the U.S. was going to shunt him aside."

Many of his fellow exiles also wanted to shunt him aside. Chalabi may have been the most energetic and capable of the opposition leaders, but he was also the most mistrusted, a legacy of his often imperious and, many exiles felt, deceitful manner of operating. They accused him of double-dealing and forever undermining the standing of others for his own personal gain. Despite the fact that the name of the organization, the Iraqi National Congress, was closely identified with him, his fellow exiles refused to take orders from Chalabi. So, in an effort to convince various opposition factions to stop fighting and work together, Ricciardone—at the White House's direction—pressured Chalabi into stepping down as head of the INC to become part of a collective leadership. He was now just one of seven leaders in the opposition hierarchy—a disheartening setback for the man who did so much to resurrect the Iraqi opposition and get the U.S. Congress behind them. It was all slipping through his fingers.

But Sisyphus-like, Chalabi once again mounted a counterattack. Working harder and longer hours than anyone else, he gradually reasserted his dominance over the INC and waged an effort to undercut Ricciardone and his other detractors at the National Security Council. Chalabi's supporters in Congress began to plant articles in the press critical of the "morning-after strategy," as Chalabi derisively called the State Department plan to marginalize his Iraqi opposition, making it responsible only for maintaining essential services the morning after Saddam fell. Senator Bob Kerrey called Ricciardone and went to his office to complain in person. And Richard Perle popped in to share his pro-Chalabi views.

But for Ricciardone, Chalabi's most brazen act was playing one government agency against the other. "I'd say to Chalabi," Ricciardone recalled, "'Don't screw around with the United States of America. Don't try to play the CIA against the State Department against the Defense Department. That's not the way we deal with people or governments. Don't do it.'" Chalabi's response? "He did it anyway."

And then he stopped returning Ricciardone's phone calls altogether. All the while, Chalabi's supporters on Capitol Hill were ramping up the pressure, making trouble wherever they could for the administration.

"There are many arenas in which congressmen can make trouble for an administration," Chalabi, the perennial student of American government, explained. "They could make trouble for them in appropriations. They could make trouble for them in health care or in any of their other pet projects. This kind of phenomenon is part of the American system." And the key was "to be right in there plugged into American politics," he said as he punched his fist into an open hand.

And so when Clinton sent his nomination for U.S. ambassador to Kuwait up to Capitol Hill, it was dead on arrival. The nominee, Larry Pope, spoke Arabic and had more than thirty years of experience as a foreign service officer, much of it in the Middle East. But he had also served as political adviser to Anthony Zinni and that, according to a *Washington Post* article at the time, proved to be Pope's undoing.

Angered by Zinni's "open scorn" for Chalabi's military plan, the *Post* reported, Jesse Helms, chairman of the Foreign Relations Committee and one of Chalabi's most powerful allies, "decreed [that] his committee would not grant Pope a hearing, sinking the nomination and prompting Pope, 55, to retire from government service."

Chalabi believes it was this same political leverage that eventually forced the administration to release $25 million in aid to the Iraqi opposition.

Ricciardone agrees: "Ahmad used the Iraq Liberation Act to bludgeon us into getting the State Department to release money and support the INC, saying we were thwarting the will of Congress."

The money and support were doled out through the same legislation the U.S. government used to provide foreign assistance to other governments—the U.S. Foreign Assistance Act. In Chalabi's eyes, to be lumped in with other "governments" represented a victory—an incremental one, to be sure, but a step in the right direction—connoting a grudging, if limited, recognition of the INC as Iraq's official government-in-exile.

Chalabi then decided to use some of the $25 million to open offices in the world capitals most crucial to the INC's success. He opened one in Washington located just blocks from the Capitol dome. "The State Department came to visit twice," Chalabi said. "It was much better than their offices."

He would also open offices in London, Damascus, and Tehran, the latter despite U.S. economic sanctions against Iran dating back to the 1979 hostage crisis. Chalabi managed to wrangle a waiver from the U.S. Treasury Department for conducting anti-Saddam propaganda from inside Iran, and—in true Chalabi fashion—he rented a large, comfortable villa there, decorated with expensive Persian carpets and brocade-covered sofas and armchairs and staffed by about a dozen Iraqi aides and security people. "All paid for by the State Department," Chalabi said with a grin.

By late 1999, Chalabi had not given up on the Clinton administration. He thought that with the 2000 presidential elections drawing near, the Democrats—and especially Vice President Al Gore—would not want to leave themselves open to attacks for being soft on Saddam. Chalabi still hoped he'd be back in northern Iraq before the end of Clinton's term.

But no matter how many rear-guard actions Chalabi and his Capitol Hill partisans pulled off, the administration limited its military aid to the opposition to nonlethal items only: $2 million worth of desks, fax machines, and other surplus office supplies from the Pentagon's vast inventory, but not a single round of live ammunition.

And whatever interest Clinton had in regime change had passed by the end of 1999. The doves had regained the upper hand by arguing that taking down Saddam—whatever the merits—simply wasn't worth the cost. And Clinton himself decided he'd rather end his presidency trying to bring about Arab-Israeli peace than making war with Saddam. So there'd be no regime change in Iraq on Clinton's watch, let alone a Chalabi-led insurrection.

The president never announced that. He continued to talk tough about

Iraq, but it was no mystery to Richard Perle what was happening. Perle invited Chalabi over to his home in Chevy Chase to talk to him about it. "I remember saying to Ahmad that we're not going to get anywhere with Clinton," Perle recalled. "And he immediately understood it. Immediately. He's very smart. And we talked about it at some length. And we talked about what can usefully be done now with the resources available to improve the prospects that the next president will do the right thing."

One thing Chalabi's allies did early on, in anticipation of just this eventuality, was to make sure there was no "sunset clause" written into the Iraq Liberation Act. That meant the law would not terminate at the end of Clinton's term and that regime change would thus remain the policy of the U.S. government when the next president took office.

But which president? Would it be Al Gore, the sitting vice president? Or would it be Texas governor George W. Bush, the eldest son of former president George H. W. Bush? Chalabi was careful to deal with both the Democrats and Republicans, since he couldn't be sure who'd win. In 2000, he and some of his fellow members of the INC met privately with Gore, while Chalabi nurtured his already good relations with Gore's running mate, Joe Lieberman, one of the Iraq Liberation Act's original sponsors.

Meanwhile, Richard Perle continued to introduce Chalabi to Republicans of consequence. He brought the Iraqi exile along with him, for example, to the American Enterprise Institute's World Forum in Beaver Creek, Colorado, the conservative think tank's annual conclave of business executives, heads of government, government officials, and intellectuals from around the world. Over the years, participants had included British prime minister Margaret Thatcher, former French president Valéry Giscard d'Estaing, and former president Gerald Ford, a regular. The three-day gathering, held every summer, was (and still is) a private, highly exclusive function. Reporters are not invited, and plenary sessions and small-group discussions involving international politics, policy, and security are conducted off the record.

In 1998, Perle spoke about the balance of power in the Middle East, and introduced Chalabi as a featured guest speaker. This is where Chalabi met Newt Gingrich, then Speaker of the House, and Donald Rumsfeld, the future secretary of defense. "Rumsfeld told me about the time he met Saddam in Baghdad," Chalabi beamed.

Chalabi also met Dick Cheney for the first time at one of the AEI world conferences. "Cheney's a man of few words, so he listened to me," Chalabi said. "He listened to me talk about the process of change in Iraq, what could be done, and what a post-Saddam Iraq would look like."

At the time, Cheney was chairman and CEO of Texas-based Halliburton, the world's second-largest oil field services company with operations in more than seventy countries—a point not lost on Chalabi, who set about wooing the man with potential opportunities should he, Chalabi, succeed in Iraq. "I told him, 'Economically we have a major interest in developing an oil industry that is in close links with the United States.' I said that we want to move forward on this. And it is natural for the United States and Iraq to have this kind of relationship. And I was very clear about it." During their meeting, Chalabi could tell Cheney was sizing him up "to see if I was an asshole or a credible person." He said he passed the test.

Chalabi met Cheney a second time at the AEI's 2000 World Forum. Cheney was still CEO of Halliburton. But by then he had taken on a new assignment: heading up George W. Bush's vice-presidential search committee. Chalabi says it was a good break to be able to reintroduce himself to Cheney and to remind him of his history fighting Saddam. He hoped it would pay dividends should the Republicans win the election, and by now that was who Chalabi was pulling for—the Republican candidate. Chalabi says he took his lead from Richard Perle, who'd had a meeting with Bush and came away convinced Bush would finish the job his father had started.

"Richard has a gift which the Arabs call *farasa*," Chalabi explained to me. "He can see into somebody's heart. And he said that Bush may not understand Iraq, but he has the temperament to do what we want—to get rid of Saddam." Perle had looked into candidate Bush's heart during a visit to the Texas statehouse in 2000. At the time, Bush was such a neophyte in international affairs that his campaign organized a circle of advisers to tutor him. Perle was among a group that day which included Paul Wolfowitz, Richard Armitage, and Condoleezza Rice, who would become Bush's national security adviser and secretary of state.

Perle says he remembers the meeting with Bush well: "We saw him in the governor's mansion. He came into the room and went around and shook hands and got introduced to everybody he didn't know. And then he said, 'I wanna thank you for coming here. You're all busy. I understand that, and I appreciate that you've taken time out to come and see me. I need your help.' Then he said, 'I need your help not to become president. I'll take care of that. I need your help to be a good president because I need to understand the things you know.' "

Perle understood that the Texas governor was a newcomer to foreign affairs, but he was taken aback by just how little Bush actually knew. "He acknowledged not knowing things that were so basic most people would have been too embarrassed to admit. For example, he didn't know Germany is a member of NATO. That was pretty shocking." The fact that Bush's own father was president when the Berlin Wall fell in 1989 and when the Soviet Union was dissolved two years later made it all the more astonishing. But at the same time Perle says he respected Bush for being so candid about his ignorance. "I was impressed by that. That's a guy," Perle said, "with a strong will and determination to learn and who is open to ideas."

And to one idea in particular, as far as Perle was concerned. Perle says while the subject of Iraq never came up during the discussion, he came away convinced Bush "was a guy you could persuade that Saddam was a menace. And he seemed to be someone you could persuade to get behind the [Iraqi] opposition."

However, Perle did not find Bush to be such a blank slate that he felt he could mold him in his own image. "You mean, turn him into a neoconservative?" Perle laughed. "No. I remember thinking that because he's not committed to another view, there is a chance that he will [embrace regime change]. But I didn't think this guy was putty in our hands." To the contrary, Perle says, he found that Bush was "a pretty tough-minded guy. He understood that there are people who were hostile to the United States, and you've gotta deal with them very firmly." And hence, Perle concluded, Bush had the "temperament" to do what neither his father nor Clinton was willing to do: take down Saddam Hussein and his regime once and for all.

Perle would soon get the chance to test his read of George W. Bush—and his own belief that a focused effort by a handful of organized individuals can make a difference.

SEVENTEEN

That coterie of anti-Saddam diehards wasted no time in setting their sights on the new administration. On January 21, 2001, the second day of George W. Bush's presidency, Richard Perle convened the midday meeting at his home in Chevy Chase, Maryland, that Ahmad Chalabi attended in his beige sports coat with blue pinstripes. There was but one item on the agenda: regime change in Iraq.

None of the Americans there—Paul Wolfowitz, Douglas J. Feith, Zalmay Khalilzad, John P. Hannah—had a job yet in the administration, but it was clear that they all would, and that they would be well positioned to influence the president's Iraq policy. There was no doubt that Wolfowitz would be offered a high-level position; the only question was where. About six weeks later, on March 2, he was sworn in as the Pentagon's second-highest-ranking official, deputy secretary of defense. "We were happy he was there," Chalabi later said. "Wolfowitz told Perle if the administration did not follow a policy of overthrowing Saddam, he would resign."

As for Perle, he was offered the number three position under Wolfowitz, that of undersecretary of defense for policy. But Perle turned it down and instead recommended Feith for the job, which Feith assumed later that summer. Perle himself took the post of chairman of the Defense Policy Board, the committee charged with advising the Pentagon's top three officials—Wolfowitz, Feith, and Secretary of Defense Donald Rumsfeld—on matters of policy. Khalilzad, an American citizen born in Afghanistan who had long supported the ouster of Saddam Hussein, would join the National Security Council as a special assistant to Bush. Meanwhile,

Hannah, an earnest, thirty-nine-year-old neoconservative with degrees from Duke University and Yale Law School, had known Chalabi for years and was a big supporter. He would be working directly for Vice President Dick Cheney and his top national security adviser, I. Lewis "Scooter" Libby. The stars were aligning for Chalabi and the constellation of policy hawks who gathered at Perle's house at the dawn of the Bush presidency. "The general mood was, 'We've got a chance now,' " Perle said of the meeting.

Perle also felt good about having Cheney as vice president. "He was someone who I thought of as sympathetic to what we were trying to do," Perle told me. "And he knew Ahmad."

Chalabi was the lone non-American at the meeting. His systematic courting of people with influence had brought him to this point, to membership in an elite group of Americans positioned to take him to the next stage of his long passage home. He was not only their coequal but the lynchpin of their strategy. "Here we are championed by very strong people in the United States," he marveled to himself as he settled in for the meeting. He had come a long way indeed.

Chalabi arrived that day with his Capitol Hill aide-de-camp, Francis Brooke, and was joined by a longtime friend of Perle's named Harold Rhode, an unassuming, but strong-willed and energetic figure who worked as a midlevel Middle East specialist at the Office of Net Assessment, the Pentagon's internal think tank. Rhode, who has a PhD in Islamic studies, shared Perle's enthusiasm for Chalabi, saying at various times that he regarded the Iraqi expatriate as "the Charles de Gaulle of Iraq" and the "George Washington" of his country. But for Rhode, Chalabi's significance extended beyond the borders of Iraq. "Once I met Ahmad," Rhode said, "I intuitively understood that there was hope. Hope for what? A better future for the Middle East."

He saw Chalabi—with his intellect and apparently liberal, pro-Western values—as a potential agent of change for the entire region, someone who could at last infuse modernity into the political and cultural deserts of Arabia. "This is a man who can create or start the beginnings of a new Middle East," Rhode had thought to himself when he first met Chalabi in 1992. "He can do it. He can introduce freedom to the Middle East." In the nine years since then, Rhode's views about the Iraqi exile had not changed one bit.

The person who introduced Rhode to Chalabi was also sitting in on the meeting that day. She was Laurie Mylroie, a quiet-voiced and somewhat frazzled-looking academic who had published extensively on the subject of Iraq. She had just written a book, *Study of Revenge: Saddam Hussein's Unfinished War Against America*, claiming Saddam had orchestrated the 1993 terrorist attack on the World Trade Center in New York City, the first act of international terrorism within the United States. She also put him at the center of a vast, anti-U.S. terrorist conspiracy, blaming Saddam and his intelligence service for just about every major, anti-American terrorist incident of the past decade, from the leveling of the federal building in Oklahoma City in 1995 to the bombings of two U.S. embassies in Africa in 1998. An American, Timothy McVeigh, had been tried and convicted for the Oklahoma City carnage, and was facing execution. And hundreds of law enforcement and national security professionals from the CIA, the FBI, and the U.S. Attorney's Office had investigated the embassy attacks and found conclusive evidence proving al-Qaeda—not Saddam—had carried out the bombings. Yet Mylroie claimed that al-Qaeda was a front for Iraqi intelligence. The vast majority of terrorism experts dismissed her theories as "specious" and "risible," some calling her a "crackpot" anti-Saddam zealot.

She would soon be brought on as a Pentagon consultant, but for the moment the agenda at Perle's house was regime change—and on that issue she was considered to be of help. "Mylroie was an encyclopedia of things on Iraq," Chalabi said, in explaining the reason for her presence. "She had detailed records of everything Saddam ever said. She monitored broadcasts that related to Iraq and to the reaction of other Arab states and how it all related to U.S. policy. She was doing this work voluntarily. She was committed. So she was very important."

Such was the menagerie of conspiracy theorists, policy wonks, and neoconservative insurgents who had gathered together that day, their crosshairs firmly fixed on Bush's foreign policy agenda. "The strategy was to get the U.S. to commit now," Chalabi recalled of that day's deliberations.

But they were under no illusions it would be easy. The new president had neither campaigned for the overthrow of Saddam nor shown himself to be a fan of nation building. In fact, nation building was something Bush had openly derided as a candidate. "Maybe I'm missing something here," Bush had said just three months earlier in his October 2000 debate against his Democratic rival, Al Gore. "I mean, are we going to have some kind of nation-building corps from America? Absolutely not."

But Perle knew the president's foreign policy team would soon be undertaking a comprehensive review of the Iraq policy it was inheriting from Clinton, the policy of containment. In other words, Bush's Iraq policy was up for grabs. "So the issue was," Perle said, "how to persuade the new administration that they should change policy."

For Perle, who led the discussion, the act of persuasion was as much science as it was art. It began with identifying and neutralizing their likely adversaries in the upcoming policy review. To him, Condoleezza Rice, Bush's national security adviser, was somewhat in the middle. He didn't expect her to oppose regime change, but he didn't think she'd argue for it. He foresaw strong resistance from much of her staff, which included many holdovers from the Clinton administration. The real heat and vitriol, however, would come from what he called "the usual list of suspects: the State Department, the CIA, and the uniformed branch of the Pentagon (as opposed to the civilians)." The key to reducing their influence, he said, was to be better organized than they were. He said it was important to get their allies inside the government to work together—and to arm them with the best information and arguments available in support of regime change. It's not that they were unable to think for themselves, Perle would later explain. It's just that they had to juggle so many complex issues at once—from U.S.-Russia relations, missile defense, and NATO expansion to Iran and the Arab-Israeli conflict—that they could use all the help they could get.

"I have been a big believer for a long time," Perle elaborated, "that the machinery of government is made up of busy people. They've got a lot to do, more than there's time to do it. People whose only experience with government is getting a driver's license renewed—or getting a building permit—think that government employees are lazy sods who have nothing but time on their hands. But when you're in the policy world, you see how hard people work—long hours under constant strain. So if they're sympathetic and you can draft the talking points for them, it's a big help for them. And it obviously is an effective way to advance your argument."

It's the first lesson he learned as a Washington intern some thirty years earlier—doing the intellectual heavy lifting for others—and one that he employed with great success throughout his government career on Capitol Hill and as an assistant secretary of defense in the Reagan administration. And, as always, for Perle it was the ideas that mattered most.

"So on the grounds that we could make the argument more intelligible than others," Perle said, "the challenge was to think through the arguments, the counterarguments, and help people inside who were sympathetic to make them more effective in advocating that position. And that's all you can ever do."

What they needed to do first and foremost, he said, was undermine the principal argument in favor of containment: as long as Saddam was hemmed in by sanctions, there was no cause for concern. "If you could show that the sanctions were in jeopardy and might even collapse," Perle explained, "then you'd have to face the question of 'What do you do then?' "

There was already growing opposition to the sanctions, Perle pointed out, among veto-wielding members on the UN Security Council, France and Russia. And while Saddam deliberately exacerbated the problem by withholding food and critical medical supplies from his own people, it became increasingly accepted worldwide that the sanctions were causing undue hardship on the Iraqi people. The images of suffering, bedridden Iraqi women and baby-sized coffins carried on the rooftops of taxis led to an erosion of support for sanctions even in the United States.

"So we had to argue," Perle told me, "[that] it was just a matter of time before the sanctions gave way. And when that happened we would face a resurgent Saddam, a Saddam who had outlasted the coalition that defeated him and drove him from Kuwait, and a Saddam who had outlasted the sanctions. He's back, he's still in power, and you don't know what he'll do next. But you knew that this was one of history's truly monstrous dictators, and therefore you had to assume bad things." Assuming the worst-case scenario, he said, the United States would face a Saddam with new nuclear, chemical, and biological weapons, and a renewed capacity to intimidate and attack his Arab neighbors.

It was not enough, however, to argue the fragility of sanctions. Perle said they also had to offer a solution to the Saddam menace. And that's where Chalabi and the Iraqi National Congress came in. They were the solution. "They were viable, and a military strategy like Chalabi's for confronting Saddam and overthrowing his regime would work," Perle said. "Those were the main issues to be argued."

Those issues had already been argued, and won, in Congress, where leaders of both the Republican-controlled House and Senate now supported the Iraqi opposition as the vehicle for overthrowing Saddam and his regime. The 2000 GOP presidential nominating convention similarly embraced the Iraqi National Congress in its party plank, as had a host of former

Republican government officials, including three national security advisers and three secretaries of defense, along with Clinton's first CIA director, R. James Woolsey. But inside the bowels of the bureaucracy, where U.S. foreign policy was hashed out one memo and one meeting at a time, and where the administration's Iraq policy review would be chewed over and debated before bubbling up to the president for a decision, Chalabi was well known—and not well liked. The policy apparatchiks would present formidable opposition to Chalabi on a personal level, and to his military plan operationally.

At CIA headquarters in Langley, for example, Chalabi was so despised that no one there wanted anything to do with him—period. At Foggy Bottom, State Department officials who had worked closely with him for years found him to be divisive, devious, and power-hungry, and they believed he had little following among either the Kurds in northern Iraq or his fellow exile leaders in Europe and the Middle East. As far as anyone at State could tell, he enjoyed even less support among the Iraqi people inside the country. His family had fled more than forty years ago, and what little Iraqis had heard of him since then had come from Jordan, where Chalabi had been convicted in absentia of bank fraud. As one American analyst put it at the time, "The INC enjoys more support along the Potomac than the Euphrates."

But Perle would put his own prestige and reputation on the line for Chalabi, as he had known the man now personally for a decade and reached an entirely different conclusion about him: Chalabi was an honorable man. He had his flaws, to be sure, and of course he coveted power. But it was power with a purpose: to rid his people of a vicious tyrant. Regarding the embezzlement conviction in Jordan, Perle thought, "So what?" Even if the charges against Chalabi were true—and Perle did not think they were—there were far deadlier sins in the Middle East than stealing money. And, besides, since when did the CIA—and the State Department, for that matter—get religion about climbing into bed with shady characters?

As for Chalabi's lack of political support in the region, Perle—along with Wolfowitz—argued that was easily remedied: all Washington had to do was put its stamp on Chalabi's authority, and America's Arab allies would fall into line, as would Iraqis from the Tigris to the Thames.

Perle was aware of the criticisms of Chalabi's military plan, too. But he knew Wolfowitz had since beefed it up with his own innovations, while

Wayne Downing, the retired four-star general, and Dewey Clarridge, the ex–CIA officer, had also tweaked it. Perle hoped to arrange a series of briefings at the Pentagon between Downing and the military brass as soon as possible. Downing passed away in 2007 and can no longer defend his plans. Perle, however, is happy to do so.

In Perle's account of the beefed-up military plan, the United States would help the INC recruit, train, and equip a highly mobile light infantry force of ten to twenty thousand troops, most of whom would be former Iraqi military personnel. They would be inserted into Iraqi Kurdistan, in the country's north, and near an air base in Basra, in the country's oil-rich south. The occupied areas would collectively be declared Free Iraq, and U.S. airpower would defend them from Iraqi army counterattack. From there, Perle was drawn to what he called the inkblot strategy. "The idea being," Perle told me, "that the inkblot covers the area that's not under Saddam's control and, like ink spilling down a blotter, it moves slowly out. As it presses up against Saddam's defensive lines, Saddam had a choice. He could either yield territory or mass his forces to contain the expansion. And if he did the latter, if he massed his forces, we could strike them from the air. So he would have to choose between accepting political losses—the loss of any territory would have been a defeat and an embarrassment for him—or using his forces in ways that made them vulnerable."

While Saddam's military was no match for America's, it seemed optimistic to believe that a rebel force of 20,000 lightly armed soldiers could wrest control of Iraq from Saddam's army of 400,000. Even with the Kurds holding the north, INC forces would have to control a military front in the south and west that stretched some six hundred miles. Perle had an answer for skeptics.

"It was also Ahmad's belief," Perle responded, "that there were units of the Iraq army that would defect to the INC if they saw a realistic opportunity to do so."

That premise was based on Chalabi's experience in 1995, when he had attached his INC militia—which numbered anywhere from five hundred to five thousand, depending on who you believed—to a much larger Kurdish force and together they took on two brigades of the Iraqi 38th Infantry Division. Many of the division's soldiers did desert. But they had come from an Iraqi military unit that was based hundreds of miles from Baghdad, consisting of soldiers whom Saddam barely bothered to train, equip, or even stock with the most basic of supplies, including boots and food. Before the

1995 military operation, Chalabi once said, the often-barefoot Iraqi soldiers would cross a river into Kurdistan and trade bullets for live chickens and other food supplies.

By contrast, Saddam's elite Republican Guard and Special Republican Guard forces, which numbered nearly 100,000, were well cared for by Saddam—and they were infinitely more disciplined than any soldier Chalabi would have encountered in the north. During the 1991 Gulf War, after thousands of sorties and thirty-nine days of nonstop, withering aerial bombardments by U.S. and coalition pilots, not one Republican Guard division cracked. And the few regular army divisions that did desert did so not because of the pounding they took from the sky, but mostly out of fear of the impending coalition ground offensive.

Moreover, many military analysts inside the U.S. government and out discounted the ultimate effectiveness of airpower alone to bring down a regime—it had never worked before. And they also were skeptical that it could protect opposition forces from a determined foe. As *Foreign Affairs* magazine asserted in a 1999 article entitled "The Rollback Fantasy":

> U.S. air support could not protect the opposition troops because Iraqi attacks could come during bad weather or simply at night, when the U.S. ability to interdict ground troops is greatly reduced. The 1996 Iraqi attack on the opposition-held northern city of Erbil is instructive here, precisely because the Iraqis were terrified that the United States would try to defend the city from the air. They therefore built up their forces carefully, attacked at night, smashed the INC and Kurdish forces before daylight, and withdrew the next day, presenting Washington with a fait accompli. The United States simply does not have enough all-weather strike aircraft to keep enough warplanes in the Persian Gulf to respond instantaneously to regime attacks on opposition units inside Iraq for the months and perhaps years that it would take to topple Saddam.

The Chalabi plan, critics asserted, would almost certainly end up with what General Anthony Zinni once called the Bay of Goats scenario, in which the United States would have to choose between allowing the Iraqi opposition to be slaughtered by Saddam's forces or rescued by the U.S. Army—that is, a direct American intervention.

Perle's response? "Look," he said, "there was certainly a danger that in pursuing the strategy of moving gradually forward out of areas covered by the no-fly zone and confronting Saddam's forces that you could get into a situation where the opposition was trapped and vulnerable. Nobody could exclude that as a possibility."

But Wolfowitz thought that risk could be minimized, arguing the United States should also be prepared to commit ground forces to protect a sanctuary in southern Iraq where the opposition could safely mobilize.

Perle denied that that was tantamount to a U.S. invasion of Iraq. "No," Perle insisted. "It is by definition a U.S. military involvement, but very different than an invasion. I think the concept then was to defend territory that wasn't already under Saddam's control." He was referring to the areas in northern and southern Iraq already under protection by the no-fly zone.

In a later conversation, Perle addressed the long-standing charge that he and his allies had always wanted to put American boots on the ground and were just waiting for an excuse to do it. "Nobody sitting around and talking about what to do next was arguing for the United States invading Iraq—no one," he said. "There's a lot of confusion on this point because the critics of Chalabi and of his friends all say, 'We had been trying to do this for years, and 9/11 gave us an opportunity to do something we wanted to do anyway.' What we wanted to do anyway, or at least what I wanted to do anyway, was get behind the [Iraqi] opposition to Saddam. Not send the U.S. Army in to topple him."

Besides, he says, prior to the terrorist attacks of September 11, 2001, any policy proposal that hinted at an invasion would have been rejected out of hand. "If you wanted to move the Bush administration in the direction of the policy that could lead to Saddam's removal," Perle said, "the worst way to do that would be to argue for an invasion, because nobody was gonna support that." So you had to argue for something short of that, he said, and that was supporting the Iraqi opposition as Congress intended when it passed the Iraq Liberation Act. "And the costs of implementing the Iraq Liberation Act," he insisted, "were pretty modest."

In the final assessment, he regarded Chalabi as both a personal friend and a reliable partner for the United States of America, one with a real plan to overthrow Saddam and his regime. That would be Perle's mantra from his perch as a Pentagon adviser, and one that Wolfowitz and Feith would try to advance from theirs inside the new administration as Bush's foreign policy team undertook its first comprehensive policy review on Iraq.

The review began in early 2001. It was waged mostly in writing through policy papers and at the deputies' level between the department's number two officials, including Wolfowitz at the Pentagon and his counterparts at the CIA, the State Department, and the office of the vice president. As Perle had anticipated, even though the Clinton administration had been replaced by the Bush administration, the same bureaucratic battles carried over and, just as before, boiled down to containment versus regime change.

The two sides also had very different views on the role of Chalabi's Iraqi National Congress. Wolfowitz and Scooter Libby, Cheney's chief of staff and top national security adviser, advocated an aggressive strategy to empower the INC, proposing that the exiles receive U.S. military training and reestablish their presence in Iraq, north and south, for future military operations against Saddam's regime.

The other faction, centered at the State Department, favored "smart sanctions," a streamlined and reinvigorated way to clamp down on Saddam's purchase of WMD-related items, while essentially lifting all remaining restrictions on civilian goods going into Iraq. This approach envisioned a greatly reduced role for the Iraqi opposition, limiting it largely to propaganda and humanitarian aid for displaced Iraqis.

Curiously, throughout the debate Chalabi's name rarely, if ever, came up. But for both sides he was the elephant in the room.

"Our sense was," one senior State Department official said, "it was too much about Chalabi."

"They really carried his water," said Richard L. Armitage, the barrel-chested, gravelly voiced number two at the State Department.

The name Ahmad Chalabi never passed the lips of the CIA's deputy director, John McLaughlin, either. McLaughlin, who had been named to the CIA's number two position in October 2000, didn't have to say anything about the Iraqi exile. Everyone knew exactly where the agency stood on him.

Beyond Chalabi, there were real and substantive differences. The CIA still argued for regime change, but by means of a coup rather than a wholesale eradication of the Ba'athist regime. The agency wanted another military strongman to take over, one who was less erratic than Saddam but who was still Sunni, Ba'athist, and committed to opposing the Islamic radicals in Tehran. To Langley, the issue was stability—and ensuring that Iraq remained a bulwark against Iranian hegemony in the region.

Wolfowitz and Feith shared those concerns, but they had no confidence in the CIA's ability to pull off a coup, given that Langley's last attempt—just five years earlier—had ended in a bloody fiasco. Nor did they view the status quo in Iraq as either orderly or stable for the long term.

But Chalabi was the fault line. His presence hovered over the policy debate, for he had essentially come to personify both the Iraqi opposition and, in large measure, the case for and against wholesale regime change.

That divide was reflected in a four-page, single-spaced fax that Perle sent to Secretary of Defense Donald Rumsfeld on February 19, 2001, a month after the new administration took office. "I have been working with Zal on Iraq," Perle began, referring to Zalmay Khalilzad, one of the men who had sat in on the meeting at Perle's home the month before, "but wanted to share a personal view with you as well. I have known and dealt with the Iraqi opposition for the last 15 years. I have come to know Ahmad Chalabi very well indeed." Perle was now getting to the point of his note. "I know he has many detractors, especially in the intelligence community." But the spy community's "30-year history of incompetence" in handling Iraq and other matters in the region was matched only by "their efforts to discredit Chalabi." Calling such efforts a "disgrace," Perle went on: "To defame him, they have resorted to lies and character assassination in a shocking scale."

Perle pointed the finger at the CIA director, asserting, "George Tenet in particular has been single-minded in attacking the INC. I like to think that as between my assessment and Tennant's [sic], you would have enough confidence in my judgment, considering the time and attention I have devoted to this matter, to come down on my side of this."

Perle detailed Chalabi's history with the CIA and the Clinton administration—from Chalabi's point of view—saying that "in the last four years, the Clinton administration has put more effort into undermining Chalabi than undermining Saddam."

Perle then outlined a seven-point proposal for implementing a new policy regarding the opposition, including reestablishing the INC's presence in northern and southern Iraq. "As INC presence widens," Perle wrote, "Saddam will be challenged politically to demonstrate he can prevent an alternative 'government' from operating on Iraqi territory. It is then that we must be prepared to use the 'no fly' zone to protect the opposition from Iraqi armor. This can be done with U.S. air assets. . . . With the INC operating in this fashion, we could expect major defections from Saddam's forces. Ultimately it is this that can break the back of the regime."

It was a major affirmation of Chalabi, personally wrapped in an Iraq policy proposal centered on him operationally—sent directly to the secretary of defense. But that was just the beginning. Over the next several months, there would be a slew of proposals and behind-the-scenes machinations that were designed to promote either Chalabi personally or the policy of regime change via the INC.

For example, in March 2001, unidentified sources at the Pentagon leaked word that it had created a new position called Iraq transition coordinator, a job that was designed to replace the one held by Chalabi's State Department nemesis Frank Ricciardone. The Pentagon's candidate for the new post was a well-known Chalabi partisan, Randy Scheunemann, the former adviser to Senate Majority Leader Trent Lott. The move was part of the Pentagon's larger strategy for wresting away control of the administration's Iraq policy.

That same month, the administration freed up millions of dollars that had been previously earmarked for Chalabi's INC but had been bottled up by the Clinton administration. The money was to be used to fund something called the Information Collection Program, under which Chalabi was to use his INC offices in Tehran, Damascus, and elsewhere in the region to collect information mostly about Saddam's war crimes and other crimes against humanity. But Chalabi decided to expand its purview and use the program to gather information that would be useful in influencing the Iraq policy debate that was now raging back in Washington. He wanted to use it to find evidence that would undermine the State Department's proposal for so-called smart sanctions and to show they "existed only in Washington policy papers—not on the ground."

To prove that, he went after the failings of a similar concept, the UN's Oil-for-Food Program. Under Oil-for-Food, Baghdad was allowed to sell $4 billion worth of oil every year to buy food, medicine, and other humanitarian supplies for the Iraqi people. Of course, it was wishful thinking to ever believe Saddam would observe the rules, let alone spirit, of the program. But Chalabi now set out to prove that Saddam had broken the rules, dispatching his people in the INC's Damascus office to fan out to Syrian pharmacies and buy medical supplies imported from Iraq, showing that Saddam's regime was reselling medical products purchased under Oil-for-Food and then pocketing the cash.

Chalabi also came up with evidence showing that the regime had skimmed some $200,000 a day over five months from an oil pipeline deal and hundreds of millions of dollars more from wheat purchases from Australia—proof that the UN was already unable to stop Saddam's larceny. "Think about it," Chalabi remarked. "Saddam's treasury was being bloated by all that."

And that was to say nothing of how Iraq exploited the Oil-for-Food Program to dole out oil sales in return for political support in the UN, rewarding those who toed Baghdad's line and stiffing those who didn't.

"Smart sanctions would never work!" Chalabi bellowed to me. "It's too much money, too lucrative, and the consequences of conducting this illegal activity were minimal."

Back in the 1990s, when the INC was funded by the CIA, Chalabi used to tell the accountants in Langley that Iraqis did not operate in a receipt culture. But, in this instance, he was extraordinarily scrupulous about keeping his records organized, including the Syrian pharmacy receipts, so that he could supply his evidence to journalists in search of a story. It was all accurate information, much of it independently corroborated in later years. But, to paraphrase Richard Perle, it was also information with a purpose: to arm his allies inside the administration with ammunition to shoot down smart sanctions. And by feeding the information to journalists, Chalabi was also able to drive the public debate occurring in the newspapers and think tanks of Washington and New York. It was a tactic that, remarkably, was all financed by the U.S. government—and one that he would soon employ again.

Meanwhile, back in Washington, Richard Perle pressed for a meeting between Vice President Cheney's staff and Chalabi's Kurdish aide, Aras Habib Karim. "Perle found Aras very impressive," Chalabi recalled. "So he pushed them to meet Aras so the administration would have some assurance who the hell I am talking about—who would be running this. It would solidify support."

In a few years' time, U.S. counterintelligence would issue a "burn notice" against Karim, declaring that he was a full-up, paid agent of Iran's intelligence service. But in 2001, Karim was only under suspicion for his ties to Iran. Given three polygraph tests by the CIA, he failed two and came up "inconclusive" on the third. But the agency nonetheless issued him a visa to enter the United States. And after arriving, he motored up to Pennsylvania Avenue and walked right into the Old Executive Office Building, next to the White House, where he met with William J. Luti, a special adviser to

Cheney for national security affairs, and John Hannah, one of the men who had sat in on the meeting at Perle's house in January.

At about the same time, Chalabi got his own special invitation from Hannah—this time, to meet personally with Cheney. Chalabi was told to be discreet. "They said no press. Nobody knows about it," Chalabi recalled. So he and Francis Brooke drove to the vice president's residence on the grounds of the U.S. Naval Observatory in northwest Washington, D.C. Brooke waited in another room while Chalabi met privately with Cheney—for what was now their third meeting in two years.

As always, the vice president did most of the listening, and when he did talk, says Chalabi, he was frugal with his words but deliberate about his message. "He said that our policy is to support a democratic Iraq," Chalabi recounted. A "democratic Iraq" was Cheney-speak for the overthrow of Saddam and his Ba'athist regime—neither a continuation of containment nor the CIA's policy of a palace coup.

Chalabi underscored that while Cheney "expressed support and sympathy" for overthrowing Saddam, with Chalabi's Iraqi National Congress as the "main engine" for doing so, he did not say explicitly that the United States would invade Iraq.

A senior White House official confirmed that Chalabi had indeed met with Cheney alone, more than once, although the official couldn't recall exactly when. The official was skeptical, however, that the vice president would have so openly endorsed the INC. "It's not how the vice president usually operates," the official said.

But to Chalabi's ears, that's the way it sounded, and he left the vice president's residence a happy man. So far, his friends in the new administration had really delivered.

EIGHTEEN

In March 2001 there was yet another piece of good news for Ahmad Chalabi: the new Bush administration had titled its as-yet-unfinished Iraq policy review "Winning the Unfinished War." It had a nice, forward-sounding ring to it.

As the policy draft circulated through the outer rim of the Pentagon, where senior military officials have their offices, and made its way into the White House complex along Pennsylvania Avenue, Chalabi settled in for the bureaucratic battle to come. He continued to commute between Washington and London, leaving Francis Brooke to attend to the details of the daily grind. Brooke had already relocated his family from Atlanta to Washington, where he now lived rent-free in Chalabi's $2 million Georgetown townhouse. The former beer industry lobbyist was living more comfortably than ever, but that hardly mattered to him. He was focused on getting the Bush administration to back his boss, and he knew he had a long way to go yet. "It was a competitive environment for foreign policy," Brooke recalled, "so we were making every effort to advance our policy."

Brooke worked around the clock, staying in frequent contact with the Iraqi National Congress's allies inside the Pentagon and at the office of the vice president. He fed them new leads that the INC was able to extract from inside Iraq—courtesy of the U.S.-funded Information Collection Program. He planted stories in the press. And he lobbied the INC's friends in Congress to weigh in on their behalf.

The Iraq policy review was supposed to be completed within a matter of weeks. But the hoped-for bureaucratic sprint quickly bogged down into a trench war between the hawks and the doves. Sometimes, Brooke says, the deliberations turned ugly. "There was no refereeing of the disputes," Brooke recalled. "There was only blood on the floor. The Bush administration was very dysfunctional. One side couldn't agree with the other, especially when it came to us. It was always 51 percent to 49 percent when it came to Chalabi. Some days we were up, some days we were down. It was a constant struggle." Unfortunately, he said, "There were only a limited number of slots for people who thought like us, and it was never enough."

Chalabi, however, remained characteristically optimistic. "It was going well," he said of the policy review. "It was not, as George Tenet said, a 'slam dunk.' But it was going well."

At a July 13, 2001, deputies meeting, Paul Wolfowitz made a big push to strengthen U.S. support for the Iraqi opposition. It was the same initiative he had been advocating for years, but one he was now presenting as "draft plans." Those plans included recognizing a provisional government and establishing a second anti-Saddam enclave in the southern Iraqi city of Basra. Along with U.S.-protected Kurdistan in the north, Wolfowitz said, the region should be designated as Free Iraq and given legal possession of the billions of dollars of frozen Iraqi assets in the United States and Europe. The protected zone in the south, he said, would serve as a base where anti-Saddam members of the Iraqi military could switch sides and then, under U.S. protection, expand to encompass Saddam's oil fields and their revenues. The hope was that capture of the oil fields would cause the collapse of Saddam's regime.

It was essentially the Downing/Chalabi strategy for overthrowing Saddam, and a near-carbon copy of the inkblot strategy Richard Perle had outlined in his February fax to Defense Secretary Donald Rumsfeld. At the heart of the plan, Wolfowitz said, was the conviction that Iraqis "needed to be able to do the fight themselves with our help, and that we should give them substantial help, including air power. But I didn't wanna see a lot of American body bags for their liberation."

At the State Department, however, Wolfowitz's plan was greeted with derision. To Secretary of State Colin Powell and his number two, Richard Armitage—both former military officers—it was one of the most strategically unsound proposals they had ever heard. It reminded them of the strategy that the United States had employed during the Vietnam War called Chieu Hoi (Open Arms). In the case of Iraq, it struck Powell and Armitage as wishful thinking, if not lunacy, to expect that all the United States had to do was liberate fourteen acres of territory in a country the size of France and then members of Saddam's army would simply rush to the side of the U.S.-supported opposition. Chalabi may have convinced Wolfowitz—and the Pentagon's other civilian leaders—of that, but Armitage and Powell, the latter a retired four-star general and onetime chairman of the Joint Chiefs of Staff, thought it was laughable. The Iraqi army was certainly unhappy with its lot, they agreed. But there had never been any such mass defections in the north, where Chalabi himself had operated for four years and where the United States had maintained a no-fly zone for ten years.

But Rumsfeld put his foot down. He was worried about Saddam's growing proficiency at evading UN sanctions and insisted that Bush hear the proposal. He urged National Security Adviser Condoleezza Rice to convene what's called a principals meeting—one chaired by the national security adviser and typically attended by the vice president, the secretaries of defense and state, and the director of the CIA, among others—on Iraq in preparation for a discussion with the president.

Later that month, Wolfowitz and the Pentagon's number three official, Douglas J. Feith—who had sat in on the meeting in Perle's living room six months earlier—prepared a memo for Rumsfeld on how to end the "logjam" on support for the Iraqi opposition.

Less than a week later, on August 1, Rumsfeld got his principals meeting, in which Wolfowitz presented a top secret paper discussing covert and other U.S. support for the Iraqi opposition groups and possible direct military action. The paper was entitled "A Liberation Strategy," the identical heading used by retired general Wayne Downing in the plan he had helped draw up for Chalabi.

Then a new high-water mark for Chalabi arrived: his allies inside the administration got to make the case to Bush directly, with Wolfowitz assuring the still-new commander in chief that the enclave strategy would succeed. Powell warned the president, however, "This is not as easy as it is being presented."

Either way, it was a remarkable milestone: Chalabi's long-held dream of regime change, and his strategy for achieving it, had made it all the way into the Oval Office. To be sure, history was his ally, as was Saddam Hussein himself, whose repeated feints, miscalculations, and provocative pretenses—directed mostly at Iran—wound up casting the dictator in the

most threatening light possible in Washington. Even so, Chalabi had overcome a great deal.

But he and his alliance had not yet made it to the finish line. As of late
summer 2001, Bush had not decided what America's policy toward Iraq
should be. I had been following the contours of the debate from a distance as
a producer for CBS News' *60 Minutes*. But on the evening of September 10,
I became privy to a new perspective on it when I had dinner near the White
House with Richard A. Clarke, Bush's top counterterrorism adviser. The
year before, *60 Minutes* correspondent Lesley Stahl and I had done a story
with Clarke about terrorism. He was a hard-liner on the subject, someone
who had been dealing with the threat since the 1980s, when he got his first
presidential appointment from Ronald Reagan. Clarke went on to serve in
the administration of George H. W. Bush, then became Bill Clinton's terrorism czar and had been held over by George W. Bush.

Over dinner, I asked Clarke about something surprising I had recently
heard: that he had asked for a transfer from his terrorism job. He confirmed
that it was true, and said it was because of his frustration with the administration's lack of focus on al-Qaeda. He asked me not to run the story—at
least not yet—and I agreed. But as he eventually would say on *60 Minutes*,
and in his 2004 memoir, *Against All Enemies: Inside America's War on Terror*, the Bush team did not take the threat of al-Qaeda seriously, despite his
repeated warnings, and those of the CIA, about the growing body of evidence indicating Osama bin Laden was planning an imminent attack on
the U.S. homeland. As Clarke would also later testify before Congress, he
encountered key administration officials who belittled the threat posed by
al-Qaeda and instead focused incessantly on Iraq. In particular, he singled
out Paul Wolfowitz and an April 2001 meeting of the deputies committee,
composed of the agencies' seconds-in-command. It was the first high-level
discussion on terrorism since Bush took office. Clarke began his brief by
saying, "We have to deal with bin Laden, we have to deal with al-Qaeda."
He outlined a series of initiatives designed to take the fight to the terrorist
leader and his organization. But Wolfowitz interjected, "No, no, no. We
don't have to deal with al-Qaeda. Why are we talking about this little guy?
We have to talk about Iraqi terrorism against the United States."

When Clarke and the deputy directors of both the CIA and the FBI
pointed out that there had been no Iraqi terrorism directed at the United
States in eight years, not since 1993, when the U.S. bombed Iraq for its

ham-handed attempt to assassinate the first President Bush while he was in Kuwait, and that the few terrorists who remained in Iraq had been inactive for a decade, Wolfowitz turned to Clarke with a scowl and said, "You give bin Laden too much credit. He could not do all these things like the 1993 attack on New York, not without a state sponsor. Just because the FBI and CIA have failed to find the linkages does not mean they don't exist."

Clarke's jaw dropped as he listened to Wolfowitz spout "the totally dis-credited Laurie Mylroie theory that Iraq was behind the 1993 truck bomb at the World Trade Center, a theory that had been investigated for years and found to be totally untrue."

Clarke's warnings would continue to go unheeded until the morning after our dinner. But with the attacks of September 11, he finally got the war against al-Qaeda he wanted—and, in the same stroke, Chalabi got a new opening to press the case for his.

In Iraq, when Saddam Hussein first learned of the September 11, 2001, attacks, he thought America's tragedy would finally put Washington and Baghdad on the path to reconciliation. Saddam had long regarded al-Qaeda and its Islamic ideology as a threat to his secular regime, and had even directed his intelligence service to locate and capture any members of the terrorist group who might be in Iraq. That's why—as senior regime figures would later tell their American debriefers—Saddam believed after 9/11 that the Bush administration would finally embrace Iraq's previous offers to combat Islamic fundamentalism. It was, however, another of Saddam's grave miscalculations about Washington.

Ahmad Chalabi, on the other hand, knew America well and he imme-diately grasped the significance of 9/11 for U.S. policy. "It made sure that they would get rid of Saddam," Chalabi said. "If these people in caves in Afghanistan could mobilize and penetrate the United States' entire security system, kill three thousand people, and hit the symbol of American capital-ism in New York, the World Trade Center, then no U.S. president could tolerate a regime like Saddam's. He's funded terrorism. He has a history of using weapons of mass destruction against his people. And the CIA is telling you he has stockpiles of biological weapons. Do you risk leaving Saddam in power? Who would leave him in place after 9/11?" Besides, Chalabi said, "We had already set the stage. The people in charge of national security had this on their mind," he said, referring to regime change in Iraq. "And, of course, to see how effective we were, the concept of overthrowing Saddam was presented as one of the first actions of the United States."

Within twenty-four hours of the attacks, the Pentagon was in fact beginning to shift its focus to Iraq—despite the CIA's determination that al-Qaeda alone had orchestrated the attacks from Afghanistan. Richard Clarke says that he was incredulous at first but that he then realized "with almost a sharp physical pain that Rumsfeld and Wolfowitz were going to try to take advantage of this national tragedy to promote their agenda about Iraq."

During a series of high-level meetings that day, Rumsfeld and Wolfowitz both recommended expanding the U.S. response to include bombing Iraq. "There aren't any good targets in Afghanistan, and there are lots of good targets in Iraq," Rumsfeld famously asserted.

Meanwhile, Wolfowitz said he was skeptical that al-Qaeda could have pulled off simultaneous attacks in New York and Washington without the help of a state sponsor. The operation was too sophisticated, he said. Iraq must have helped them, he said, again echoing Laurie Mylroie's thesis.

In fact, Iraq had nothing to do with the attacks, and Clarke and CIA director George Tenet told Rumsfeld and Wolfowitz that—repeatedly. But the administration's previous debate over regime change had almost immediately morphed into a new, and more contentious, rift over whether to include Iraq in the United States' response to 9/11. The battle lines remained essentially the same, with the State Department on one side arguing for narrowly targeting al-Qaeda to keep the international consensus together and the Pentagon on the other side leading the charge for also confronting Iraq.

On September 15, during a meeting of top officials at Camp David, Wolfowitz told Bush (erroneously) that there was "a 10 to 50 percent chance" Iraq was involved in the 9/11 attacks and that the United States would have to take down Saddam's regime if rogue nations and terrorist groups were to take the war on terrorism seriously. At the same meeting, Rumsfeld said this was a good time to attack Iraq, since there was going to be a large buildup of forces in the region and, again, because Afghanistan lacked "good targets."

On September 19, Richard Perle convened a two-day meeting of the Defense Policy Board, the Pentagon advisory committee, during which Chalabi was a featured speaker. The board comprised a who's who of foreign policy heavyweights, from Henry Kissinger to James Schlesinger and Harold Brown (former secretaries of defense), Newt Gingrich, and General Jack Keane.

"I wanted to connect Chalabi with these people. Absolutely," Perle said later. "So that he would establish his own relationships with them, follow-up conversations, all toward enhancing his ability to develop his ideas and to share his information with influential decision makers."

Chalabi was introduced by Bernard Lewis, who said that the United States had to respond to 9/11 with a show of strength. Doing otherwise, he warned, would be viewed as a sign of weakness in the Islamic world—and would invite more attacks against America. At the same time, he said, it was America's support of Arab dictatorships that fueled the people's rage there against the United States. Washington should support democratic reformers in the Middle East. "Such as my friend here," he said, "Dr. Chalabi."

Chalabi then proceeded to make the case he'd been making for years: that as dangerous as Saddam was to American national security, the strongman was actually a paper tiger and could easily be defeated. Chalabi presented his enclave strategy, asking that the United States "help us create a military force of ten thousand Iraqi soldiers." He also said that if the United States decided to invade Iraq itself, then this envisioned INC army of ten thousand should be part of the effort. Chalabi was looking into the future, and hedging his bets.

Following the meeting, one of the Defense Policy Board members, James R. Woolsey—the former CIA director whose law firm represented Chalabi's INC—flew with a team of Justice and Defense Department officials on a government plane to London. Their assignment was, in a nutshell, to chase down Laurie Mylroie's theory—specifically, to find evidence that Saddam had been involved with both the 9/11 attacks and the 1993 World Trade Center bombing. Both Wolfowitz and Feith supported the mission.

Woolsey would soon return empty-handed. By then Bush had already decided to postpone the question of what to do about Iraq.

But Chalabi remained buoyant. The battle over Iraq was joined, and his friends inside the administration remained as determined as ever. "Our friends were energized that we had to do something," Chalabi told me.

They shifted into yet a higher gear when letters containing deadly anthrax powder started showing up in the U.S. mail—and killing people. The first death due to anthrax inhalation was publicly confirmed in Florida on October 4. Then a letter containing anthrax spores was opened at NBC News headquarters in New York City. Letters were also sent to CBS News, ABC News, the *New York Post*, and the *National Enquirer*. Finally, envelopes containing anthrax arrived in the Washington offices of two U.S. senators. They contained anthrax that was far more potent than what had been found in the previous letters—a highly refined powder consisting of one gram of nearly pure spores. U.S. Army scientists initially (and incorrectly) concluded the anthrax in the Senate letters had been "weaponized."

That was good news for Chalabi—or, as he put it, "It was not inimical to our cause when the Senate was hit with anthrax." That's because Saddam Hussein was immediately and widely—though, as later proven, erroneously—identified as the prime suspect. The anthrax crisis was taken as a new round of ammunition in the campaign for overthrowing Saddam. As one British newspaper noted at the time, "[S]keptics fear American hawks could be publicizing the claim [of Iraqi involvement in the anthrax attacks] to press their case for strikes against Iraq," adding, "[T]he pressure now building among senior Pentagon and White House officials in Washington for an attack may become irresistible."

The pressure continued to mount as thirty-one people on Capitol Hill tested positive for the presence of anthrax, including twenty-three members of Senate Majority Leader Tom Daschle's staff. The mail-processing facilities for Congress, the CIA, the State Department, the Justice Department, and the Supreme Court were all shut down, as were all six major congressional office buildings, including the Senate Hart Building. President Bush said the nation had been hit by a "second wave of terrorist attacks."

In early October, amid this maelstrom of fear and panic, Chalabi says, he received a phone call from John P. Hannah, one of Cheney's national security aides who reported to Scooter Libby. Hannah asked Chalabi to meet him at 11:30 that morning at a Starbucks near the White House. When they arrived, the shop was largely empty. They ordered coffee and sat down to talk. Hannah, Chalabi said, quickly got to the point. "The administration is looking for people who know about Iraq's weapons of mass destruction, Iraqis who know about these weapons firsthand. Can you introduce us to any?" Hannah asked. "It's critical that you have some people who know about WMD."

Despite the timing, Chalabi did not get the impression that administration officials believed Saddam was behind the anthrax attacks; nor were they worried that he might be plotting an attack. "No," Chalabi said flatly. "It was to push forward the policy. Hannah said, 'The administration needs information about weapons of mass destruction so we can move forward with this agenda.'" In other words, the goal was to strengthen the policy hawks' position internally—*inside* the Bush administration—in support of overthrowing Saddam. The meeting, he said, lasted less than half an hour.

When asked about it, Hannah didn't specifically recall the encounter, according to a former senior administration official close to Hannah. But he doesn't deny that it took place and, in fact, thinks it likely did occur just as Chalabi described. "I'm sure," Hannah recalled. "I certainly—yes—would have wanted the help of Ahmad and the INC in terms of building this case against Iraq and why Iraq needed to be taken care of, a serious factual brief [on Saddam's WMD program]."

At the time, Hannah's boss, Cheney, was growing increasingly alarmed about America's vulnerability to a large-scale biological weapons attack. He had seen the data on the number of people who could be killed and injured by a bioweapons incident. And he knew that Iraq in 1995 had admitted to mass-producing purified biological toxins, including 19,000 liters of concentrated botulinum toxin, 8,500 liters of anthrax, and 2,200 liters of aflatoxin. Iraq also told weapons inspectors that it had destroyed all of its deadly biological agents. And that was true. But in the fall of 2001, the United Nations could not verify Baghdad's claims, while Saddam had proved himself to be a serial liar when it came to his WMD stockpiles. In addition, while U.S. intelligence had strongly and specifically disputed any links between Saddam Hussein and al-Qaeda, Cheney knew that the CIA in other instances had been wrong before—sometimes with catastrophic consequences. How much of a risk could America afford to take now? The anthrax letters, coming so closely on the heels of 9/11, played into the vice president's conviction that it was just too dangerous to leave Saddam in power. In his view, the administration needed to "pull out the stops in developing an aggressive policy to get rid of this guy," one former senior administration official said.

The Bush administration also approached the Kurds and at least one other Iraqi opposition party about introducing them to defectors. But Chalabi—always the most determined, energetic, and organized of the Iraqis in the opposition—was the only one to deliver.

Chalabi refutes the widely held criticism that he and his aides "came and actively pushed the weapons of mass destruction issue on the United States, so that cynically we could create the pretext for why the United States would go to war, and that we manipulated and lied to the United States government to promote these notions." He asserts, "We didn't go to the Bush administration. They came to us." They also came to him on a separate occasion, he says, asking for defectors who could link Iraq's intelligence service to international terrorism.

It was Chalabi, however, who went to the press (as well as to the U.S. intelligence community) with the defectors he would soon find. He acknowledges part of the reason was to sway public opinion in favor of attacking Saddam. He wanted to "influence the case that Saddam was a bad guy, that he had terrorism connections and was bent on revenge" against the United States by moving public opinion more in line with the anti-Saddam factions inside the Bush administration.

But the overriding purpose for publicizing the defectors, he says, was to send a message to another audience: the policy makers themselves inside the administration. Chalabi wanted to give his allies there—and in Congress—ammunition to show how effective he was. "We were responding to the continual claims by our adversaries in the Bush administration that we were useless," he explained, "that the INC was not capable on the ground. We wanted to demonstrate the contrary, that we were capable on the ground." He hoped that by showing they "could get significant people to give important information about Iraq," it would negate that criticism and help his partisans secure a leading role for him and the INC should Bush—as was widely anticipated—decide to take down Saddam.

And thus was born what would become perhaps the signature scandal in the lead-up to the 2003 invasion of Iraq: the procurement of Iraqi defectors whose bogus tales of WMD and Iraqi-sponsored terrorism permeated the press and circulated at the highest levels of the U.S. government.

NINETEEN

William Safire, the former *New York Times* columnist, once wrote, "Veteran reporters and creaking commentators have a single goal in writing about great events: advance the story. Unearth facts that policy makers do not know, do not want to know, or do not want the public to know they know."

Few outside the profession comprehended that mission, or ambition, as well as Ahmad Chalabi. He grasped the imperatives and impulses of American journalists with an acumen equaled only by his understanding of the U.S. political system. He had spent a lifetime cultivating access in both worlds, and now, with America reeling from two cataclysmic attacks—9/11 and the anthrax mailings—he made the most of it. When administration officials approached him about Iraqis who might know of Saddam Hussein's continued possession of weapons of mass destruction and his ties to international terrorism, he scoured the world looking first for Iraqis who could link Iraqi intelligence to al-Qaeda and, by extension, to the attacks of 9/11.

Chalabi told me he himself actually believed that Osama bin Laden operated alone. "Operational security of bin Laden implied he would not tell anyone," he said. But that didn't stop Chalabi from pursuing defectors who suggested otherwise, and then introducing them to members of the media and makers of government policy who were ripe for what he had to offer.

The suspicion that Iraqi intelligence was in league with al-Qaeda, and had actually masterminded the attacks of September 11, went to the top of the administration, to George W. Bush himself. The president raised the subject on the evening of September 12 when he pulled his terrorism adviser,

Richard A. Clarke, aside into a conference room in the White House, shut the door behind them, and said, "I want you to find whether Iraq did this."

"Mr. President," Clarke responded, "we've been looking at this. We looked at it with an open mind. There's no connection."

"Iraq, Saddam—find out if there's a connection," the president shot back, telling Clarke to "go back over everything" to "see if Saddam did this. See if he's linked in any way."

Clarke went back to the raw data and, together with analysts from the CIA and FBI, took a fresh look. His conclusion remained the same: Iraq had no involvement with 9/11. When he sent the finished report to Stephen Hadley, then the deputy national security adviser, it got bounced back.

Do it again, Clarke was told.

In those words Clarke heard, "Wrong answer." But that's not the way Hadley says he intended it. "I asked him to go back and check it again a week or two later," Hadley would later explain to *60 Minutes*, "to make sure there was no new emerging evidence that Iraq was involved. That's what I was asking him to do."

By that time, however, Bush had already decided to focus the U.S. response to 9/11 on Afghanistan. But he told his war cabinet he was looking at Iraq as a possible phase two of the response, setting off a furious debate within his administration over the merits of attacking Iraq. And into the breach stepped Ahmad Chalabi, hoping to create what Richard Perle once called "a climate of opinion and set of perceptions about Saddam" that would lay the groundwork for action.

Just as the policy feud inside the administration was getting under way, Chalabi put the word out to his "talent spotters," as one aide called them, to find Iraqis who had recently fled the country. In less than two weeks, they came up with the first of a batch of defectors in neighboring Turkey: a former Iraqi military officer who, like others who would follow, told stories that seemed to link Saddam Hussein to international terrorism—and the attacks of 9/11. Their accounts began to ripple through the U.S. intelligence community, resulting in hundreds of highly classified reports and analyses. Thanks to Chalabi, the information also reverberated across the country on the front pages of America's leading newspapers and in broadcasts, including my own. Whether the defectors influenced the thinking of policy makers or merely confirmed what they already thought, their stories played a major role in throwing suspicion on Iraq at a crucial time.

Chalabi's first defector made his public debut a month and a day after 9/11, in an October 12, 2001, *Washington Post* column written by Jim Hoagland. The piece reported on a former Iraqi army captain who said he had served as a military instructor in the elite militia known as Fedayeen Saddam (Saddam's Fighters). The defector, Hoagland wrote, outlined details of "training given for airliner hijacking and assassinations in the Salman Pak area of Baghdad while he was there." Hoagland went on to describe a second INC defector who "as recently as September 2000" had personally seen Islamists trained in hijacking on a Boeing 707 parked in the Salman Pak camp. The column was widely reported on CBS News' *Face the Nation* and in newspapers in New York, Seattle, Los Angeles, London, and Vancouver. The defectors themselves appeared on PBS's *Frontline*.

Three weeks later, Chalabi's Iraqi National Congress set up another defector interview with the *New York Times*. The resulting story, "Defectors Cite Iraqi Training for Terrorism," published on November 8, 2001, quoted two former Iraqi intelligence officers who spoke of Islamic militants trained at the Salman Pak camp, where they performed drills on how to hijack a plane without using weapons. (It was widely reported at the time that the 9/11 hijackers may have seized control of the planes using box cutters, small tools consisting of a retractable razor blade in a thin metal sheath. Commonly used for crafts and do-it-yourself work, such items had not previously been considered weapons by airline security officials.) As the *New York Times* observed in the story, "The assertions of terrorism training by the Iraqi defectors is likely to fuel one side of an intense debate in Washington over whether to extend the war against Osama bin Laden and the Taliban government of Afghanistan to include Iraq." Precisely, Chalabi thought.

Then on December 20, 2001, the *New York Times* ran a front-page story involving yet another defector, Adnan Ihsan Saeed al-Haideri. The *Times'* Judith Miller had flown to Bangkok earlier that month to interview Saeed. In a hotel room overlooking a country club, the reporter and the defector spent several hours sipping hot tea and coffee as Saeed told his story: that he was a civil engineer who as recently as the year before had personally worked on renovations for what he believed were "secret facilities for biological, chemical and nuclear weapons [located] in underground wells, private villas and under the Saddam Hussein Hospital in Baghdad."

Immediately after the interview, two of Chalabi's aides, who had brokered the meeting with the *Times*, handed Saeed over to agents working for the Defense Intelligence Agency (DIA), the Pentagon's in-house intelligence outfit. As Miller returned to New York City, the DIA agents drove Saeed to a beach resort two hours outside of Bangkok, where they met up with a team of analysts from throughout the U.S. intelligence community and spent the next two days vetting and debriefing him. They gave Saeed a polygraph test, which he passed. "He's the mother lode," one DIA official commented to Chalabi's deputies.

The debriefing in Thailand resulted in more than 250 reports, which were disseminated throughout the U.S. intelligence community and sent on to two foreign intelligence services.

"If verified," the *Times*' Miller wrote in her December 20, 2001, article, "Mr. Saeed's allegations would provide ammunition to officials within the Bush administration who have been arguing that [Saddam] Hussein should be driven from power partly because of his unwillingness to stop making weapons of mass destruction."

Administration hawks relished this ammunition, so fortuitously supplied by Chalabi, who was connecting the dots between Iraqi support for international terrorism and Iraqi WMD. This same coupling had become the focus of policy makers at the Pentagon and the office of the vice president during the anthrax attacks: Was Saddam behind them? What was the possibility he might furnish al-Qaeda with weaponized VX or some other deadly nerve agent?

That concern, accompanied by a growing frustration with the CIA's (accurate) disbelief of such a scenario, led the Pentagon to set up its own intelligence unit. It was manned by two analysts, both close associates of Richard Perle, who spent their days in a windowless, cipher-locked room—fifteen by fifteen feet—poring over reams of classified material, much of it raw, uncorroborated data from the CIA. They were searching for evidence of links between terrorist groups and host nations in general and, in particular, between al-Qaeda and Iraq.

In December 2001, Perle asked Chalabi to provide the Pentagon analysts with information gleaned from the defectors, information that reinforced the hypothesis of the administration hard-liners: that there was a connection between al-Qaeda and Iraq, Saddam Hussein and Osama bin Laden. The unit then reported its conclusions to senior members of the Bush administration, including Paul Wolfowitz and Doug Feith.

By this time, the CIA's Counterterrorism Center had grown wary of Chalabi's defectors and their information. In one case, the agency concluded that a defector lacked firsthand knowledge of his allegations. In another, the Iraqi was deemed to be "under the influence/control of the Iraqi National Congress (INC) and is not considered to be very credible." And in a third instance, the agency suspected a defector had been coached to lie by the INC.

The CIA and its suspicions, however, were disparaged inside the Bush administration by senior Pentagon officials, who regarded Chalabi as a valuable conduit of information with a track record that was far and away better than the agency's. And Richard Perle was openly derisive of the CIA, telling reporters that Langley had consistently misread developments in the Middle East, from the 1979 revolution in Iran to the rise of radical Islam. Its analysis, he told the Knight Ridder news service, "isn't worth the paper it's written on."

Nor did any of the red flags raised by the CIA about the defectors make it into the press coverage during the lead-up to the invasion of Iraq. To the contrary. As the year 2001 drew to a close, defectors had become one of the hottest stories in town. Chalabi no longer had to pitch or cajole reporters into giving them a listen. Journalists were now banging on *his* door, pressuring the INC for access to fresh defectors. Chalabi had provided defector allegations to just about every respectable news outlet in the country, including the *Wall Street Journal*, *Time*, *Newsweek*, *Vanity Fair*, the *New Yorker*, *USA Today*, UPI, and Fox News. The defectors' stories got wide play in the British press as well. Ahmad Chalabi was at the top of his game.

Even before this barrage of allegations, I had begun to wade into the Iraq story for *60 Minutes*. Lesley Stahl and I, along with a camera crew, traveled to Baghdad in October 2001 to interview Tariq Aziz, Iraq's deputy prime minister and one of Saddam Hussein's closest advisers.

Aziz was a short peacock of a man, with large horn-rimmed glasses, thinning white hair, and a trimmed, graying mustache. Greeting us at an ornate palace with massively high ceilings and long barren hallways that echoed our every footstep, he escorted us into his large private office, where the floors were covered with scruffy old Persian rugs and both CNN and Al Jazeera were blaring on his TV—he was constantly monitoring the news.

Before the cameras rolled, we sat down and got acquainted over sweetened hot tea as he lit up one of his freshly imported trademark Cuban cigars. He represented a brutally repressive regime, but he was gracious, polite, and urbane. Fluent in English, he spoke softly with a slight lisp.

During the interview, Aziz scoffed at the notion of any connection between his government and al-Qaeda, saying that Iraq was a secular state that did not tolerate bin Laden's brand of Islamic fundamentalism. He pointed out that al-Qaeda's declared goal was to replace governments like his in the Middle East with religiously pure Islamist states and eventually restore an Islamic caliphate. Aziz said that al-Qaeda and Osama bin Laden were as much Iraq's enemy as ours.

"We have a different ideology," Aziz told us. "If [we] caught anyone from al-Qaeda in Iraq," he said, "we put him in prison and persecute him." We immediately understood that the Iraqis had wanted *60 Minutes* to come in order to deliver the message that they had not been responsible for 9/11.

We asked Aziz if we could visit Salman Pak, the military base outside Baghdad where Chalabi's defectors said terrorists were being trained in how to hijack planes.

"You can go and visit the whole of Salman Pak," Aziz offered. "Take your cameras, and we will take you to Salman Pak."

But when we got there, the promised access was denied. Much of the base was off-limits—which had the effect of diluting Aziz's message.

During the same trip, Stahl and I also interviewed Amer al-Saadi, the architect of Saddam's chemical and biological weapons program. Al-Saadi acknowledged on camera that Iraq had manufactured tons of anthrax, botulinum toxin, and other deadly agents and that at one time his scientists were trying to weaponize them. "Trying, exactly," he told us. "That's the operative word. It never got to more than that."

He said the regime had destroyed its stockpiles of chemical and biological agents and had long ago shut down its WMD program altogether. That also happened to be true. But Stahl and I didn't believe him, given the regime's well-documented history of lying about its WMD program.

"Your government won't allow inspectors in to verify," Stahl jabbed. "Nobody believes you."

"Thousands of inspections [have taken] place," he replied. "There's nothing left, absolutely nothing left."

That was the first, but not the last, time Saddam Hussein's regime tried to use *60 Minutes* to deny Chalabi's allegations about terrorism and WMD. I returned to Iraq six months later, in April 2002, during the celebration of Saddam Hussein's birthday. I went without cameras to try to land an interview with Saddam, but that wasn't what the Iraqis had in mind. In my meetings, first with Tariq Aziz and then with Hassan al-Obeidi, the chief of Iraqi intelligence's foreign operations, I was asked to deliver a message to my contacts inside the Bush administration: that Saddam was now willing to do whatever it took to avoid war. They said they realized there was a "campaign" in the United States to link Saddam to 9/11 and prove that he had weapons of mass destruction. Both Aziz and al-Obeidi insisted the charges were untrue and that Saddam was now prepared to satisfy Washington's concerns by offering weapons inspectors unfettered access, including surprise visits, to any of Iraq's suspected WMD sites—and to open Salman Pak up for inspection as well. They asked if I would deliver that information to Washington. I told them the administration would probably be suspicious of such an informal approach, but I agreed to pass on their communiqué; I was curious to hear what the Bush administration would say.

In the meantime, they invited Stahl and me back to Baghdad to explore—and refute—another of the administration's, and Chalabi's, accusations: that of a link between Saddam Hussein and the first attack on the World Trade Center in 1993. Because one of the perpetrators, an Iraqi named Abdul Rahman Yasin, had fled to Baghdad after the bombing, everyone from Laurie Mylroie and Ahmad Chalabi to Paul Wolfowitz and Dick Cheney had suggested that Iraq probably had a hand in the 1993 attack. At the time of our trip, Bush had just put Yasin on a new most-wanted list of terrorists, with a bounty of $25 million on his head.

When we arrived in Iraq, our government minders brought us to a large military compound called the White Ship, the main interrogation center in Baghdad. We set up our cameras in a large dark room that had the dank odor and stony look of a medieval dungeon. Armed guards of the Mukhabarat, Saddam's feared intelligence service, perp-walked Yasin to where we were waiting. He was handcuffed, wearing striped prisoner's pajamas, and looked shell-shocked, if not terrified. He was a meek and vulnerable shadow of the armed and dangerous fugitive described by the FBI's most-wanted poster. Stahl questioned him at length, and between that interview and another one with Aziz, we left with the strong impression that, rather than being a terrorist who returned to Baghdad under government orders, Yasin had made his way back to Baghdad on his own. Once there, he was taken into custody for fear he was part of a U.S. sting operation—deliberately sent by the United States to create a pretext for an attack against Iraq. Aziz even described his government's failed efforts to turn Yasin back over to the United States—and offered again to turn him over.

The Iraqi government had a well-deserved reputation for deviousness, to be sure. But even the FBI and the U.S. attorney who prosecuted the 1993 World Trade Center case told us they had looked closely for any Iraqi government involvement in the bombing, or sponsorship of Yasin, and had found none. Our *60 Minutes* story reached nearly 15 million households on June 2, 2002, but barely caused a blip in the growing belief in Iraqi culpability.

My delivery of Iraq's message to the Bush administration made as little impact. I spoke to senior officials at the White House and the CIA. Both came back to me with essentially the same reaction: the time for trusting the Saddam regime had long passed. The administration viewed the Iraqi offer of unrestricted access to WMD sites as just another ruse—an attempt not to come clean, but to divide Washington from its allies in the hopes of forestalling an American invasion.

In addition to reporting on the Iraq story from Baghdad, Lesley Stahl and I also turned our attention to Ahmad Chalabi and his intrigues. By January 2002, George W. Bush was already publicly discussing a rationale for possible military action against Iraq. And Chalabi—with his string of high-profile defectors—was ramping up his effort to win support for his INC, should the U.S. take out the Iraqi dictator. We wanted to document Chalabi's U.S.-financed public relations offensive, including his use of defectors.

I flew to London to meet Chalabi and discuss the idea. My appointment was scheduled for January 21, 2002—coincidentally one year to the day after his meeting at Richard Perle's home with Paul Wolfowitz, Douglas Feith, and the other neoconservatives to map out a strategy for getting the new Bush administration to adopt regime change as its policy.

Chalabi's office—the INC headquarters, really—was in Knightsbridge, an affluent neighborhood in West London—not far from Hyde Park and down the street from Harrods, the high-end department store. It was a most improbable setting for the command post of a would-be insurgency in a Middle Eastern country. Then again, it was quintessential Chalabi to enjoy luxury even as he pushed for war.

Three chain-smoking Iraqi guards, armed with pistols and protected by bulletproof glass, directed me up a flight of stairs and into a beehive of activity, with Chalabi at the center. He was barking out orders in Arabic to his aides as he pored over a printout of the Iraqi army's order of battle, which listed all of Saddam's military units, including their equipment and locations. During our conversation, he took repeated phone calls from Harold Rhode, the Pentagon analyst who had attended the meeting at Perle's house the year before. Chalabi kept scribbling something on a piece of paper. Amid the hubbub, I saw, he was working out the solution to an elaborate algebraic equation from an old math book that was lying open on his desk.

Not surprisingly, Chalabi agreed to participate in a story for *60 Minutes*, and over the next several weeks our team chronicled his public relations campaign, which stretched from Knightsbridge across the Atlantic to Washington, to the San Diego home of the ex–CIA official Dewey Clarridge, and back to the mountain roads of Jordan where we met up with one of the INC's defectors.

Our filming began in Washington, where Chalabi arrived the day after Bush delivered his 2002 State of the Union speech. "Our war against terror is only beginning," Bush said, and warned that Saddam's regime—part of a dangerous "axis of evil"—continued "to flaunt its hostility toward America and to support terror."

The next morning we followed Chalabi as he made the rounds on Capitol Hill, touching base with supporters like Senator John McCain, the Arizona Republican who told him, "This is a pleasant time, given the president's speech last night. We hope that very soon that can turn into some significant help for you."

Chalabi moved on to the American Enterprise Institute, the neoconservative think tank, where he spent time with Richard Perle. We visited the offices of Burson-Marsteller, the high-priced public relations firm Chalabi had retained (with U.S. government funds) to promote the INC. Francis Brooke told us Chalabi was in touch with the president's and vice president's friends in the oil industry, promising executives of both ChevronTexaco and ExxonMobil preferential treatment in a post-Saddam Iraq if they lobbied the White House now on his behalf. From there, we joined Chalabi and a few aides on the Metro to the Pentagon, where they had a meeting with Paul Wolfowitz (we had to wait outside).

At the time, Wolfowitz was working multiple angles behind the scenes to keep Chalabi in play. For instance, the State Department had just cut off INC funding because Chalabi had failed to account for about $2.2 million in expenses. Wolfowitz—and a battery of Chalabi supporters in Congress—put the squeeze on the State Department's number two man, Richard Armitage.

"These guys beat me up pretty regularly," Armitage recalled. "Paul Wolfowitz and the others would call me on the phone and say, 'We—you—gotta fund the INC.' And I'm saying, 'Look, I'm not asking something unreasonable. I just want a general idea of where the money's going.'"

Eventually, Chalabi hired an accountant who straightened out his books. But Wolfowitz sought more friendly quarters and arranged to put the INC under the purview of the Pentagon's Defense Intelligence Agency. "Oh shit!" the DIA's then acting director, Jake Jacoby, told his deputy when he got news of the Chalabi assignment.

Meanwhile, the CIA's opposition to Chalabi and to the idea of an INC-led army of insurgents so rankled Wolfowitz that he demanded to know why. John Maguire, the CIA case officer with the Fu Manchu mustache who first butted heads with Chalabi in the mid-1990s, was sent to deliver the brief. "Right off the bat," Maguire recalled, "Wolfowitz asked me, 'Why do you hate this guy?'"

There were a lot of reasons why the CIA didn't like or trust Chalabi, starting with the assessments of a twenty-page psychological profile of him—classified secret—that concluded Chalabi was a classic narcissist—brilliant and patriotic, but someone who conflated his own role and ambitions with the best interests of Iraq. In Chalabi's mind, they were inseparable. The profile suggested that his tendency to see himself and his ideas as the answer to everything undermined his ability to be an effective leader.

Maguire, however, believed there was a much more basic reason for rejecting Chalabi, one that he says he tried to explain to Wolfowitz as candidly and dispassionately as possible. "I was very matter-of-fact with him," Maguire told me. "I said, 'This isn't personal and I don't hate Chalabi. It's not about me. It isn't about him. It's about results. Can this person achieve the things that we want in the furtherance of U.S. foreign policy goals? And the answer is no, because we have a documented track record of failure along the way. We know what Chalabi is capable of doing. We worked closely with him, and he is not able to deliver things that he has promised in the past. The best indicator of future performance is past performance. There is no reason to believe that anything that we have witnessed in the past has changed. There's no reason to believe that he would be able to deliver any more today than he was able to deliver six or seven years ago.' " What Chalabi had failed to deliver, Maguire said, was one substantial or verifiable piece of intelligence about Saddam's regime. Put simply, Maguire told the deputy secretary of defense, Chalabi had no following inside Iraq.

Despite their knifelike edge, Maguire's words, as far as he could tell, had no effect at all. "Wolfowitz wasn't interested in anybody else's opinion," Maguire recalled. "He had his own conclusions. He was only looking for information that would confirm what he wanted to believe."

And what Chalabi wanted Wolfowitz—and everyone else—to believe was that the INC *was* a viable organization and *did* have a network of support inside Iraq and around the Middle East that would enable it to shoulder a major role in deposing and replacing Saddam. The securing of defectors was supposed to demonstrate just how effective Chalabi was.

Another one of those defectors surfaced in February 2002. Chalabi dispatched a top lieutenant to the Middle East to interview him, evaluate his credibility, and then make sure the whole operation got publicity, beginning with *60 Minutes*.

We at *60 Minutes* approached the story with two minds. On the one hand, we were leery of defectors in general, knowing they often embellish, sensationalize, and fabricate information to get what they wanted: usually money or a visa to live in a Western country. On the other hand, we were determined to do due diligence on the man the INC supplied.

A CBS News crew and I left ahead of Lesley Stahl for Jordan, where we met the defector, described to us as a major in the Mukhabarat named Mohammad Harith. We were first introduced to him out on the street—actually, on an isolated dirt road somewhere high in the hills overlooking Amman, not far from neighboring Iraq. A chain-smoker, he was a bony, nervous man in his early forties. After a quick handshake, he ducked into a dusty old sedan chauffeured by an INC official that followed our car on a long drive through one-lane mountain passes and isolated villages. We arrived at a safe house—actually, an office building on Mecca Street on the west side of Amman, where Harith was debriefed by two INC officials, interviews we were allowed to videotape. Harith was then moved to a second location for more questions over the next two days about his supposed knowledge of weapons of mass destruction. He wore a red-and-black Arafat-style keffiyeh to hide much of his face while we recorded the questions and answers.

Throughout the questioning, I tried to assess Harith's credibility. At one point he insisted that our translator—a longtime CBS News employee and trusted friend, Amjad Tadros—leave the room, claiming Tadros worked for Jordanian intelligence. I refused to let Harith call the shots, threatening to cancel the whole shoot unless my own independent translator remained present. Harith backed down. At another point the two INC officials conducting the debriefing began arguing in Arabic. Tadros told me they were disagreeing about whether it was appropriate to broadcast Harith's remarks on American television instead of preserving them exclusively for U.S. intelligence.

What Harith told his INC debriefers—and later Stahl during her interview with him—was that in order to evade UN weapons inspectors, Saddam Hussein made his biological weapons laboratories mobile, putting them in refrigerated trucks that Harith said he personally purchased from Renault, the French automaker.

Before our broadcast, I checked Harith's allegations with a senior UN official who had detailed knowledge of Saddam's WMD program. The UN source told me Harith's information was credible, which was to say not that Harith was telling the truth but that his statements dovetailed with other evidence weapons inspectors had developed.

As we would soon learn, Harith's claims would be used by the Bush administration to support allegations about Iraq's biological weapons programs. When Secretary of State Colin Powell addressed the United Nations in February 2003 to press the case for war, he used testimony by Harith—and other INC defectors—to bolster his argument. By that time, the administration—unable to reach a consensus on Iraq's terrorist ties—had turned its focus to Iraq's weapons of mass destruction as the central rationale for war. And Chalabi's defectors were crucial in appearing to corroborate allegations about Saddam's purported WMD arsenal and thus in making the administration's case for war.

· · ·

George W. Bush would launch Operation Iraqi Freedom, the U.S.-led invasion of Iraq, on March 19, 2003. A charge led by U.S. boots on the ground was not the way Ahmad Chalabi had envisioned the downfall of Saddam Hussein. He had always dreamed that Iraqis would liberate Iraq, with his INC in the lead and the Americans in support. But that was all beyond his control now. This was America's show.

"It was unfortunate, but necessary," Chalabi reflected. "But what can we do? We are going to get rid of Saddam. Let's try to work it."

What mattered to him most now was what kind of government would follow the certain and swift collapse of Saddam's regime. "We began to say, 'Let's have a provisional government.' That was our answer," he said.

It was Chalabi's answer, but not necessarily Washington's. The Bush administration was deeply divided over the idea of establishing an emergency government composed of Iraqi exiles to lead post-Saddam Iraq. And so, in December 2002, as the United States announced that it would be sending tens of thousands of troops to the Persian Gulf region for a possible military strike against Baghdad, Chalabi hedged his bet. He traveled to the capital next door, Tehran, where he met with top Iranian government officials to discuss the coming invasion and his plan to form a provisional government—whether or not the Bush administration went along.

For Chalabi, who had spent the past forty-five years contemplating and devising the end of his long exile, the endgame was fast approaching. Now it was time to play the Iran card.

TWENTY

Ahmad Chalabi had always believed that he would need the support of both Iran and its powerful archenemy, the United States, to remove Saddam Hussein from power. They were going to be the big players in Iraq's future, he knew, and getting these two implacable foes to align their interests over Iraq was at the heart of his grand design.

Making himself indispensable to both countries was also central to his strategy. He would be the T. E. Lawrence of Iraq, the one person who was acceptable to two unyielding adversaries. And, in making himself the essential liaison, he would ensure his own path to power. Indeed, Chalabi had long looked beyond the coming war. Removing Saddam Hussein and his regime was only half the equation; his ultimate goal—though he'd never admit it—was to lead post-Saddam Iraq himself. He realized he would never get there through the will or passion of the masses. He had neither the mentality nor the feel for that kind of politics. For him, it would be through the politics of power. That's what he knew and understood, what he had been imbued with since childhood, and what he recognized would finally return him to Iraq in glory. That's why the formation of a provisional government was so central now to his master plan; it would be his vehicle to power. He'd be a leader selected not by the fervor or conviction of the Iraqi people, but by decree—handpicked according to the national interests of Iran and the United States. How and why he would eventually turn away from Washington toward Tehran for support was a function of how his standing in each capital evolved over time.

Ironically, Chalabi's initial rise in Tehran grew in large measure out of his falling-out with the CIA. That's what convinced his fiercest skeptics in Iran that he was not what they at first suspected: a stalking horse for the American spy agency. Coming out from under that shadow was difficult yet crucial.

Next Chalabi had to convince the mullahs in Iran that the United States was more likely to go after Saddam Hussein than to go after them. "The Iranians never believed the Americans were going to get rid of Saddam," Chalabi recalled. "They always believed that the Americans were going to make up with Saddam and then turn him against them again," he said, referring to the U.S. tilt toward Iraq during the Iran-Iraq War of the 1980s. "That was the prevalent thinking" in Iran in the nineties. "And it would've been a self-fulfilling prophecy if they had continued to proceed in this vein. They would have behaved in such a way toward the United States that it would have made it more palatable for the United States to make up with Saddam."

But over the years Chalabi worked feverishly to prevent that from happening. He did so by giving the Iranians a unique window into Washington. In the late 1990s, in one meeting after the other with Iranian government officials, he stressed the significance of the Iraq Liberation Act, which made regime change in Iraq official U.S. policy. After the attacks of September 11, 2001, he described to them the mood in the United States and explained that Bush's bellicose remarks toward Saddam weren't just posturing or misdirection. They were real, a reflection of Bush's true character and a signal that the politics of war were aligning in favor of overthrowing Saddam and his regime. And that was key, he told Tehran, because in Washington politics were king—even the politics of foreign policy. So, while the State Department was opposed to taking down Saddam and the CIA was anti-Iranian, those U.S. agencies weren't the real players. Those whose opinions mattered most, Chalabi assured Tehran, included just about everyone else in the U.S. political constellation—from the Republican leadership in Congress to the vice president, the secretary of defense, the top policy makers, the press and pundits, the think tanks—and an ever-growing number of Democrats.

Chalabi's sheer staying power in Washington also helped. Initially, many Iranian leaders—like some of their American counterparts—were wary of Chalabi, given his myriad manipulations and evident self-interest. But over time they could see that he actually did enjoy a close and trusted relationship with leading members of Congress and senior administration officials, and thus was in a position to give them a reliable reading of what the Great Satan was truly thinking. It all added up.

So did Chalabi's tangible achievements. He persuaded the U.S. government to waive its prohibitions against spending money in Iran so that his Iraqi National Congress could conduct anti-Saddam operations from Iranian territory. That impressed Tehran. Then there was the matter of funding for the Supreme Council for the Islamic Revolution in Iraq, the umbrella group of Iraqi opposition parties based in Tehran, loyal to Iran, and openly calling for an Islamic government in post-Saddam Iraq. And yet, because of Chalabi's influence, SCIRI became eligible for U.S. funds under the Iraq Liberation Act. That really made Tehran sit up and take notice.

Chalabi also got Senator Jesse Helms and other U.S. senators to write letters to Ayatollah Abdul Aziz al-Hakim, the head of SCIRI, urging him to join the United States in overthrowing Saddam. And after much personal prodding and wooing, Chalabi persuaded al-Hakim to fly from Tehran to Washington for a high-level meeting with senior Bush administration officials on August 9, 2002.

Bringing the ayatollah to Washington was an important milestone in Chalabi's plan for getting Washington and Tehran on the same page. On the one hand, he persuaded the Bush administration that SCIRI was not a proxy for Tehran. He explained that this hard-line Islamic party—though composed of Shiites based in Tehran—was Arab at its core, not Persian. That meant, he told them, that SCIRI's interests were not making Iraq a satellite of Iran, but keeping it firmly in the Arab fold. That would be an important leap of faith for the Bush administration, especially since the president had lumped Iran into the same "axis of evil" as Iraq. By the same token, by getting al-Hakim, Tehran's favored Iraqi, to Washington, Chalabi was able to nudge Iran into more openly identifying with the U.S.-backed process—despite the risk of alienating its anti-American base in the region.

As for the meeting itself, it could not have gone any better for Chalabi. Al-Hakim was showered with attention, while doubts about America's intentions were eliminated. Doug Feith and his counterpart at State, Mark Grossman, greeted their Iraqi guests in a conference room on Mahogany Row—the executive suite on the seventh floor of the State Department. Representatives of the CIA also attended. Colin Powell dropped by to greet al-Hakim and the other Iraqi opposition leaders in attendance. Rumsfeld received them the following day, and Cheney spoke with the group by videoconference from Wyoming. The U.S. message throughout the two-day conference was clear and emphatic: Bush was committed to removing Saddam Hussein and his regime. That news shot straight back to Tehran, and it proved decisive, Chalabi says, in bringing the Iranians around to finally believing the United States was serious about removing Saddam from power.

But Chalabi then had to contend with a new wave of anxiety as the Iranians realized an invasion of Iraq meant a quarter-million U.S. soldiers would be stationed right next door. "The debate now was," Chalabi recalled, " 'What is the cost to us if the U.S. does take out Saddam? Will they use Iraq as a base of operations to hit us? Will they use Iraq as a base of operations to destabilize us? Will they use Iraq to carry out espionage activities? And if they do that, would it be still worthwhile for the U.S. to remove Saddam? Or are we better off with a weak Saddam remaining in power?' "

Tehran was tied up in knots all over again while Chalabi contemplated the risks of Iranian opposition to a U.S. invasion. Tehran's special forces could easily wreak havoc on an American assault by blowing up convoys, attacking supply lines from Kuwait, and plastering the roadsides with improvised explosive devices—all of which would divert a huge amount of American resources from the main mission. So Chalabi tried to defuse the Iranians, playing up the virtues of a provisional government. "I told them, 'If we have a provisional government in Iraq, then it will be composed largely of people who are friendly to you. We're not gonna let this happen to you. And if the U.S. doesn't permit a provisional government of Iraq and instead occupies [Baghdad], then it's going to be such a bloody mess the Americans will have no time to deal with you." In other words, Chalabi told them, the Iraqi people would not stand for occupation and would revolt. "And either-or was a plus for them," Chalabi pointed out.

It was a masterful analysis by Chalabi, helping provide the rationale for Iran's embrace of the coming U.S. invasion. While Tehran never formally announced its support of a U.S. invasion, Chalabi said, "You could surmise it from their behavior. By September or October of 2002, they began to put a lot more effort into what we were doing."

Chalabi had finally gotten Iran on board. Now the Americans had to come through with a policy favoring a provisional government.

As Chalabi was mapping out his plans to Tehran, Paul Wolfowitz and Doug Feith were proposing the same approach inside the Bush administration, arguing for the creation of a provisional government consisting of

Iraqi exile leaders who would govern in the immediate post-Saddam period. The exiles would lay the foundation for the future governance of Iraq.

The State Department and the CIA, however, strongly opposed the plan, warning that the exiles were too fractious and unskilled to properly run a government—even on an interim basis. Moreover, the "externals" lacked legitimacy, they said, and allowing them to structure the new government would alienate any "internal" Iraqi political class that would emerge after the fall of Saddam. The "internals" would resent the United States for having imposed the exiles on them. Instead, the State Department proposed creating a U.S.-led "transitional civil authority" that would nurture the development of a "credible, democratic leadership" from within Iraq's "internal constituencies" and gradually transfer power to them.

Those were the official battle lines of the debate, anyway. Unofficially, the divide came down to Chalabi and the role he and his Iraqi National Congress would or wouldn't play in the post-Saddam era. And, again, the dispute pitted Chalabi's allies in the Pentagon against his nemeses at the State Department and the CIA.

"Throughout the United States government," Richard Perle would later complain, "there were people who would do anything they could to prevent the INC from emerging out of all of this in a leadership position. The animosity toward Ahmad, including a sort of personal hostility, mean-spiritedness, and deep abhorrence of Chalabi, led people—particularly at State and the CIA—to make serious mistakes about how to handle the postwar period. It blinded them to the benefits of working with the INC and led them to reject proposals to do that."

Indeed, whatever the merits of a provisional government, the State Department and the CIA believed the Pentagon's real purpose for proposing it was to help Chalabi gain power, and they were determined to stop that from happening. "It was clear they were pushing Chalabi," says Richard Armitage, the State Department's number two official at the time. "There are no questions. Feith, Wolfowitz, and the rest of them."

The rest of them also included Cheney, according to another senior State Department official who asked to remain anonymous. "I remember sitting in one principals' meeting with the vice president," the State Department official recalled, "and like a typical diplomat, I dutifully made the argument about the [political] legitimacy of exiles who hadn't lived in Iraq for years versus those who had stayed and suffered under Saddam. And the vice president looked across the table at me like I was from Mars and said that the only legitimacy we need here comes on the back of an Abrams tank. Now, the problem with that, in my view, is the notion that Chalabi would be perched on the tank. And our concern was always that that would just be really, really hard to sustain in Iraq."

In this diplomat's view, Chalabi had done so much to shape the thinking of Wolfowitz and Feith that their policy proposals always seemed to put him at the center of everything. "He was the answer personally. I mean, they clearly saw Chalabi, in my view, as the 'anointed one.'"

Feith, the undersecretary of defense for policy at the time, denied that, both during the give-and-take of the debate and later. He wrote in his memoir, published in 2008, "I never heard anyone at the Defense Department make an argument or suggest a plan for putting Chalabi into power in Iraq."

Not specifically anyway. But even Perle acknowledges that Feith and Wolfowitz were clearly "fighting for options that were consistent with the idea of turning things over to the INC—for example, raising an army of Iraqi exiles" under the INC umbrella and forming a provisional government. The idea was to engineer an outcome that favored Chalabi without Wolfowitz and Feith having to show their cards.

"They were eager to work with the INC," Perle says of Feith and Wolfowitz. "Doug was pushing the idea that the INC had a lot to offer. And Paul's view was, 'Chalabi is as good as it gets. Why throw the dice when there's somebody who shares our values, who's smart, and whom we know and trust?'"

As for Perle, he makes no bones about it: Chalabi *was* the anointed one. "I believed we should have handed things over immediately to Ahmad and the INC," he told me.

Only Donald Rumsfeld had the clout to overcome the State Department's and the CIA's opposition. But Perle says, "Rumsfeld was never a big Chalabi supporter. Never. And, in fact, he was very explicit. He said, 'We shouldn't be picking winners and losers. It's up to the Iraqis to do that. In the circumstances that are going to exist, cream will rise to the surface.' I heard him say it."

Perle remembers that Wolfowitz felt "very frustrated at his inability to get Rumsfeld behind a program in which we would have worked much more closely with the Iraqis, including the government in exile before the war."

Eventually, not only Rumsfeld but also Secretary of State Colin Powell and CIA director George Tenet would oppose Feith and Wolfowitz's proposal for a provisional government—and by the end of 2002 it was clear, though not yet official, that Bush would decide against it.

This was a pivotal setback for Chalabi and his designs. It also led to an epiphany, Chalabi now realizing that "the neocons were unable to deliver" what he called "the instruments of our common conception." Wolfowitz, Feith, and Perle simply couldn't do it on their own and had to rely on others. "Their main assets in the administration were two," he said. "Cheney and Rumsfeld. And Rumsfeld was the more critical. Cheney was supportive, but Rumsfeld was not interested in getting into Washington bureaucratic battles to influence the debate."

And so Chalabi's tilt to Iran began. In December 2002, he traveled back to Tehran. Along with other members of the Iraqi opposition, he met with senior government officials, including Brigadier General Qasem Soleimani, commander of the Quds Force, the special operations division of the powerful Islamic Revolution Guards Corps, to push his plan. "We took several days," Chalabi recalled. "But we ironed out a program to establish a provisional government in Iraq."

A month later, Chalabi returned to Iran—to put the final touches on the provisional government before going on to Iraqi Kurdistan for a meeting between members of the Iraqi opposition and Bush's special envoy, Zalmay Khalilzad. Khalilzad had once been in the Perle/Wolfowitz camp of Chalabi supporters—but no longer. And Chalabi knew it. "Khalilzad was specifically charged by the White House to prevent us, at all costs, from forming a provisional government," Chalabi recalled. "The U.S. was against it. We knew."

In Iran, however, it was a completely different story. When Chalabi arrived in late January 2003—less than eight weeks before the U.S.-led invasion of Iraq—it was to red-carpet treatment. He and his personal entourage of twenty-five were put up in government palaces, VIP suites, and government-owned apartments. They were hosted by the commander of Iran's elite Islamic Revolutionary Guard Corps. And on their flight into Urumieh, a provincial town near the Iraqi border, Chalabi was treated as if he were a veritable head of state. Porters scurried to carry his luggage, local dignitaries invited him to drink tea, and his Revolutionary Guard hosts took him to their local headquarters, where they slipped off their shoes and snacked on bread, sweet water-buffalo cheese, and honey. "When the

Iranians like you, as they seem to like Chalabi," noted Charles Glass, an American journalist who was traveling with Chalabi at the time, "they kill you with hospitality."

Chalabi crossed into U.S.-protected Iraqi Kurdistan later that day, and within twenty-four hours a top INC official traveling with him announced to reporters that the Iraqi opposition would be declaring a provisional government. It would include a leadership council of seven to eleven members and twenty-one ministers, with Chalabi as prime minister.

But if his intention was to present Khalilzad with a fait accompli, Chalabi's gambit failed miserably. Khalilzad ignored the Chalabi pronouncement and then proceeded to present the Iraqi opposition with Bush's official, final word on the subject: there would be no provisional government. In fact, there wouldn't even be a transitional civil authority administering post-Saddam Iraq. Instead, there would be a U.S. military occupation, presided over by a proconsul—or military governor.

Chalabi always knew this was a possibility. But he could never bring himself to believe the Americans would actually do it. Now that he heard it officially, he was despondent—and furious. "The U.S. screwed us!" he fumed. "The Americans broke the covenant."

The decision also confirmed Iran's "worst fears that [the U.S.] wanted to use Iraq as a base to hit them," Chalabi said. "In a sense, the U.S. set us up," he added, his voice now rising in anger. "We were now seen by Iran as doing the Americans' bidding and helping them into occupation."

Chalabi contacted his friends in Congress and the Bush administration, looking for help. But even many of them, he says, were dismissive: " 'We are going to liberate you.' 'Be grateful.' 'Tow the line.' That was their attitude."

He warned there would be a "day of reckoning" for U.S.-Iraqi relations unless the U.S. reversed its decision. "I told them Iraq is a difficult place," Chalabi said. "Iraqis welcome liberation, but they will oppose occupation. You will lose the moral high ground. I kept using this phrase."

In a February 19, 2003, *Wall Street Journal* editorial, he wrote, "We are a proud nation, not a vanquished one. [Iraqis] welcome Americans as liberators. But we must be full participants in the process of administering our country and shaping its future."

After the editorial was published, Doug Feith called him to say there would be a "partial reversal." "We will convene a body of Iraqi leaders who will be advising the military government," Feith told him.

"No, not enough," Chalabi shot back. "We need a provisional government."

But there would be no provisional government, and inside Chalabi a slow-burning fuse of resentment was ignited. "They thought that if they have this huge military presence here they're king," he said of the Americans. "Nobody could do anything about them and then they could shape Iraq into their own image like it was Silly Putty or plasticine. They wanted life to imitate art."

What they wanted, Chalabi believes, was for post-Saddam Iraq to comply with the so-called Arab order favored by America's allies in the region—oil-rich Saudi Arabia and the Arab Emirates, as well as Jordan and Egypt—where the Sunnis dominate. Whereas Chalabi envisioned a Shiite ascendancy, with the Shiite majority of Iraq emerging as oil-rich kingpins who were free to challenge Sunni power in Saudi Arabia and elsewhere in the Middle East.

"An Iraq where the Shia have the upper hand would be a threat to them," Chalabi asserted. Especially, he says, if he were the Shia in charge. "The fact that I was able to come and do all this work in the United States without having a country or a power base" terrified America's Sunni, Middle East allies, he told me. "Imagine what I could do if I had a country and a power base like Iraq."

But with his hopes for a provisional government giving way to the reality of an impending U.S. military occupation, Chalabi had to alter his calculations: After America had purged Iraq of its dictator and his cadre of torturers, Chalabi would increasingly tack toward Tehran. He had always believed that no Iraqi Shiite government could succeed without at least the acquiescence of Iran. And now, with his longing for redemption and his aspirations for history-making hanging in the balance, Iran would increasingly eclipse America as the repository of his ambitions.

Chalabi insists to this day that he never sought or coveted power in post-Saddam Iraq, let alone via some sophisticated strategy that would make him Washington's and Tehran's anointed one. But to know Ahmad Chalabi is to know he is no Cincinnatus, no aristocratic patrician who would walk away from the lure of power after the crisis his country faced had passed.

And any doubt about his shift in strategy was dispelled on the eve of the U.S.-led invasion of Iraq, when Chalabi uncharacteristically tipped his hand in a private conversation with one of his closest confidants, telling him, "You do realize we're going to have to go into opposition against the Americans the moment we enter Baghdad."

"What do you mean, 'Go into opposition?'" the confidant asked.

"That's the only way to gain credibility and legitimacy in Iraq," Chalabi answered.

Chalabi echoed that same message in another conversation with Aras Habib Karim, the Kurdish aide-de-camp who had been his closest adviser for more than a decade. "Ahmad told me," Karim recalled, "that after Saddam was gone we should separate ourselves from the Americans."

In those two exchanges, Chalabi acknowledged privately what soon became apparent in his actions: a gradual, strategic, and irreversible shift away from Washington and toward Tehran as his main patron.

TWENTY-ONE

Long before Ahmad Chalabi turned toward Tehran, his ties to the Islamic Republic of Iran had been a source of concern and controversy in Washington. His frequent trips to the country and his countless meetings with top government officials—including those in the Ministry of Intelligence and the Iranian Revolutionary Guard Corps—raised all sorts of questions, the principal one regarding his true loyalties: Was he a friend of America or an Iranian provocateur trying to lure the United States into doing the mullahs' bidding? Chalabi managed to fend off those suspicions for the better part of a decade thanks to his neoconservative allies.

Over the years, they argued (accurately) that Chalabi never made a secret of his dealings with Tehran and, besides, anyone involved in Iraqi politics had no choice but to break bread with the Iranians. It was a reality in that part of the world. But that line of reasoning went only so far; it was his close association with the neoconservatives that gave him legitimacy. "It makes a lot of difference, this atmosphere of who your friends are," explained Francis Brooke, Chalabi's Washington aide. "And we are friends with really seriously anti-Iranian activists—people like Richard [Perle] and Paul [Wolfowitz] and Stephen Solarz—all Jews who are all publicly opposed to Iran but who are still prepared to be friendly with Ahmad. Just by the fact that these guys are our friends, it's understood we cannot be pro-Iranian. I mean, who do you think leads the anti-Iranian charge in the United States? Same guys. Exactly the same guys. So, just by association, we were able to square that circle."

As for the neoconservatives, they had known Chalabi since 1991 and, based on their own personal experience, had come to trust him entirely—none more so perhaps than Harold Rhode, the Middle East specialist at the Pentagon who was among Chalabi's most ardent supporters. Over the years, Rhode—who has a PhD in Islamic history—got to know Chalabi on a personal and intellectual level. "We were in touch all the time," Rhode said.

They often engaged in long and sometimes heated philosophical discussions about a variety of subjects—from Iraq and Middle East culture to Israel and, most especially, Iran. Rhode said that he needed to know for himself where Chalabi stood on the Islamists in Iran and that in time he grew to understand and accept what he calls the push and pull of Iran on Iraqi Shiites like Chalabi. "There's an Arab proverb that says if you break open the bone of a Persian, shit comes out," Rhode said. "That tells you what Arabs think of Persians. At the same time, Arab Shiites for centuries have been persecuted and slaughtered by the Sunnis. This history of suffering is infused in the passion plays of Shiites—and seared into their souls. So they feel they need protection. That's where Iran comes in. Iran is the largest Shia country in the world. And in time of need they can come to the aid of Iraqi Shiites. That is the basis of Ahmad's relationship with Iran. It's not to any specific government, whether it's the ayatollahs or the shah. His connection is to the country, the idea that Iran is there as a last resort, almost as a big brother."

Rhode, an Orthodox Jew, views Chalabi's kinship with Iran through the prism of his own heritage. "The Arab Shiites are the Arab world's stepchildren. They don't really belong. The Jews are the stepchildren of the Western world. It's part of a mentality where someone like myself, because of my own historical experience, can intuitively understand what he has suffered. It's the Jewish response. Many Israelis believe they need America's protection because of what is gonna be done to us by this 'other.' The Shiites experience the same thing toward Iran."

Rhode says it often fell to him to drive up to Capitol Hill or visit with members of Cheney's staff when concerns arose about the nature of Chalabi's relationship with Iran. "My role was to be the cultural interpreter, if you will, of how to understand this man," Rhode told me.

But at Langley, CIA officials thought they understood this man pretty well themselves—based on their own years of experience with him, along with classified information from electronic intercepts, informants, and friendly intelligence services in the region. And when it came to the question "Was Chalabi an ally of America or an instigator working in Iran's interests?" their answer was "Neither." To them, Chalabi was strictly out for himself, playing both sides against the middle in pursuit of his own self-interests and, in particular, his desire to lead Iraq.

That assessment dated back to 1995 and the joint U.S.-Iranian assault on the Iraqi army he had tried to orchestrate from his CIA base of operations in Kurdistan. Chalabi misled Iran about the degree of U.S. support for the attack, while he kept Washington largely in the dark about what was happening on the ground.

"People in the White House knew less about an American intelligence operation to overthrow a foreign government than their counterparts in Tehran, and that's because they had Ahmad Chalabi telling them what was going on," said Bruce Riedel, a top CIA analyst for twenty-nine years and special assistant first to Bill Clinton and then to George W. Bush for Near East affairs. "I'm not saying Ahmad is a controlled asset or agent of the Iranian services," Riedel added. "I'm saying the agency has a long history of doubting this man's reliability, his integrity, and his loyalty."

The nature of Chalabi's relationship with Tehran, he said, soon evolved from slippery to sinister. In 2001, the proof of that was still yet to come, intelligence officials now say. But already by the eve of the Iraq invasion, there was a bundle of "soft intelligence" indicating—though not proving conclusively—that Chalabi was talking out of school to the Iranians. Based on his conversations with Perle, Wolfowitz, and others, Chalabi knew a great deal about U.S. decision makers and their plans for post-Saddam Iraq and was able to give Tehran valuable insight into how to position itself tactically and strategically for the coming war and its aftermath. In addition, there were suggestions from time to time that Chalabi had indeed played "fast and loose with U.S. sources and methods" of intelligence—all in a bid to curry favor with Iran. And yet, CIA officials say, Chalabi remained untouchable.

"We were telling people Chalabi's playing both sides of the table," recalls Rob Richer, the then director of clandestine operations for the CIA's Near East Division. "But you can't beat the Pentagon's front office. They believed Chalabi walks on water."

And so, after Bush launched the invasion of Iraq on March 19, 2003, and U.S. Central Command (CENTCOM) decided ten days into the conflict that it needed to put an Iraqi face on the invasion, Ahmad Chalabi's name immediately rose to the fore. Chalabi had always claimed that, given the will and the support of the U.S. government, he could raise an army of exiles. And during the lead-up to the invasion, Paul Wolfowitz and Doug Feith had pushed for just that—to recruit and train Iraqi exiles in Hungary. But for a variety of reasons, including CENTCOM commander General Tommy Franks's disdain for the idea, the proposal never got off the ground. But now, in the heat of battle with no sign of mass capitulation by Saddam's forces, CENTCOM thought it would be easier for the Iraqi army to surrender if it were to fellow Iraqis.

One of Doug Feith's deputies, William Luti, immediately put CENTCOM in touch with Chalabi, who had previously entered northern Iraq from Iran. Chalabi said he could quickly pull together a force of one thousand. Meanwhile, Wolfowitz and Luti briefed Cheney on this seat-of-the-pants operation—but not the National Security Council, the State Department, or the CIA.

The plan called for flying Chalabi's so-called Free Iraqi Forces to the south of Iraq to help turn around the situation there. But before Chalabi's ad hoc posse could board the C-130 transports, the whole scheme nearly unraveled. Chalabi was able to raise only about six hundred of the one thousand soldiers promised, and many of them turned out to be Iranians. "Some of these guys couldn't even speak Arabic," Rob Richer recalls. "They spoke Farsi."

The agency also was "reporting," Richer says, that perhaps as many as a half dozen or so of the Iranians either belonged to or were affiliated with the Iranian Revolutionary Guards Corps. The rest of Free Iraqi Forces—a hodgepodge of Kurds and Iraqis who had spent their exiles in Iran—were paid $5,000 each by Chalabi. In other words, Chalabi had amassed a band of mercenaries with Iranian agents sprinkled among them. When CIA director George Tenet discovered what was unfolding, he exploded. "You're flying Iranian agents into a country we just spilled American blood to invade," he yelled. "The Iranians must be tickled pink to see how this is working out," another CIA official remarked.

The "soldiers" were ultimately allowed to board the C-130s—but without any of their weapons. Then, once the airlift got under way, a new controversy erupted: Chalabi insisted on joining them for the flight into southern Iraq. CENTCOM pushed back, arguing the United States should not appear to be taking sides in Iraq's future politics by putting a would-be candidate for president of Iraq on an Air Force plane. But in a terse conversation with CENTCOM's deputy commander, General John Abizaid, Wolfowitz would not back down. And on the morning of April 5, 2003, Ahmad Chalabi and his men were issued shoulder patches for the now-official Free Iraqi Forces and flown from Iraqi Kurdistan to Tallil Air Base, 190 miles south of Baghdad.

When they landed at the bombed-out and abandoned air base, there was no welcome and there were no provisions. CENTCOM had soured on the mission and decided to provide no logistical support—no water, food, electricity, toilets, or beds. It was a harbinger of a relationship with the United States that was increasingly bipolar, alternating between that of friend and adversary.

Chalabi and his group took up residence in a filthy, deserted warehouse on the air base and remained there for the next ten days. But Chalabi was determined to claim some measure of credit for overthrowing Saddam. He had his nephew Faisal Chalabi drive in from nearby Kuwait with a convoy of supplies: everything from mangoes and canned sardines to disposable toilet seats, a dozen GMC and Mitsubishi sport-utility vehicles, and more than $300,000 in U.S. currency stuffed into backpacks. The money was a cash advance from the Chalabi family, equal to the INC's monthly Pentagon stipend.

Once Chalabi's men managed to procure side arms and AK-47 assault rifles from local merchants, the entourage proceeded to the nearby town of Nasiriya, where Chalabi picked up a bullhorn and addressed a gathering crowd of three thousand in Arabic, yelling, "Your government. Your country. Your Iraq."

"Ya Hussein! Ya Hussein!" the crowd chanted back, invoking the name of their ancient Shiite martyr.

From Nasiriya, Chalabi sped north to Baghdad, giving himself—he hoped—a head start over the other exiles, who would soon be arriving and trying to establish their own power bases in the new Iraq. As Chalabi's convoy of soldiers, INC lieutenants, and relatives raced toward the capital, a call came in on Chalabi's Thuraya satellite phone. It was CENTCOM. "They wanted to know why I was going to Baghdad," Chalabi said. "They were worried I would announce the formation of a provisional government when I arrived. They asked me, 'What are your intentions?' I answered them, 'What are my intentions? I am going home, thank you. Bye.'"

And on the afternoon of April 16, 2003, amid a driving sandstorm,

Ahmad Chalabi did just that, arriving home in Baghdad after forty-five years of exile. There were no welcome signs, no celebrations, no Iraqis lining the sides of the streets to greet him and throw flowers. Instead, the roads were barren but for the garbage that blew in the wind. The air was hot, and the bright desert sun was dulled and ruddied by the cloud of dust and sand enveloping the city.

As Chalabi surveyed his beloved Baghdad for the first time since age fourteen, a rush of conflicting emotions swept over him. On the one hand, he felt a deep sense of pride. He had spent a lifetime fighting to get back home—and he had actually *done* it. He had accomplished what he set out to do—and not as a bystander, but as someone deeply involved in the wave of history that ended with the downfall of Saddam Hussein. It was a personal victory and a family triumph. And the Shia of Iraq were on the cusp of seizing their destiny. It was a great achievement. Still, he felt anxious and apprehensive about the chaos and the challenges ahead: cementing the defeat of Saddam, eradicating the remnants of the dictator's Ba'ath Party, rebuilding Iraq, and most of all recalibrating his relations with Tehran and Washington. Politically, he would have to generate a following inside Iraq, among the locals. But his dealings with America and Iran—those were key if he was to emerge as Iraq's next leader and reclaim his and his family's name.

TWENTY-TWO

Ahmad Chalabi was the first exile leader to reach Baghdad after the collapse of Saddam Hussein's government. He and his entourage of Kalashnikov-toting militiamen pulled into the old Iraqi Hunting Club, a walled compound of empty fountains, drained swimming pools, and fly-infested meeting salons that once served as the playpen of Saddam Hussein's erratic and sadistic son, Uday. "It was such a disgusting place," Chalabi recalled. "Low buildings, badly furnished rooms, cheap furniture, and fitted carpets which were grimy. The gardens were dying. Altogether, it was very disappointing." But it would have to do. Over the next few weeks, the decaying social club—located in the posh Baghdad neighborhood of Mansour—would serve as the INC's new headquarters.

Chalabi's first order of business—which he executed immediately on the afternoon of his arrival—was to send a detail of operatives across the capital in search of internal files from Saddam's principal instrument of terror, Mukhabarat, the intelligence service. "We wanted to know how to dismantle the regime," he said. "What are the keys?"

His men first targeted the office of the Mukhabarat director, then the deputy director. From there, they moved on to the Special Security Organization, which had been responsible for Saddam's personal security. They hit Ba'ath party offices, secret police stations, and Iraqi army buildings. In time, Chalabi's men gathered up an estimated twenty-five tons of internal intelligence documents, enough to fill a basketball court from one end to the other a meter high. And then Chalabi set up an analysis center to pore through the files, one page at a time. If information is power, Chalabi was amassing his own brand of weapons of mass destruction—not only to destroy the remnants of Saddam's regime but also to arm himself with information about his political rivals, all of whom had been closely monitored and reported on by Saddam's intelligence services.

Politically, Chalabi wasted no time getting organized, either. While he insisted he was not a candidate for office, Francis Brooke dubbed himself Chalabi's "campaign manager" and supporters plastered the walls of the city with pro-Chalabi signs. And like a man running for president, Chalabi granted audiences to a long procession of Iraqis—from the mayor of Baghdad to retired businessmen, lawyers, university professors, Shiite clerics, Sunni leaders, women wearing veils, and tribal sheikhs dressed in flowing robes and sandals, thumbing their worry beads. Dignitaries like Massoud Barzani, the Kurdish leader, dropped in, and Chalabi held court on a daily basis with reporters from around the world.

He also visited the house where he grew up, the bank his uncle once owned, and the hometown of his father. It was a dizzying first few days back. As he processed it all, he recognized some stark realities of his homeland: the disrepair of the country's infrastructure; the backwardness of its commerce, culture, and education; and, most significantly, the tragic legacy of thirty-five years of Ba'athist rule.

He witnessed that legacy firsthand in May 2003, one month after his return, when he visited a mass grave near Hilla, fifty miles south of Baghdad. He watched in stunned silence as ordinary Iraqis, using shovels and their bare hands, dug up shards of bones and body parts. They came across a wristwatch, a pair of black-and-gold slippers, a comb, fragments of torn clothes—the details of ordinary lives ended in horror. A mini-bulldozer arrived on the scene and began scooping up mounds of dirt filled with skulls, limbs, and a rib cage, dumping them randomly on the sand, where they were then placed in plastic bags. It looked like a scene out of hell. "One woman clad in black," Chalabi recalled, "she was probably fifty, but looked eighty. She was sitting on the sand surrounded by rows of plastic bags full of bones. She looked at me and said, 'Which one is my son?'"

As more and more bodies were unearthed—three thousand in all were exhumed from the site—a wave of rage and vindication swept over Chalabi: rage at the evil of Saddam and absolute vindication for having done whatever was necessary to liberate his country.

He would apply that same standard—doing whatever was necessary—as he waged his battle for personal power. The immediate challenge was the new U.S. occupation authority in Baghdad and its policy of sidelining so-called externals like him in favor of Iraqis who had opposed Saddam but had not gone into exile. He spoke out against the policy, repeatedly denounced the American occupation, and sided with the French in their efforts to pressure Washington into granting Iraq its sovereignty. He also worked to sabotage the administration's plan to let the United Nations choose an interim government for Iraq.

Chalabi was engaged in open political warfare with the White House. And yet he could still count on his patrons at the Pentagon for a hand up. Over the next year, they would continue to wage a rear-guard insurgency on his behalf from inside the Bush administration, and there was no detail too minor to merit their attention. For example, when the initial administrator of the U.S. occupation, retired lieutenant general Jay Garner, denied at a press conference that he was a supporter of Chalabi and rejected the suggestion that he would ease Chalabi into power once the occupation ended, Garner says he got an immediate earful from Doug Feith. "Feith called me that night very upset and said I had done a great deal of damage to both Chalabi and the INC," Garner recalled in an interview. "I told Feith, 'I don't give a damn and if you don't like it, you can fire me.' About a half hour later, Wolfowitz called to smooth things over and say that I should be more careful of what I say to the press. Then I was embargoed from talking to the press." Garner was incredulous. "Here I am the guy who was going to be in charge of rebuilding Iraq and I couldn't talk to the press!"

Shortly thereafter, Wolfowitz organized a direct line of communication to Chalabi, directing the CIA to issue him a secure telephone unit (STU), a highly restricted technology with channels classified up to top secret. The STU was developed by the National Security Agency and was mostly reserved for use by U.S. government officials and those involved in covert operations. No one could remember the last time a foreign national not working for the CIA was given access to one. When Langley got the order, CIA officials weren't sure what concerned them more: the idea of Chalabi having access to so sensitive a piece of equipment or his having unfettered and unfiltered access to so senior a policy maker as Wolfowitz.

"Senior policy makers make decisions affecting Americans' lives," explained a former case officer who was assigned to the CIA's Baghdad station at the time. "And, remember, we were still in a very tense situation. There had been massive looting. Ba'athist insurgents were killing and wounding our soldiers. And Iranian irregulars were on the loose all over Iraq. Now, as an intelligence officer, you're supposed to run intelligence through channels that are known and constantly evaluated to make sure the information and picture that is crafted for policy makers is as accurate and timely as possible. You never want unvetted information from an uncontrolled source making it to senior policy makers, especially if the source is someone like Chalabi, who we know is out to influence as well as inform. We also know he has a documented, proven connection to a hostile government, Iran. And from a counterintelligence perspective, there's the risk of a two-way flow of information. And we know Chalabi wasn't doing all of the talking. He did a lot of the listening."

In addition to issuing the STU, the Defense Department had its in-house intelligence agency, the DIA, set up shop under the same roof as Chalabi after he and his top lieutenants moved out of the Hunting Club into a private compound in Mansour. The thought of a U.S. intelligence cell sharing space with Chalabi's INC horrified agency officials even more than the issuance of the STU had.

Meanwhile, Chalabi's supporters sought to bolster his standing in the region. In December 2003, a senior administration official asked King Abdullah of Jordan during a state visit to Washington if the king could see his way toward "resolving" Chalabi's 1989 Petra Bank conviction. To His Majesty, the implication was clear: he was being asked to set aside Chalabi's guilty verdict. King Abdullah was said to have been both angered and offended by the approach, telling his American interlocutor that there "was much to be resolved between Chalabi and Jordan, and Chalabi and the royal family," according to a source close to the king. In Washington, the king's reply amounted to a classic "nonresponse response," the royal equivalent of no. Nothing came of the overture.

Chalabi's benefactors, however, were nothing if not relentless in trying to give their man in Baghdad an upper hand. On January 20, 2004, they somehow managed to slip Chalabi into the House of Representatives Chamber to hear George W. Bush's State of the Union address. Not only that, they got him the seat of honor right behind the First Lady, Laura Bush.

When Rob Richer, the CIA's top spy in the Middle East, saw Chalabi there—grinning, with his pursed lips and cat-ate-the-canary look—he just shook his head at what Chalabi's friends in the administration had managed to pull off. "It was a statement," Richer says. "You don't put someone up there in the gallery next to the First Lady knowing he's going to be all over worldwide TV the year after the invasion of Iraq in one of the most critical State of the Union addresses ever unless you've thought it through. No one just said, 'Hey, by the way, we don't have Chalabi on the guest list this week.' It's a statement. What someone said is, 'Let's show people who we want. Let's show the Iraqis who we support.' And in the Arab world, putting a man behind his wife while her husband speaks conveys complete trust in him. That was the indication to everyone in that part of the world that Chalabi was 'The Man.'"

He wasn't Bush's man, however, and the president had been outspoken about that among his top advisers. "Our president refused to put his thumb on the scale for Ahmad Chalabi," Richard Armitage, the then assistant secretary of state, says. "Refused. He said, 'I'm not gonna do it. I won't put my thumb on the scale for any Iraqi. Let the Iraqi people figure this out.'"

It turns out that Bush was as surprised as anyone else by Chalabi's appearance in the gallery during his State of the Union speech, Armitage says. He also was furious. The morning after the address, the president brought up the subject of Chalabi's seating arrangement during a meeting in the Oval Office. "What was Chalabi doing there?" the president asked angrily. "What was he doing in the box?"

"Everybody looked around," recalls Armitage, who was present at the meeting, "and they looked at their shoes and they looked at their fingernails. Well, I was interested myself in the answer to the question. I didn't see the vice president in the room. But I'm sure it was the vice president who did it. He was the only one who could have arranged it."

Armitage says that when no one answered the president, Bush demanded to know, "Is anybody talking to Chalabi?"

Scooter Libby, Cheney's representative at the meeting, said nothing. Wolfowitz answered, "Well, we've talked to him once or twice."

Armitage couldn't believe it. "We know these guys are talkin' to Chalabi all the time. And no one says a word? When someone is asked a direct question by the president of the United States and they don't answer him honestly, well, I'll tell you, that doesn't happen very often."

As for Chalabi, he was grateful for the continued loyalty of his friends, capitalizing on their State of the Union sleight of hand to insinuate himself into some of the most powerful positions available in occupied Iraq. After the new U.S. administrator, L. Paul Bremer III, created the advisory Iraqi Governing Council, Chalabi became head of its economic and finance committee. As such, he oversaw the appointment of the oil minister, the minister of finance, the central bank governor, the trade minister, the head of the trade bank, and the managing director of the nation's largest commercial bank, filling many of the posts with his relatives and political allies. Chalabi also became head of the De-Ba'athification Commission with the mandate to purge former members of Saddam's regime and his Ba'ath Party from the government. The backbone of Chalabi's commission was those secret documents he had seized from Saddam's files, which gave Chalabi crucial ammunition in deciding who got to keep their jobs and who didn't. He padded his portfolio of positions just as the United States announced that it would be returning sovereignty to Iraq by the end of June 2004. "Ahmad is positioning himself," a fellow cabinet minister told *Newsweek* at the time. "He is a master tactician."

By that spring, Chalabi seemed to be at the pinnacle of influence in Washington and on the cusp of power in Baghdad: the Iraqi exile who returned home victorious and the Pentagon favorite who would run the country once the U.S. occupation ended. His life's dream seemed to be within grasp. But the ground beneath him was already beginning to crumble, and the pattern of his life—attaining power followed by controversy and then scandal—was about to swallow him up again.

On January 24, 2004, four days after the State of the Union address, the U.S. government's chief weapons inspector in Iraq, David Kay, resigned from his post, announcing that after scouring the country for nine months his team had found no evidence that Saddam was stockpiling weapons of mass destruction before the war. Meanwhile, a separate analysis found that all of Chalabi's defectors were wrong—not only about WMD but also about Saddam Hussein's links to al-Qaeda. Their claims—fed to the Pentagon and other senior Bush administration officials—were exaggerated in some cases and invented in others, the analysis found. In one instance, it appeared that Chalabi's Iraqi National Congress had coached a defector to lie. That defector: Mohammad Harith, the one Lesley Stahl and I had interviewed in Jordan.

It's true that Chalabi did *not* offer up the Iraqi defector code-named Curveball, whose false information proved to be the most pivotal of all in providing the rationale for war. And Chalabi certainly wasn't alone in arguing, or believing, that Saddam had WMD. But his high-profile promotion of the defectors had come back to haunt him, as the press that once had so assiduously courted him now turned the tables and began to crank out withering analyses of him and his stable of deceitful defectors.

Then in February 2004, Chalabi told a British newspaper that it didn't matter if his defectors had provided faulty or fabricated evidence to the U.S. government. What was important, he said, was that he had achieved his aim of getting America to overthrow Saddam. "We are heroes in error," he told the *London Daily Telegraph*. "As far as we're concerned we've been entirely successful. That tyrant Saddam is gone and the Americans are in Baghdad. What was said before is not important."

Chalabi's quote "really frosted" the president, according to L. Paul Bremer III, the head of the U.S. occupation in Iraq. It seemed to lend credence to the allegation then ravaging Bush's presidency, namely, that the war had been based on lies.

Chalabi's supporters defended the remark as a typical smart-ass Chalabi comment that had been misinterpreted by the reporter. And Chalabi, who understood how damaging the *Telegraph* interview was, called the White House to explain how his comments had been misconstrued.

But the *Telegraph* interview added to a long list of growing tensions. For one, Chalabi was already engaged in open political combat with the White House. He and Bremer were barely on speaking terms. And in the view of senior U.S. government officials, Chalabi played a cynical and dangerous game in the way he executed his duties as head of the De-Ba'athification Commission, using it for personal political gain while fueling the growing sectarian war between Iraq's Sunni and Shia populations.

The controversy centered on his draconian implementation of Bremer's order dissolving the Ba'ath Party and excluding from government service former leading members of the party hierarchy, most of whom were Sunnis. Some thirty-five thousand civil servants lost their jobs as a result of his order. Thousands of them were teachers, doctors, and nurses—clearly people who bore no responsibility for the Ba'ath Party's reign of brutality. The U.S.-led occupation authority devised an "exception" to the De-Ba'athification order that allowed many of the fired workers to be reinstated; but, U.S. officials say, Chalabi dragged his feet in implementing it.

"He was a big factor in slow-rolling the 'exception' policy," according to a senior military official in Iraq. "He stood in the way, and did so at a crucial period. This happened in the fall of 2003, when we still had considerable support among the Sunni Arabs. That evaporated, however, by the end of the year when it became clear there would not be large exceptions to the original De-Ba'athification order, and that happened because we weren't getting straight answers from Ahmad Chalabi."

Chalabi's motive for opposing the exception policy was in part simple vengeance: The Sunnis once had the whip hand. They had the power to make deals and make money. Now it was the Shiites' turn. But it was also about raw politics, positioning himself as the avenging angel of post-Saddam Iraq. "[It was] to establish his Shia credentials," the military official explained. "Remember, he was an expatriate and aristocrat with no street cred. But what he did reverberated throughout Iraq. It affected tens of thousands of Sunnis, each of whom had a family of five to ten people. So the result for them was the loss of hope and faith, that they didn't have a stake in the success of Iraq. It fueled the insurgency."

And while Chalabi played politics with Iraq's security, U.S. and Iraqi authorities accused him of also enriching himself through a series of corrupt schemes. One involved charges of counterfeiting. U.S. and Iraqi government officials believed that, in addition to Mukhabarat documents, Chalabi's men had seized Saddam-era money plates and begun printing Iraqi dinars. Chalabi allegedly did so while chairing the committee that oversaw the exchange of Saddam-era dinars for new Iraqi currency. "So he was printing old money and selling it to the committee he chaired for new money," according to a former U.S. embassy official in Baghdad. "He was literally minting money. It's brilliant. He's an evil genius."

There were also charges that Chalabi was getting a piece of *every* transaction that flowed into, out of, or through the bank he put his cousin in charge of, the Trade Bank of Iraq, including letters of credit, wire transfers, and U.S. government funding. Chalabi's alleged take: up to 1.5 percent of every transaction. By the end of 2004, the United States alone had funneled billions of dollars in aid through the Trade Bank of Iraq.

Furthermore, Kurdish officials told the U.S. government that Chalabi had "significant interests" in the trading and smuggling of every conceivable product from Iran, from oil and gas to cigarettes, carpets, and pistachios. In 2004, imports from Iran topped $800 million.

And, finally, there was the very serious allegation that Chalabi had shared some of his seized Mukhabarat documents with Iran. That charge came from the intelligence service of a U.S. ally in the region, one with extensive tentacles inside Iraq. "The Iraqi Mukhabarat had a proven clandestine network for purchasing the component parts used to build weapons of mass destruction," a senior official in that intelligence service explained to me. "The Iranians wanted to know about that. The Iraqi Mukhabarat files also contained the names of a number of secret Mukhabarat agents operating undercover in the Iraqi Shiite community. We know that after the fall of Baghdad, Iranian-backed agents had a 'hit list' of Shiites and Sunnis, and we believe that many of the targets came from the files Chalabi gave to Iran."

And what would Chalabi's motive have been for sharing such sensitive information with Tehran? "Chalabi understands the surging role of Iran in Iraq, and he wants to exploit that for his own gain," the intelligence official explained.

The CIA deemed this information to be "credible," according to several former U.S. intelligence sources. But the evidence against Chalabi was murky. "We believe that Chalabi gave the Iraqi Mukhabarat files to Iran," the foreign intelligence official said. "But we don't have ironclad proof."

And that absence of proof was enough for Chalabi's supporters to keep their man in the game—even as Washington's patience with him was growing short. And so, despite a long winter and spring of mounting tensions, the Pentagon spigot remained open, with $340,000 a month flowing into Chalabi's INC, while the Defense Intelligence Agency continued to operate its intelligence-gathering cell from inside his Mansour compound. That arrangement, however, was a ticking time bomb that would soon explode. Chalabi's balancing act between Washington and Tehran was about to come crashing down.

TWENTY-THREE

By the spring of 2004, free elections had been scheduled for early the following year. The U.S. occupation was winding down. And Tehran was ratcheting up its strategy for extending its influence into Iraq.

The ayatollahs' goal was to make sure that neither another Saddam-like strongman seized power in Iraq nor a U.S. client-state hostile to Iran emerged. Toward that end, they kept an eye on the upcoming Iraqi elections. The CIA estimates that Tehran was spending $11 million a week on a grassroots political campaign that included sending two thousand religious students and scholars, about a third of whom belonged to Iranian intelligence, to the holy cities of Najaf and Karbala. Their job was to infiltrate Shia shrines in an effort to influence voters ahead of the elections.

The Iranian regime kept another eye on the burgeoning sectarian violence in Iraq, where a deadly mix of foreign fighters and homegrown militias—former Ba'athists embittered by their ouster from power, Iraqi nationalists, and Sunni Islamists drawn from the Arab region, as well as Shia fighters from the urban slums of Baghdad and southern Iraq—battled one another. The carnage was particularly gruesome. Car bombs and gunmen, suicide bombers and ambulances packed with explosives targeted bus stations, markets and mosques, funerals and wedding parties. Loosely organized fighters also ambushed coalition troops, kidnapped and beheaded foreign contractors and aid workers, and sabotaged Iraq's infrastructure and other U.S. efforts to reconstruct and stabilize the country. Over the course of 2004, the insurgency grew in size and sophistication, as did the number of attacks, from about twenty-five a day to approximately sixty—mostly in Sunni-dominated central Iraq.

Iranian hard-liners tasked the Quds Force to turn up the fire in what would soon become a full-fledged civil war. Quds was to Iraq's Shia militias what al-Qaeda in Iraq was to the Sunni insurgent groups—the foreign enabler and escalator of violence. The Quds Force furnished Shia insurgents with money, arms, and ammunition, including Katyusha rockets, newly designed rocket-propelled grenades, and explosively formed penetrators—a new kind of roadside bomb covered with copper that melted on impact and pierced through armored vehicles. The Quds Force also flooded Iraq with thousands of foreign fighters—as many as thirty thousand, by some estimates—to kill Sunni fighters and Ba'athist loyalists, as well as coalition troops. The CIA verified their presence by visiting local morgues.

"You'd see all of these dead bodies lined up in the morgues," recalled John Maguire, who was the CIA's deputy chief of station in Baghdad at the time, "and you could tell which ones were Iraqis and which ones were foreign fighters. The Iraqis were buried right away. The other ones each had a little tea cup placed next to their head, and in the tea cup was a tiny piece of paper with a traveler's prayer written on it." Those bodies, Maguire says, were tagged for return to Iran and Lebanon. It turns out that many of the dead were fighters from Hezbollah, the Iranian-backed Shia militant group based in Lebanon. And the group was also sending its best leaders into Iraq to assist and train members of the militia loyal to Moqtada al-Sadr, who had become the Shiite community's leading voice for violence against Sunnis—and for fighting American soldiers.

All told, Iran's presence in Iraq was beginning to wreak havoc on the U.S. occupation, igniting a surge in the death and maiming of American soldiers. "In the spring of 2004, the number of deaths and casualties began to increase dramatically," Maguire recalls. "We'd lose thirty guys in a month, but we'd have three hundred critically wounded—or more."

One of the senior Iranian field commanders most responsible for that carnage was Ahmed Frouzanda. He oversaw Revolutionary Guard operations in central Iraq, an area that encompassed all of the capital and stretched southwest to the Euphrates River (in the Sunni-dominated Triangle of Death) and north to Samarrah. "He was an aggressive guy," Maguire says. "He killed a lot of Americans."

Knowing that made it all the more bitter when U.S. officials discovered that Chalabi was not only meeting with Frouzanda but betraying the United States by revealing to him one of America's most closely held secrets.

According to multiple senior U.S. intelligence officials, Chalabi met

Frouzanda in March 2004 in the Diyala province of Iraq, near the Iranian border. Joining them were three other Iranian intelligence officials, including the Baghdad station chief for Iran's Ministry of Intelligence and Security. Also present was Chalabi's closest confidant and chief of intelligence, Aras Habib Karim. During the gathering, Chalabi barely uttered a word, according to U.S. sources. Karim did most of the talking, telling the Iranians he had just learned that the United States had broken Iran's secret code for transmitting confidential messages to its posts all around the world, including those between Baghdad and Tehran. When asked how he knew, Karim said he had pried the information from a drunken American official with access to sensitive information.

Frouzanda turned to Chalabi, who nodded, confirming that indeed the United States knew how to read Iran's most sensitive of messages. U.S. intelligence officials surmised that Chalabi wanted Iran to tighten up its security to ensure that his own secret communications with Iran would not be exposed.

The Iranians didn't know whether to believe Chalabi, so in their report to headquarters detailing the encounter they wrote, "We've seen no indication that we've been compromised." Incredibly, they then cabled the report over the very channel Chalabi had just told them was compromised.

And that's when the National Security Agency (NSA)—America's giant ear in the sky that collects and deciphers foreign communications and signals intelligence—learned of Chalabi's purported treachery. They were stunned. "This was huge, just huge," says one former U.S. intelligence official. "It's impossible to overstate the damage that would be done by compromising our ability to crack this code."

It was the one channel the Iranians believed was sacrosanct. "It gave us the only insight we had into their unguarded conversations," the intelligence official says. "It was the only information we trusted. To protect this capability, the NSA only shared the information it got from its code-breaking with the Defense Department. It didn't go to the CIA or the FBI. In order to read it at the State Department, you needed a special dispensation from God. This was the crown jewel. And losing it would be a terrible, terrible blow. U.S. lives are at risk when you compromise something like that."

As NSA cryptographers continued to monitor Iran's communication over the next few days, they detected a steep drop-off in the volume of electronic traffic between Tehran and Baghdad. "It slowed to a trickle," another former senior U.S. intelligence official told me. "We were worried that we had lost that intercept capability."

But no government changes its communications system overnight—or without rock-solid proof of a compromise—because doing so is such an elaborate, time-consuming, and hugely expensive proposition. Tehran would have to devise a new algorithm for encrypting its messages—no easy feat—and then replace its communication systems in all its embassies and stations around the world, an undertaking that could take as long as a year, if not more. So, for the time being, Iran was stuck with the system it had. That's why U.S. intelligence officials were immediately skeptical when a new message was sent over the compromised channel. It was so "suspiciously juicy"—laying out the specific time and place in Baghdad for a weapons exchange with anti-American insurgents—that the United States deemed it a setup. "It was obviously going to happen at a place they could watch and observe either directly or through a surrogate,"the senior U.S. intelligence official told me. "So we didn't act on it."

As a result, U.S. officials believe, Tehran concluded that its code had not been broken—at least for the time being. It would not change its worldwide communications system based solely on the word of Ahmad Chalabi, whom the Iranians trusted little more than many of their American counterparts.

In Washington, meanwhile, news of the Chalabi treachery circulated within only a small circle of senior Bush administration officials. And immediately Chalabi's supporters started to push back. At the Defense Department, they asked, "How reliable is this information? Are the Iranians trying to embarrass or set up Chalabi?" Scooter Libby from the office of the vice president raised the same question: "How credible is this?"

The information was supposed to be highly restricted, classified executive secret level gamma, meaning it was top secret information gleaned from an electronic intercept that could be read only by the top two or three executives at each of the designated agencies, which included the Defense Department, the DIA, the CIA, the NSA, and the State Department.

But word began to leak out almost immediately. I first heard about Chalabi's purported breach of faith on April 21, 2004. When I called a contact at the CIA, he refused to say anything about it—period. Then he told me to sit tight and remain at my desk.

About a half hour later, my phone rang. It was a senior U.S. intelligence official—not with the CIA—who said he wanted to talk to me, but not on an open line. He told me to leave my office and head to a specific address in northwest Washington, D.C., where someone would be waiting to meet me.

When I arrived, I was escorted into a nondescript office building and across a totally empty lobby until we approached a marble wall. At that point, my escort pushed the wall. It popped open, and behind it sat an armed guard at a desk. It was like being in a James Bond movie. He wrote down my driver's license information and told me to take the elevator up to the tenth floor.

The elevator opened to a plain office door with an opaque white window. I proceeded through the door to a cramped office—an office within the larger office—where, I was told, the bare white walls were lined with lead, making it impervious to electronic eavesdropping. The room was empty except for an oversized wooden desk and a telephone, which suddenly rang.

I picked up the line, and it was that same senior U.S. intelligence official who had called me at my office. He apologized for not coming to meet me in person but said that we were now talking over a "green line," the kind of telephone line that government officials use to discuss top secret information. The intelligence official then proceeded to confirm how Ahmad Chalabi, the man who brought America to Iraq, had betrayed the United States' ability to eavesdrop on the world's biggest state sponsor of terrorism, Iran. The official added, however, that Iran didn't know whether to believe Chalabi and was therefore still using the code. For that reason, the official asked CBS News not to run the story, which we agreed to do (as long as no other news organization was about to publish the information).

In the May 10, 2004, edition of *Newsweek*, reporter Mark Hosenball came close to scooping us, revealing that "top Bush administration officials have been briefed on intelligence indicating that Chalabi and some of his top aides have supplied Iran with 'sensitive' information on the American occupation in Iraq." The story made no mention of cracking secret codes, but that day it became the central focus of conversation during a National Security Council meeting at the White House.

"What the hell is this?" Bush asked, referring to the charges in the *Newsweek* article. He was visibly upset, said one participant: first there had been Chalabi's "heroes in error" interview, and now here were allegations that he was divulging secrets to Iran. The president wanted to know what was behind the story.

Among those attending the meeting were Vice President Dick Cheney,

National Security Adviser Condoleezza Rice, Secretary of State Colin Powell, Deputy Secretary of State Richard Armitage, Secretary of Defense Donald Rumsfeld, Paul Wolfowitz, and CIA director George Tenet. The CIA's Rob Richer and NSC staffer Frank Miller were back-benching, sitting in chairs along the wall. It was left to three-star general Michael Hayden, director of the National Security Agency, to brief the president on what happened.

Hayden explained that the NSA had cracked Iran's secret codes and that there was an intercept indicating Chalabi had divulged that capability. "This compromise could impact our ability to read Iranian communications," Hayden told the president. "But this could involve much more than the Tehran-to-Baghdad code." Hayden explained that much of the Iranian government, including its military, used a variation of the code—as did its proxies, such as Hezbollah. By breaking this one code, the NSA was able to crack everyone else's, Hayden explained. "So this is a compromise of potentially significant ramifications," he added.

Then Wolfowitz said, "Make sure this is not something the Iranians are using, one, to discredit Chalabi or, two, to test if we are reading their traffic."

At this point, the president pointed out a piece of information in the *Newsweek* article that bothered him: that the U.S. government was still paying Chalabi's group $340,000 a month. Turning to Rumsfeld, he asked, "Who does Chalabi work for? Who pays him?"

"I don't know," Rumsfeld replied. He then turned to Tenet and asked, "George, who does he work for?" implying that perhaps Chalabi worked for the CIA.

"He doesn't work for us," Tenet replied testily. "Isn't that right, Rob?"

"He works for the DIA," Rob Richer answered. To Richer, it seemed like Rumsfeld genuinely didn't know that Chalabi was on his payroll.

"If we're paying this guy and he's giving away our secrets," Bush said firmly, "it needs to stop. Condi, look into it!"

At the next NSC meeting, Bush brought up Chalabi again. "What exactly is our relationship with him?" the president asked.

This time, Stephen Cambone, the undersecretary of defense for intelligence—the Pentagon's intelligence czar—said that Chalabi's information collection program was providing intelligence that was saving U.S. soldiers' lives.

Turning to Tenet, the president asked, "George, is that right?"

"Sir, I have not seen, nor am I aware of, one piece of information that came from Chalabi or the INC alone that has any value," Tenet answered, seizing the opening provided by the president and plunging in the knife.

The president then turned back to the group at large and said that the U.S. government's relationship with Chalabi had to be severed—immediately. He instructed Rice to "take care of it."

After the meeting, Rice gathered Rumsfeld, Cambone, Tenet, and a few others together. "I need an evaluation of Chalabi's intelligence," she said. Then, looking at Cambone, she added, "I want to know when and how you'll terminate the relationship with him."

By the next NSC meeting, however, Cambone still had not gotten back to her. When Chalabi's name came up—this time about how he was speaking out against U.S. policy in Iraq—the president turned to Rice and said, "We are done with Chalabi, aren't we, Condi? That relationship is cut, right?"

Rice looked over at Cambone, who said, "We're still evaluating that, Mr. President."

At which point, the president became visibly angry—again. "His face turned to stone," recalls Rob Richer. "The president has been discussing this over three—three—NSC meetings throughout the spring, and Chalabi's INC is still on the payroll. The president's order to pull the plug continued to be ignored. He was not happy. He kept looking at Condi, who was supposed to take care of this. But she couldn't take on the Defense Department. That was the problem."

And beyond the matter of Rice's influence with Defense was the Pentagon's stubborn allegiance to Chalabi, Richer felt. "Backing Chalabi was more important to them than following the direct orders of the president of the United States," Richer says. "To them, the neocons—Perle, Wolfowitz, Feith, Vice President Cheney, Scooter Libby—their political vision and their ideology superseded any direction from anyone else. To them, if it didn't fit their vision, it could be ignored or stonewalled."

Following that meeting, the evaluation of Chalabi's information came in: while the Defense Intelligence Agency said it was saving the lives of American soldiers, a full and independent evaluation by the U.S. intelligence community at large—which includes military and civilian intelligence agencies alike—looked at the Pentagon's summary of reports supplied by Chalabi's network and concluded that the material was "unremarkable, barely tactical in nature, and did not warrant any continued support of the Iraqi National

Congress," Richer said, paraphrasing. "This was the intelligence community's finding to Cambone."

On May 19, 2004, Wolfowitz announced that after ten years and $33 million in aid, Chalabi's INC would no longer receive U.S. funding. It would be "inappropriate," Wolfowitz explained, for the Pentagon to continue funding an Iraqi political party in light of efforts to set up a new Iraqi government. But that was all political camouflage designed to conceal the true thrust of events: after Chalabi's Iranian betrayal, his Pentagon patrons no longer had the juice to protect him.

The following day, May 20, American authorities—including the White House—signed off on a raid of Chalabi's home and office in west Baghdad. While U.S. soldiers cordoned off the street, seven Iraqi police officers burst through the front door of his home looking for seven of his lieutenants who had been charged by Iraqi authorities with car theft, currency fraud, and other crimes. Down the road, a group of Americans dressed in civilian clothes looked on as a second contingent of Iraqi cops burst into the headquarters of Chalabi's INC office, ordering Chalabi's guards to load their police vehicles with the office's computers, documents, and other files. They were looking for evidence of Chalabi's leak to Iran.

Chalabi denounced the raids and said the accusation was a lie. "This was a manufactured charge—untrue, false, unfounded," he told me, echoing remarks he made at the time. It was trumped-up, he said, political payback for his principled opposition to Bush administration policies. As evidence, he cited a meeting in Baghdad with Robert Blackwill, a senior White House official who, he says, threatened him. "He said to me, 'Do you know who I am? I am the special envoy of President Bush. Your situation is very precarious in the White House. If you continue to oppose the policy of President Bush, we will bring the full weight of the United States to bear against you.' I told him his warning didn't persuade me, and I stood up and left." The threat turned into reality, Chalabi claims, with the raid of his house on May 20.

That same day, word of his alleged betrayal of NSA code-breaking began to leak out into the press. And, immediately, his boosters in Washington distanced themselves from him. "There's all this stuff about his advising us on policy and his being highly influential, and it's wildly overstated," Doug Feith told *Time*. "The stuff that's been reported about us being very close is just wrong." Cheney also made a few choice leaks, letting it be known through surrogates that in the run-up to the war he viewed Chalabi as merely "one of many" exiles who could aid the United States. Cheney ordered his staff to cut off all communication with Chalabi. And Paul Wolfowitz remained mum, letting Chalabi twist in the wind.

Only Richard Perle continued to defend his friend, telling the *New York Times* that the charges against Chalabi didn't pass "the laugh test." He said it defied logic that a seasoned Iranian intelligence operative would use the same communication channel Chalabi had just warned him was compromised. "You have to believe that the station chief blew a gift from the gods because of rank incompetence," Perle told the *Times*. "I don't believe it, and I don't think any other serious intelligence professional would either."

The directors of the CIA and the NSA pointed out that bureaucracies make mistakes similar to the Iranian use of the compromised channel all the time. The CIA certainly had a long list of its own to prove the point. It was clear to U.S. intelligence officials that the explanation was simply that Iran was not taking Chalabi's word at face value. And they weren't about to start hand-carrying messages from Tehran to its posts around the world when there were no other indications that their communication system had been compromised.

In May 2004, the CIA and the NSA asked the FBI to look into how Chalabi had obtained the highly classified code-breaking information. The bureau sent a small army of special agents from its foreign counterintelligence branch to Baghdad, while dispatching investigators from its Washington field office to polygraph civilian employees at the Pentagon. They concluded that the source of the leaked classified information was a DIA analyst in Baghdad who had been assigned to the Pentagon's intelligence-gathering cell inside Chalabi's compound.

"There were about ten guys assigned to the cell," a former U.S. intelligence official explained. "It was a tactical 'humint,' or 'human intelligence,' team that was living in the Chalabi compound. And they'd sit around and get drunk with Karim [Chalabi's chief of intelligence] and the other guys working for Chalabi. Our guys forgot who they were talking to. Friendships formed, they drank together, and before you knew it, the DIA guys were talking out of school. They let their guard down. They left their laptops [containing top secret information] open. They grew undisciplined. It wasn't deliberate. There was no intent to hurt the United States. It was a breakdown of counterintelligence discipline. That happens when the Pentagon has you living with the guys you're supposed to be watching."

U.S. intelligence officials now believe that Karim compromised more than just the United States' code-breaking capabilities. Among other things, they believe he also gave Tehran the U.S. army's order of battle, or military profile, in Iraq, and its strategy for countering the growing insurgency.

John Maguire, the CIA's former deputy chief of station in Baghdad, blames the Pentagon's civilian leadership for what he calls an intelligence debacle. "They strapped their wagon to the wrong guy," Maguire said. "He had a track record with documented counterintelligence problems, especially with Iran, and they ignored it. It's beyond explanation."

After the raid on Chalabi's house, CIA analysts took another look at Chalabi's relationship with Iran. They now believe that Karim was "a full-up, recruited, and paid asset" of Iranian intelligence. That meant he was tasked by Tehran and reported back to them.

Intelligence analysts think Chalabi had a different kind of relationship with Iran. For one, they believe Iranian intelligence would have had as little success in controlling him as the CIA did. "Ahmad Chalabi is not a controllable asset," says former CIA analyst Bruce Riedel. "He's an independent actor. He's an Iraqi patriot—and an opportunist—who uses everybody for himself."

Riedel's thesis is that Chalabi was for Iran what people in the spy business call an agent of influence. "An agent of influence is someone who can push a certain policy direction and do so in a way that there is plausible deniability that he's doing it for a foreign power," Riedel explained. "And in Ahmad's case, he's a perfect person to be an agent of influence for the Iranians, because—like them—he wanted to get rid of Saddam. He didn't want money to do it, other than for the purpose of accomplishing the goal. And the Iranians would have seen him as someone who was in a position to influence American policy, and therefore it was in their interest to support him covertly and to exchange information with him."

Riedel believes that Chalabi probably started out as an informant for Iran: What is the Clinton administration doing about Iraq? How serious are they about trying to overthrow Saddam? Is the CIA attempting a coup? "When the Bush team comes in, and he's cultivating all of these Republican relationships, he now becomes not just a useful informant," Riedel said, "but a mechanism to encourage them in what they already wanna do. Which is go to war, invade Iraq."

Chalabi was by no means the only impetus to war. But he stoked the desire, making it not merely a priority but an obsession, raising the stakes by supplying defectors who bore false witness to Saddam's nonexistent ties to al-Qaeda and the regime's phantom stockpiles of WMD. He lobbied Congress, met privately with the vice president, and fed faulty intelligence directly to senior Defense Department policy makers, bypassing the process for vetting raw data.

After the U.S. invasion, Chalabi was able to help Iran in other ways, Riedel says: "He can also give Iran some pretty good insights as to what the Americans are gonna do when they get to Iraq, which is surprisingly little in terms of how they're gonna run the country. They have no imperial designs on Iraq. And that there's a lack of consensus inside the administration. The State Department wants to do one thing. The Defense Department wants to do something else. And the Defense Department's gonna call the shots here, 'cause they're really in charge. He's telling Iran something very, very important now: Who matters in the U.S. government. Reading about it in the newspapers is one thing. But knowing that kind of information from a source as well-connected as Chalabi would have been a gold mine for Iran."

It was always clear that once the United States removed Saddam, there would be a struggle for dominance in Iraq, and that the two key players in that struggle would be the United States and Iran. Riedel says Washington and Tehran bet on the same horse, Ahmad Chalabi. But it didn't work out so well for the Bush administration. "Here is our principal interlocutor on the Iraqi side—the man who sits next to the First Lady [at the State of the Union address]—and he is double-dealing on behalf of America's adversary," he explained. "And to be fair to him, he's not even hiding it. Now, he's hiding, perhaps, how badly he's screwing us. But he's not hiding that he's in bed with them. And we're just ignoring it."

Riedel acknowledges there are other Iraqi leaders supported by the United States with nefarious ties of their own to Tehran. "But," he adds, "they didn't have the kind of influence in Washington that Ahmad did. Ahmad Chalabi is really unique. He's a unique character in contemporary American foreign policy. What other foreign individual has had the access to power that he did?"

TWENTY-FOUR

The raid on Ahmad Chalabi's house on May 20, 2004, nearly erupted into a deadly firefight. When the Iraqi police burst through the front door wearing flak jackets and waving pistols, Chalabi's private security detail—a team of armed guards as ferocious as a pack of pit bulls—sprinted to the front of the house, their guns drawn and in the firing position. Chalabi, who had been upstairs asleep in his bedroom when the commotion started, hurried down the stairs of the two-story house to the main level, where—after a tense, screaming standoff—he got his men to back down. "We narrowly avoided a massacre here," Chalabi recalled. "My guards were ready to shoot."

They holstered their weapons, while the Iraqi police handcuffed and took several members of Chalabi's entourage into custody. Violence was averted.

But the raid marked the end of Chalabi's American era—the final act in a near-biblical fall from grace. It was as bitter and tumultuous as Chalabi's undoing in Jordan after the collapse of Petra Bank and his father's in Baghdad when Iraq's monarchy fell. Chalabi was humiliated and, seemingly, washed up: defrocked by the Americans, under investigation by the Iraqis, and accused of spying for Iran. However, even Chalabi's fiercest critics agree that he may be the shrewdest and most resilient politician alive. He is the ultimate survivor, a nervy risk taker with Houdini-like staying power. And in the short term that's how it played out. "They thought they could write my obituary," Chalabi said in 2005. "But they were wrong."

As in previous crises, Chalabi became calm as he engineered the twists and turns of his latest resurrection. The first thing he did was to use the raid to undo his image as an American invention. "I recognized this was a great opportunity for me to show people I am not America's stooge," he said. "And that was an important thing. The Americans did [me] a great favor, because while they did liberate the country, their presence here, and their behavior subsequent to the liberation, made it a big, huge stigma to be working with them. And I was the Iraqi face of the American occupation—no matter what I did and spoke about. But by this one act of theirs, this raid—which showed deep hostility toward me—they cleaned the slate. And I immediately recognized that."

He held a press conference that afternoon, likening the raid on his house with the U.S. occupation of Iraq.

"Let my people go," he bellowed.

"Like Moses," he later remarked, with a wink and a flash of his mischievous smile.

He then went about his comeback methodically, employing the same strategy he had once employed in Washington: identifying centers of power and then either ingratiating himself with them or insinuating himself into their good graces. And so a few days after the raid he traveled to the Shiite holy city of Najaf to meet with Moqtada al-Sadr, Iraq's most prominent anti-American cleric, whose Iranian-backed militia was engaged in a violent showdown with U.S. forces. After two months of escalating combat, more than 350 Shiite insurgents and 20 coalition soldiers had been killed. "I didn't know what was waiting for us in Najaf," Chalabi recalled, "whether we were going to be shot by the U.S. Army or by the Sadr people."

Chalabi stayed in Najaf for nine days and helped negotiate a cease-fire. But he infuriated the U.S. Army by championing al-Sadr, who had called on his followers to "terrorize the Americans."

Chalabi went on to play an important role in persuading his fellow Shiites to join Iraq's political process, becoming something of a mentor to al-Sadr, coaching him and providing him with strategy and analysis. In the process, the aristocratic external—Chalabi—was able to attach himself to the most potent of internal figures to emerge in post-Saddam Iraq. This was the genius of his courting al-Sadr.

Chalabi denied there was even a whiff of opportunism to his new political bent. And yet this self-proclaimed secularist suddenly started making public appearances at religious Shia commemorations, engaging in ceremonial chest-beating and other rituals as a display of devotion to Husayn ibn Ali, the great Shia martyr. Chalabi was hardly convincing in this new role, as his wardrobe at these rituals was an expensive black, two-piece Italian suit and designer T-shirt. He never grew a beard or bothered to wear a turban or traditional Islamic dress, like the ankle-length white *thoub*. But he knew he needed to make the gesture if he was going to convince Iraq's major Shiite groups, including hard-line Islamists, to join together in a political coalition, the United Iraqi Alliance. His crowning achievement: he managed to get the country's most revered religious leader, Grand Ayatollah Ali al-Sistani, to endorse the ticket in the country's upcoming election, scheduled for January 30, 2005. It would be Iraq's first since the invasion.

When the votes were tallied, the ticket led by Ayad Allawi, the Bush administration's preferred candidate, finished a distant third, with 13.8 percent of the 8.5 million votes cast. The Chalabi-engineered coalition came in first, with more than 48 percent of the vote—not enough to win an outright majority of the transitional National Assembly, but far more than necessary to dominate it.

It was less than a year since his break with America, and Ahmad Chalabi was already back. He swaggered with renewed confidence, and wasted no time making his move. "Ahmad thought that since we delivered the Shiite Alliance, we should get prime minister," recalls Nabeel Musawi, one of his closest lieutenants at the time.

The members of the newly elected parliament would select the prime minister. In the end it came down to Chalabi and Ibrahim al-Jaafari, a doctor and the leader of one of Iraq's major Shiite religious parties. Chalabi was the much more qualified candidate, but Jaafari had closer ties to Iran. He had lived in Tehran during much of Saddam Hussein's reign and belonged to a religious party that had long favored an Islamic state in Iraq.

As the vote came down to the wire, with only two days to go, Iran's top diplomat in Baghdad, along with a senior Iranian intelligence official, paid a visit to Chalabi at his compound. Musawi, the Chalabi aide, attended the meeting and said that the Iranian ambassador was blunt, even rude, in telling Chalabi to drop out of the contest. "I saw Ahmad's face," Musawi recalled. "It was red. He was furious—a cocktail of emotions running through him. I could see clearly, though, that Ahmad wouldn't say anything."

Chalabi was angry not because Iran's leaders presumed to choose Iraq's first democratically elected prime minister, but because they didn't choose him. Musawi, on the other hand, was outraged by the Iranians' meddling.

"As the ambassador was taking us through all the reasons why Ahmad should drop out," Musawi says, "I interrupted the conversation and said, 'Mr. Ambassador, excuse me, but on what authority do you tell us how to run *our* country?' The ambassador was shocked to hear my words. He said, 'I have a list of quotes from Dr. Chalabi saying he would never seek the prime minister position. Why the change of heart?' I said, 'This is an internal decision that we don't have to explain to anyone.'"

After the meeting, Chalabi withdrew his nomination, insisting publicly that he did so for the sake of unity. "I would be blamed for ruining the Shia ascendancy," Chalabi told me, "because of my personal ambition. I said no. And I withdrew."

But Musawi says Chalabi backed out because he was afraid: "Look, this is a man who lives in a country occupied by the United States, which now despises him. So he couldn't afford to piss off the Iranians. There are only two forces on the ground in Iraq, and if Ahmad ignored the ambassador's wishes, this would be something the Iranians would not forgive. He would be dead in two days, and he knew it."

After withdrawing his nomination, Chalabi became one of the country's four deputy prime ministers. He was also named chairman of two powerful committees, one that gave him authority over the country's oil industry and the other over approving all government contracts worth more than $3 million. Over the next several months, he played an integral role in hammering out Iraq's new constitution. By all outward appearances, he was on top of the world, moving around Baghdad in thirty-car motorcades and a much-expanded security detail. But for Chalabi, the role was the consolation prize—and one that came with a glass ceiling. He now realized the limits of his strategic tilt toward Iran: without a lot more leverage, he would never be acceptable to the turbans in Tehran. He was secular and, for them, that was a near-insurmountable obstacle.

"The Iranians wanted an Islamic Shia to be prime minister," Chalabi said. "It was a point for them to get an Islamic prime minister who lived in Iran [during their exile], who worked with them, and who subscribed to their Islamic view of the world. It was a very important point to Tehran." Chalabi was disappointed, but he didn't give up. The wheels kept turning.

Something else also became clear in 2005, as observed by Dexter Filkins, the *New York Times* foreign correspondent: By siding with Iraq's Islamists and by organizing the January elections around the country's Sunni/Shia divide, Chalabi had "thrown his weight behind a number of trends that were only then becoming dominant: the Islamization of Iraqi society, the division of Iraq into sectarian cantons. Those trends later spiraled out of control, into the de facto civil war" that nearly tore the country apart. From late 2005 through the end of 2007, tens of thousands of Iraqi men, women, and children—all innocents—were maimed or killed, to say nothing of the thousands of casualties suffered by U.S. and Iraqi armed forces.

No one imagined that Chalabi wanted that. And, of course, far greater forces than he galvanized the violence—forces both ancient and extant, foreign and domestic. But in his drive for power, and in his hubris, believing that he could manage, while exploiting, the chaos he knowingly stoked, Chalabi helped arouse passions that were beyond anybody's ability to harness. As Iraq descended into near apocalyptic violence—with kidnappings, targeted assassinations, suicide bombings, and the murder and mutilation of Sunni Arabs by Shia death squads, their bodies punctured by holes from electric drills and left uncollected on the streets—even some of Chalabi's closest friends could not forgive him.

"It's not even that I'm angry," said Tamara Daghistani, his lifelong friend. "I'm heartbroken. All my life my dream was to go back to Iraq and live the end of my days in my own country. And suddenly, I can't do that anymore. We're back to more bloodshed and more deaths than even Saddam can claim."

As the body count climbed, Chalabi sought opportunity where he could find it. And in late 2005, it came from the most unlikely of places: Washington. Faced with the chaos and violence, an increasingly desperate Bush administration began to reach out to anyone who might help, including—in a head-snapping reversal—Chalabi. The administration set aside the allegations of spying for Iran that had preceded the raid on Chalabi's compound eighteen months before and, in November 2005, invited the Iraqi back to Washington.

Ostensibly, Chalabi went to meet with the secretary of the treasury, John Snow, to discuss trade issues. But while there, Chalabi met with Cheney, Rice, and Rumsfeld. The second round of elections in Iraq was just a few weeks away, and Chalabi had another shot at becoming prime minister, or so it seemed to administration officials. They wanted to make sure they could work with him, and vice versa. And he wanted to know if the administration would support him for prime minister in the upcoming election. No one made any promises, but a rapprochement seemed afoot.

That same month, Chalabi also traveled to Tehran for meetings with Ali

Larijani, the national security adviser who reported directly to the country's supreme leader, Ayatollah Ali Khamanei, who in turn had the final say over national security questions. Chalabi also met with Mahmoud Ahmadinejad, the Iranian president. Would the Iranians support him in his bid for prime minister this time around? Did his apparent reconciliation with Washington give him the leverage in Iran that he now needed? Chalabi didn't have to wait long to find out.

When he returned to Iraq in the lead-up to the December 2005 elections, the Shiite coalition he had organized offered him and his party a paltry 3 seats out of the 128 it expected to control—and no prime ministership. The tender seemed designed to insult, and it did. Chalabi demanded no fewer than 10 seats and when he didn't get them—ultimately, the offer came up to 6—he pulled out of the coalition and ran in the election on his own as an independent, a secular, and as the lead candidate on the Iraqi National Congress's ticket. Some of his aides predicted he would win as many as 50 seats, but he got demolished. In his hometown of Baghdad, he pulled in an embarrassing 8,645 votes out of the 2.5 million cast. Nationwide, it was no better: slightly more than 30,000 votes out of 12 million. That amounted to one-quarter of 1 percent—not enough to win even a single seat in the parliament.

Today, Chalabi says he wasn't surprised by the results. "I expected it," he insists.

But his closest aides say he's either lying or in denial. "At the time, he was speechless, absolutely depressed," recalls Musawi.

"He got angry a lot," remembers Aras Habib Karim, Chalabi's closest of lieutenants. "He lost his temper over silly things. But it gave him an excuse to explode and vent his anger." Karim says that for weeks Chalabi's mood swung from quiet and sullen to resentful and bitter. "He felt rejected and betrayed. He felt that he was the man responsible for liberating Iraq and for getting rid of Saddam. Why didn't he get *one* seat? He was crushed. I told him that Churchill won the war and lost the election. But it didn't help."

Chalabi may have done more than any other Iraqi to rid the country of Saddam Hussein and to make the election possible, but he underestimated the depth of his unpopularity. He was well-known in Iraq, but most everyone there—from taxi drivers and housekeepers to his fellow elites—had heard of his Petra Bank conviction and associated him with corruption. Many also derided him as an American patsy, while still others disliked his ties to Iran. In a 2004 poll, he ranked as the nation's least-trusted public figure, lower than even Saddam. That hurt.

Then there was the question of Chalabi the politician. In person, behind closed doors, he was a commanding presence: charming, brilliant, and irresistibly likable. But on the campaign trail he was stiff and awkward—even insecure. "Ahmad had gotten so used to making dark moves and back room deals," his aide Nabeel Musawi says, "that when it came time for him to be on a platform and talk directly to the public and connect with them, he just couldn't do it. He tried. He honestly tried. But he was so uncomfortable and it showed. For those who know Chalabi like I do, you could see he was just so out of his natural environment. He's more comfortable making deals in back rooms and making big decisions away from the public. So it wasn't for lack of effort on his part. It just wasn't him."

In the end, Chalabi was a power politician, carved from a different era—from the time of his father and grandfather, when men of means and rank gathered to cut deals and hatch schemes over cups of hot tea in the parlors of their large estates. That's what Chalabi had been steeped in as a child, at the knee of his father. One of his boyhood heroes had been Nuri al-Said, a close family friend who was first appointed prime minister of Iraq under the British mandate in 1930. From then until the end of the monarchy, al-Said had brokered many of the key policy decisions that shaped modern Iraq—without ever standing for election. That is what appealed to Chalabi: to be not exactly king, but somebody who could stand above the political fray and guide Iraq into the modern era through a series of backroom deals that he conceived and commanded by fiat. That was the true nature of Chalabi, and it dictated to a large degree the way he navigated his life from exile back to Baghdad. But his country had become a much different place from the Iraq of his childhood. It was sliding into civil war, and power increasingly rested not with politicians or powerbrokers, or even with occupying armies, but with the likes of Moqtada al-Sadr, populist firebrands with large street followings and ruthless militias. Iraq had passed Chalabi by.

Over the next year and a half, as the violence in his country exploded, Chalabi remained in Iraq. Leaving the country never occurred to him But he entered a kind of wilderness period. He talked of reinvigorating the INC and met with people to plan a comeback. But he never followed through. He

remained one of the hardest-working and most competent Iraqis in Baghdad, as he continued to chair the De-Ba'athification Commission, his lone
remaining tentacle to political power. But there was something different
about him now. He seemed unmoored.

"He basically had no plans for not being in power," Musawi says, "and he
just sort of lost focus. The idea that he would not be the leader of Iraq never
occurred to him. And when that didn't materialize, he lost direction."

He gravitated to new relationships, which strained some long-standing
ones, like those with his wife and many of his closest confidants. Musawi
left Baghdad and returned to live in London. Others resigned or drifted
away. And the U.S. and Iraqi governments basically shut him out of power.
Many of his peers simply disliked or distrusted him. Worse, they could now
safely ignore him.

Chalabi said at the time that this interlude would pass, and that his
detractors would come back to him. They always did. But for nearly two
years, he sat mostly on the sidelines of his country.

Then in November 2007, Iraq's prime minister, Nouri al-Maliki, created a new, high-profile post for restoring basic government services in
Baghdad—health and electricity, sewage and potable water. The government's failure to deliver those amenities had made life in the capital virtually
unbearable for most Iraqis, which in turn contributed mightily to both the
breakdown in civil society and the people's alienation from their government. The hope was to bolster the recent security gains made by the U.S.
military "surge" with improvements in the quality of life. It was classic
counterinsurgency strategy, connecting the government to the well-being
of the people and, in the process, winning over their hearts and minds.

The man in charge of implementing that strategy in Iraq, General David
Petraeus, thought Chalabi was just the person to cut through Iraq's crip-
pling bureaucracy to get the job done. The commanding general had gotten
to know Chalabi well and found him to be both a first-class opportunist and
perhaps the single most intelligent, capable, energetic, decisive, and effective person in all of the country. Harnessing the needs of the Iraqi people
to Chalabi's remarkable, can-do skill set and his enormous, me-first well
of ambition struck Petraeus as a masterstroke. Thus, Chalabi was reborn
and reincarnated—as Iraq's indispensable Mr. Fix-It. Just as Chalabi had
predicted, his detractors had come to back to him, and they did so with the
blessing and encouragement of the U.S. military.

"Why is it that the U.S. can't cut the cord with Chalabi?" one former

CIA official marveled at the news of Chalabi's latest political comeback. "It's like a horrible marriage: why can't we break up? One of the reasons is, Chalabi actually does have these skills. He's very Western, and the U.S. military likes working with him."

Chalabi was given his own office inside the International Zone (less formally known as the Green Zone), the highly guarded enclave in Baghdad where the seat of power for the U.S. and Iraqi governments resided. He conferred with everyone from Maliki and Iraq's minister of electricity to Petraeus and Ryan Crocker, the U.S. ambassador in Baghdad. "Until you put a bullet through that man's heart," the incredulous ex-CIA official remarked, "don't count Ahmad Chalabi out. He will always come back."

Over the next six months, Chalabi made little progress improving the quality of life in Baghdad. But he returned to political prominence, while reviving and repairing his relationship with the United States—so much so that there was even talk of revisiting and possibly "reinterpreting" the NSA intercepts that suggested he had spied for Iran. But as Kurdish leader Jalal Talabani once said of him, "Ahmad Chalabi is brilliant, but he is not wise," and Chalabi once again torpedoed his own ascendancy by demonstrating what a ruthless and diabolical opportunist he can be. In the spring of 2008, when a major battle erupted in the southern city of Basra between the Iraqi army and Iranian-backed fighters loyal to Moqtada al-Sadr, he did the unthinkable: he betrayed the Iraqi government and sided with al-Sadr.

As the battle began, al-Sadr's forces took the initiative, seizing control of wide swaths of the city and battering government forces with quick hit-and-run assaults. The violence spread to Shiite districts of Baghdad where al-Sadr's militiamen held sway. They began lobbing a seemingly unrelenting barrage of mortars and rockets over the walls into the Green Zone, killing and injuring Iraqi and American workers. They were so successful that al-Maliki's government teetered on the brink of collapse. Such a fall would have been a staggering blow to the overall U.S. effort in Iraq and to the gains Petraeus's surge had been making in tamping down the insurgency.

It was a time of national crisis, and everyone understood the stakes. Leading members of al-Maliki's parliamentary coalition called to pledge their support, saying they would bury their considerable differences with him and stand with the government of Iraq. "It was a huge and important gesture," a senior U.S. military commander remarked at the time.

Chalabi, on the other hand, tried to exploit the crisis for his own political gain. According to senior U.S. officials, instead of pledging fealty to Maliki, he egged on al-Sadr's key military commanders. "Chalabi told them not to ease up," a senior U.S. military official told me. "To keep pressing their military advantage. That they were succeeding, and the Maliki government was crumbling. Maliki cannot withstand the onslaught for much longer. The continued attacks will cause his government to fracture and the parliament, which was literally under rocket and mortar attack in the IZ [the International Zone], will call for his removal. There'll be a vote of no confidence, and Maliki will be gone."

To make matters worse, U.S. intelligence officials learned that Chalabi was also talking to top Iranian intelligence officials in Baghdad, urging them to use their influence in Baghdad to get Iraq's political leadership to rally around him and Jaafari, the former prime minister, so that they could lead the country when the Maliki government fell. "Chalabi told the Iranians he expected Maliki's government to fall," the senior U.S. military official recalls, "and that Tehran would find a 'very favorable' friend in Jaafari and himself if they were to replace Maliki."

Ultimately, the U.S. Army and Special Forces sent in reinforcements to Basra and the Sadr City section of Baghdad and—after weeks of sometimes pitched battle—turned the situation around. Moqtada al-Sadr's fighters stood down, while the thirty-five-year-old cleric remained safely sheltered in Iran. Maliki's government survived. Chalabi had bet on the wrong horse.

"He's way smarter than I am," Ryan Crocker said of Chalabi at the time. "But for all the wattage, he does make mistakes. He made the judgment early on in Basra that Maliki had made a bad and possibly fatal mistake and it was the time for him to leap into this and position himself to replace Maliki."

Instead, al-Maliki disbanded the government services committee Chalabi chaired—essentially firing him and leaving him with no official duties. The United States also declared him persona non grata. "He was dead to us," said Colonel Steven Boylan (now retired), who was Petraeus's public affairs officer at the time. "Nobody would return his phone calls. E-mails went unanswered. He was cut off. We severed all ties and communication with him. As far as we were concerned, he didn't exist anymore."

Boylan sat in on some of the classified briefings where Chalabi's duplicity was detailed, and he says the feeling on both the Iraqi and American sides was that Chalabi had completely gone over to the dark side. "What he did was tantamount to treason," Boylan says. "He was a member of the current government at that time. He had significant power at that time. And here he was talking to the enemy of the state and telling them how he thought they could win. From our eyes, he was trying to engineer a coup. For a while, I thought he might be arrested."

Just as bad, Boylan says, was the personal nature of Chalabi's disloyalty: "Maliki hired him. General Petraeus and Ambassador Crocker lent the weight of their offices to help him. And how does he repay that confidence? By betraying them. What he did was not for the good of Iraq. It was for the good of Ahmad Chalabi."

I asked Crocker why he thought Chalabi had made such a reckless gamble when his relations with the United States had improved so dramatically. "Chalabi made a strategic decision some time ago," Crocker said, "that he was determined by hook or by crook—or mini hooks and mini crooks—to reclaim the family heritage of leadership in Iraq and that everything else is tactics. He has seen the Iranians as helpful to him in this regard. And the Iranians, no doubt, see him as helpful to them."

Chalabi denies any wrongdoing. But by the summer of 2008, he found himself in a familiar place. He was out of power, a man alone on the outside looking in. He put on a brave face, however, saying, "This is the second time they say I betrayed the United States. There was a comeback the last time."

TWENTY-FIVE

When a soldier clears the chamber of his or her M-16, the weapon is said to be "on green," while "red" means that a rifle is locked and loaded and ready to fire. That terminology was applied to the division of Iraq after U.S. forces rolled triumphantly into Baghdad in April 2003: the 5.6 square miles of heavily fortified and relatively secure territory in central Baghdad along the Tigris River, officially called the International Zone, became known as the Green Zone. By the spring of 2008, it had become the country's seat of power; the U.S. embassy was located there, as were the offices of Prime Minister Nouri al-Maliki, several government ministries, and the Iraqi parliament.

Everything outside that compound, where bombs exploded and gunfire crackled almost incessantly, became known as the Red Zone. And it was there that Ahmad Chalabi carved out his own little empire, an eight-square-block area in the Mansour district of west Baghdad. "Ahmad set up his own personal Green Zone," Francis Brooke says. "He just did it. And when the Iraqis and Americans complained, it was already too late. We call it our Yellow Zone."

The perimeter of Chalabi's compound was surrounded by blast walls, concrete T-walls, and concertina wire, with access available only through entry control points manned by the Iraqi army—a perk extended to him as a former deputy prime minister. Another six hundred soldiers—the equivalent of an Iraqi battalion—lived in the compound year-round and were assigned to protect him. Chalabi brought in an additional three hundred private guards and a team of South African–trained guard dogs to afford

extra protection for him and the twelve hundred people who also were resid-
ing within the boundaries of his realm. By May 2008, Chalabi had not been
selected prime minister or even voted into parliament. But he had erected
his own city-state, where he was sovereign and everything existed to serve
his needs and propel his aspirations forward.

He had a chef, a manservant, and two tea boys. There were aides who
opened and closed doors for him, shined his shoes, and helped throw on
his coat. When it rained, he walked under an open umbrella held by a valet.
Someone else carried his cell phone, while yet another person held on to
his reading glasses until he needed them; he even had staff clean his lenses.
"Here," he would command, holding out his arm and handing them to
another of his servants.

It was a most extraordinary and extravagant life, one reminiscent of his
father's and equally immune from the daily hardships of Iraq. While people
in Baghdad got only a few hours a day of running water and electricity, those
amenities were available to Chalabi—Iraq's erstwhile Mr. Fix-It—around
the clock. He trucked in his own ready-to-drink water tanks and kept as
many as three massive generators—each the size of a trailer—rumbling
next to his house, supplying all the light and air-conditioning he could possibly need on a blistering Baghdadi day.

It was easy to tell when Chalabi was present in the Yellow Zone. The
pounding roar of the generators reverberated through the hot, dry air like a
hovering helicopter. When Chalabi left the compound, the air grew still and
silent—the generators turned off to cut down on his $900-a-day cost in die-
sel fuel (about $300,000 a year). Everyone else who lived there—from the
soldiers protecting him to his top aides, cousins, nephews, and neighbors—
all had to do without power or running water in his absence. This was Chalabi in full pasha mode.

He lived alone (his wife and children having stayed in London) in a comfortable two-story house at the epicenter of the Yellow Zone, a house that
had belonged to his sister before the 1958 revolution. Under Saddam, the
Ba'athists had used the house as a party headquarters. But Chalabi reclaimed
it as his own and decorated it with exquisite and typically expensive taste:
the walls of his main parlor were lined with original oil paintings, some
distinctively Muslim, others French, English, and Danish, from a pensive,
bespectacled cleric reading the Quran to abstract art. The mantle of his fire-
place was framed by tall, curving ivory tusks. And upstairs he maintained a

vast personal library filled with books on mathematics, philosophy, history, Stalin, Goethe, the Renaissance—and his nemesis, the CIA.

Every night at about nine o'clock, he emerged from his study on the second floor, a solitary figure descending a flight of marble stairs to the house's main level, where dinner was served. The evening meal was a ritual of food and conversation, with plates of hummus, fattoush, grilled fish, and chicken kabob passed around as Chalabi held court with six to eight guests, usually relatives and his closest aides. It was here that Chalabi was often at his most unguarded. "I'm in Baghdad. Saddam is gone, and I'm living like this," he boasted one evening as he waved his arm across the dinner table. As rich and plentiful as it all was, however, being sultan of the Yellow Zone was not what Chalabi had in mind when he returned to Baghdad after forty-five years of exile.

I was among Chalabi's guests over a nearly three-week period in May 2008, just when the U.S. and Iraqi governments had severed ties with him and dealt another body blow to his aspirations. For the most part, he was his usual gregarious and entertaining self. But it was clearly a difficult time for him. He often seemed unsure of his footing, something I'd never observed before. And he frequently let fly with outbursts of anger and resentment over his latest run-in with Washington, as though it were he who had been betrayed. Sometimes he turned the dinner conversation into a bitter critique of the United States. "American culture is like pornography to a teenager," he said. "You can't get enough of it. Then you're bored by it."

He complained that Americans simply didn't understand the Arab culture. "They don't have servants. Can you imagine! The few who do, try to make them members of the family. Can you believe it! They think it's humiliating to have a tea boy. It's humiliating to be homeless in New York City."

He didn't mean any of it—he's as big an Americaphile as there is. But it was a measure of the bitterness he harbored over his stunted stature in Iraq. He blamed the United States, especially those he felt had let him down personally, people like Paul Wolfowitz. "My relationship with Wolfowitz terminated in 2004," he said coldly during one of our dinners. "He condoned the raid on my house. He never defended me. And when he came to Baghdad afterward, he never came to see or even call me. Wolfowitz thought it was counterproductive to be associated with me, and he never said or did anything in my defense."

Wolfowitz and the U.S. government were continuing to shun Chalabi the last time I saw him in Baghdad, in December 2010, as were the Iraqi people for all intents and purposes. Earlier that year, Chalabi had run for parliament—back on the Shia ticket this time—and pulled in eight-tenths of 1 percent of the vote in Baghdad: 20,000 votes out of more than 2.5 million cast. Because of a quirk in the country's byzantine election laws, however, his party was awarded one seat in the new legislature—and Chalabi took it. But that's all he got. He was given no ministry to run, no portfolio to oversee, no delegation to lead. Chalabi was a party of one in a parliament of 325.

The CIA was right, after all: In Iraq, he had no constituency. And the dreams he had for himself and his country remained stuck in the Yellow Zone, trapped behind the cement blast walls and concertina wire of his makeshift empire. And that's where they're likely to stay, for it now seems clear that history has passed him by.

From the beginning, that was Chalabi's game: to deal himself into history. He had devoted his life to engineering the ouster of Saddam Hussein—or, more precisely, to getting the United States to do it for him. But overthrowing Saddam was just a means to the greater glory he sought. History was in Chalabi's blood. He read it. He absorbed it and understood its flow of events. He could talk for hours about the influence of Aristotle and Plato on Iran or the idea of Zoroastrianism and how it changed the Persian Gulf or how the Arab conquest of Spain tied into medieval European history. What animated Chalabi the mathematician more than anything else was the idea of becoming a man of history himself—as the liberator of Iraq, the man who overthrew the murderous thug from Tikrit; as the Shia's great emancipator, the person who freed the long-embattled Shiites from the shackles of their realm and the history of their oppression; and as the region's first true polymath, or Renaissance man, the Middle Easterner who bridged the traditional and the modern, the sacred and the secular, and who pointed the Arab world back in the direction of human achievement as an economic power and a leader in the arts and sciences.

That was his grand vision for Iraq and for himself—and he would do anything to achieve it, fair or foul. He would manipulate the Americans and use the Iranians—he was no one's puppet. And he would spend his own money and risk his life. Such was the scope of his ambition—and the depth of his need for redemption: to absolve the shame of his father's fall from power after the 1958 revolution, to atone for the stain of his own Petra Bank conviction and, later on, to redress the ignominy of the 2004 raid on his house. For years, Chalabi had managed to foist his psychological compulsions and personal ambitions onto the world stage, conquering Washington and insinuating himself into the inner sanctums of Tehran. He had a shot. He was on the cusp of winning it all. But then, ironically, history dealt him the queen of spades, the unluckiest card of all.

"I think he would have been a much larger figure in history if we had not had 9/11," Richard Perle said, reflecting on how the terrorist attacks altered the trajectory of Chalabi's rise. "What he managed to accomplish before 9/11 was without precedent. He came to Washington and developed the idea that Saddam could and should be removed from power, and he persuaded a bunch of people to pass legislation changing the foreign policy of the United States. So when 9/11 happened, there already was quite a lot of steam behind bringing down Saddam's regime. And up until that point, Ahmad was the only show in town.

"But after 9/11, the institutions that became crucial were CENTCOM, Tommy Franks [the commanding general], the CIA, and the State Department. Ahmad became relatively minor, which is why the Bush administration was perfectly comfortable kicking him to the sidelines. Far from regarding him as essential to their plans, administration officials left him on the sidelines. Ironically, 9/11 made it more likely that we would do what Chalabi wanted done. It made it less likely that we would do it with him."

Paul Wolfowitz sees it differently. He believes that the CIA and the State Department's enmity toward Chalabi had a greater impact on history than anything Chalabi himself did. "What I hadn't adequately appreciated at the time," Wolfowitz said, "was how much the hostility to Chalabi drove the hostility to the exiles—the so-called externals—and that in turn drove us into an occupation policy instead of a liberation policy. Which is why I think the most interesting questions about Chalabi aren't the ones that are usually asked. It's, 'Why did major elements in the U.S. bureaucracy hate him so?' And 'Why did it dominate U.S. policy to the extent that we didn't train an army of Iraqi exiles before the war, or that we didn't establish a provisional government made up of Iraqi exiles?' We set up an occupation because of that. It really had a huge impact, this distrust of him."

Ken Pollack, who had his share of run-ins with Chalabi as a national security adviser during the Clinton administration, says Chalabi has only himself to blame: "Imagine how much stronger Ahmad's stock would've been had he been a straight shooter. Had he played the long game. 'Cause he is so smart and he is capable of persuading people of all kinds of things. If he had said to himself, 'I'm gonna move the United States over a much longer period of time, and the key thing is to really convince Americans that I am the George Washington of Iraq,' he could've ridden into Baghdad on the back of an M-1 tank and been made the first president of Iraq by the United States. But by being Machiavellian—and by being Machiavellian with an incredibly short time horizon—he screwed himself over and over and over again, to the point where it took a small cabal in the vice president's office to do anything with him in Iraq, 'cause every other part of the U.S. government had gotten burned by him and wanted nothing to do with him."

Chalabi is now sixty-seven, and for the first time in the decade I've known him he seems weary—perhaps from the toll of age, but I suspect more from the all-consuming burden of his relentless quest. He insists, however, that he is not slowing down and that he remains undaunted by the setbacks he's suffered. "I am not made euphoric by success or despondent by failure," he said. "That explains why I continue."

And if anyone can conjure up yet another cunning comeback, it is Ahmad Chalabi. He won't stop trying until he either succeeds or is returned to the ground with his ancestors. I asked him how he hoped history would remember him when that time comes.

"That I was true to my original aims in life," he said. "I am from this country. I am from this land. And I want to live here and die here."

History will also remember him as the great bluffer of Baghdad. Never has anyone parlayed such a weak hand into such a momentous outcome as he. When Chalabi embarked on his long journey home, he commanded no army, led no tribe, and hailed from Iraq's lowest caste, the Shia. Sometimes he had no money, either. All he had was his guile and his genius, and a single-minded determination to lure the world's last standing superpower into invading Iraq in a war of choice—to send its soldiers to fight and die and to spend upward of a trillion dollars of its national treasure—so that he could go home. It's really quite remarkable. And from an Iraqi point of view, who is to say Chalabi was not justified in doing whatever was necessary to rid his country of a genocidal dictator, someone who had killed, raped, and tortured more than a million people?

But for America, what Chalabi maneuvered us into may turn out to have been the biggest foreign policy disaster in a generation: an ill-planned, poorly executed preemptive war that employed torture and gave us the devastating images of Abu Ghraib prison, undermining the region's confidence in both our country's competence and moral authority. Perhaps the greatest irony of all, it fortified an ascendant Iran by eliminating its nemesis next door, Saddam Hussein and his Ba'athist regime.

In one of my last interviews with Chalabi, I asked him about his relationship with his fellow travelers in Washington, the neoconservatives. "Who used whom?" I asked. "In looking back, did they use you as an instrument of their designs, or was it the other way around?"

"It was a commonality of interest, a convergence of conceptions about the future," he said. "But if you look at the situation now, their influence is shattered, Iraq is liberated, and I am sitting home." In the Yellow Zone.

ACKNOWLEDGMENTS

Many people helped give life to this book, beginning with my friend Jim Risen, who spurred me to write it in the first place, and Zaab Sethna, who helped sway an initially reluctant Ahmad Chalabi to talk to me. Once Dr. Chalabi decided to go along with this endeavor, he was characteristically difficult to pin down, sometimes cantankerous, and often impatient with my persistent questioning. But, ultimately, he was—in true Iraqi fashion—unsparing with both his time and hospitality, opening the doors of his home in Baghdad and allowing me to spend up to two and three weeks at a time with him. Dr. Chalabi is a complicated man, and most certainly he had his own reasons for cooperating with this project. But he also undoubtedly knew he would take some hits in this book. To his credit, once he committed to this venture, he kept his word and fielded all questions, allowing me to interview him, re-interview him, and then to interview him yet again—for more than sixty hours in all, without any guarantees about how the information would be used. *Arrows of the Night* would not have been possible without Dr. Chalabi, and for that I am deeply grateful to him.

This book also could not have been written without the cooperation of numerous other sources, many of whom are identified by name in both the text and the source notes. I am most thankful for their time and trust, to say nothing of their patience. If there are any errors in fact or interpretation in what I have written, they are completely my responsibility and those who have helped me should bear no blame. There are also a handful of people who asked not to be identified in the book; they, too, have my sincerest thanks.

The two other people who most gave life to this project are Jeffrey Fager, the chairman of CBS News and the executive producer of *60 Minutes*, and Lesley Stahl. From the moment I approached Jeff about my interest in writing this book, he could not have been more enthusiastic or supportive, never wavering despite the varied burdens this opportunity for me put on him, the broadcast, and, most especially, his correspondent Lesley Stahl.

As for Lesley, she has been my boss, my partner, and my friend for the better part of fifteen years now, and the degree to which she backed this project, and tolerated my long absences from the office so that I could properly pursue it, has been nothing short of breathtaking. She never complained to me once, and in fact took the time to read over, comment on, and edit every one of my twenty-five chapters before I submitted them to the publisher. In terms of word count, this book is the equivalent of more than forty-five *60 Minutes* segments—and Lesley provided crucial encouragement and suggestions throughout every step of this undertaking. Her support and generosity, along with Jeff's, made all the difference.

Many others at *60 Minutes*, my professional home since 1984, contributed greatly to the book. This whole adventure began under Don Hewitt and Phil Scheffler, who commissioned my first story on Chalabi in 2001 and then allowed me to continue to explore this saga as it continued to unfold over time and across the world, from Washington to Europe to the Middle East. Joining me in those early years was Adam Ciralsky, my former associate producer. Together we blazed our first trails into Saddam's Iraq, then into Chalabi's world of exile, and, finally, into the neoconservatives' perch in the Pentagon. Bill Owens has supported this effort, as has CBS News' Linda Mason. Amjad Tadros, my friend and CBS News colleague in Jordan, got me into and out of Baghdad safely, while introducing me to some of Chalabi's past associates in Amman. Kathy Liu, Tadd Lascari, and Jennie Held contributed research, while George Crile, one of my early mentors at *60 Minutes*, taught me the joy of reporting from war zones like Iraq, where most everything is painfully difficult to do but ultimately an experience well worth having.

Beyond CBS, Ranya Kadri in Amman provided ideas and insights, along with a large measure of enthusiasm, as she introduced me to former members of the Royal Court of Jordan and the country's military and financial establishment. She is an ace, and a most generous one at that.

Speaking of generosity, I am particularly indebted to two dear friends who were essential to this project, one at the beginning and one at the end: Tammy Kupperman Thorpe and Chris Rickerd. Tammy is a first-rate journalist whose reputation for fairness and integrity helped open many doors for me at the Pentagon, while Chris kept the pipeline of research flowing with indefatigable good cheer. I can't imagine writing another book without either of them.

In Baghdad, I am grateful to Entifadh Qanbar for both his time and cheerful arguments, Faisal Chalabi for his keen perceptions into his uncle's character, and Kamaran Ahmed for befriending and protecting me in ways that I could never repay. I am also deeply appreciative to Nabeel Musawi for all his recollections and nights of good fun.

One of my goals in this project was to fill in the gaps of history surrounding Chalabi and his march through Washington. I believed that in drilling down into his story, there were not only untapped headlines (one hopes!), but also matters of nuance and interpretation that would help explain how Washington works and why the United States wound up in a war with Iraq. From our first conversation, Bill Thomas, Doubleday's publisher and editor-in-chief, shared my aims and enthusiasm for this book. Along the way, he went beyond a publisher's call of duty as he had to cope with the delays and tribulations of a first-time book writer. I am grateful for his support and patience. Thanks also to Steve Rubin, Doubleday's former publisher, and to Kris Puopolo, whose skillful editing and energizing enthusiasm contributed greatly to this effort.

Every author should have an agent as fiercely loyal and empathetic as Tina Bennett at Janklow & Nesbit Associates. Whenever the going got tough, she seemed to sense it across the 250 miles that separate our offices and, invariably, called me with exactly the right words of support and assurance that kept me going. She never wavered in her conviction about this project—or about me. Thank you, Tina.

As is evident in my source notes, I relied on many previous works of journalism and scholarship. *Newsweek*'s Chris Dickey provided important documents from his personal archives. Mark Hosenball, Michael Isikoff, and Evan Thomas wrote early and incisively about Chalabi, as did Andrew and Patrick Cockburn. Bob Woodward and Karen DeYoung had a direct line into the war council advising President George W. Bush, while James Risen of the *New York Times* consistently turned out some of the most original and in-depth reporting there was on the Bush administration. I am indebted also to the National Security Archive at George Washington University for the extraordinary lengths it has gone to in order to get information declassified and then to make it available to members of the public like me.

I also benefited greatly from Vali Nasr and his research on Islam and the conflicts within that great religion. Fouad Ajami has written extensively and eloquently on Iraq, Lebanon, and what he once called "The Arab Predicament"; while Les Gelb, the president emeritus of the Council on Foreign Relations, provided vital instruction on how to understand and delineate the historical significance of Ahmad Chalabi in the making of U.S. foreign policy. I am also most grateful to Ambassador Frank Ricciardone not only for his time and expertise, but also for introducing me to a book called *First Great Triumph: How Five Americans Made Their Country a World Power*. Written by Warren Zimmerman, it tells the story of how the United States exploded onto the world scene at the turn of the twentieth century and became an imperial power thanks to the vision, audacity, and arrogance of five remarkable Americans. They, and a brilliant French engineer whose single-mindedness and skill at lobbying Congress helped persuade the United States to build a canal across Panama, bear an uncanny resemblance to Ahmad Chalabi and his neoconservative allies a century later.

Finally, there is my family. They lived through every twist, thump, strain, and success of this experience, showing me a depth of love and support that defy description. My daughters, Olivia and Abbey, were amazing, as they patiently and (mostly) quietly racked up a list of IOUs that I shall soon redeem. Ron and Jane Schmiedekamp repeatedly came to my rescue, helping with the children, looking in on my mother, and making me feel a part of their family. I am forever indebted to them. My sister Monica pitched in often, giving generously of her nurturing and loving nature to both me and my girls. My big brother, Andrew, was my sounding board and biggest booster throughout this experience. He is incredibly smart and a good writer in his own right. I'd owe him big-time except that he is totally selfless in his love and support of me. This book would simply not exist without him. Last but not least is my mother, Mary. She has always been there for me through thick and thin, and, if that weren't enough, she has been a wonderful role model for my children. Her love will cling to me all my life.

NOTES

CHAPTER ONE

3   *As one of the participants:* Francis Brooke (a top aide to Ahmad Chalabi), interview with the author, March 9, 2009.

CHAPTER TWO

6   *"The sons of the sultan": Chalabi* stems from the Turkish *Celebi,* which also means "gentleman," "sage," and "prince." Originally, the title signified nobility, but later it came to include well-bred, educated men as well.

7   *Chalabi's father helped out:* Hanna Batatu, *The Old Social Classes and the Revolutionary Movements of Iraq* (London: Saqi Books, 2004), 315–16.

7   *The following year:* On April 4, 1939, King Ghazi, the successor of Faisal, died in an automobile accident while under the influence of alcohol.

8   *In short, Abdul Hadi had mastered:* Batatu, *Old Social Classes,* 316.

8   *On hot summer nights:* In January 2008, Chalabi gave the author a tour of his childhood residence.

9   *such was the milieu of Chalabi's youth:* Ahmad Chalabi, interview with the author, May 11, 2008.

10   *She and the rest of the Chalabis:* Fouad Ajami, interview with the author, February 2005; Fouad Ajami, *The Foreigner's Gift: The Americans, the Arabs, and the Iraqis in Iraq* (New York: Free Press, 2006), 229–32.

10   *The younger generation:* Phebe Marr, *The Modern History of Iraq* (Boulder: Westview Press), 67.

14   *Immediately, the Chalabi men gathered:* For a thorough and engaging exploration of the Chalabi family history, see Tamara Chalabi, *Late for Tea at the Deer Palace: The Lost Dreams of My Iraqi Family* (New York: Harper, 2011).

CHAPTER THREE

15 *Abdul Hadi now had to prepare:* Ahmad Chalabi, interview with the author, May 21, 2008.

16 *"Ahmad told me that his father":* Entifadh Qanbar, interview with the author, June 12, 2007.

16 *"To Middle Easterners, the family name":* Tamara Daghistani, interview with the author, June 2007.

24 *Al-Sadr was the flip side:* In 1978, Musa al-Sadr traveled to Libya, where he disappeared, a victim of Muammar al-Gaddafi's foul play. To the Shia faithful, al-Sadr became the iconic "vanished imam," the Twelfth Imam, who did not die but who was hidden by God until the end of time when he would return to punish the wicked and bring peace and justice to the world.

26 *"I found him not only very, very interesting":* Thomas Carolan, interview with the author, June 18, 2009.

CHAPTER FOUR

30 *"Within minutes":* Tamara Daghistani, interview with the author, November 4, 2007.

30 *Nabulsi immediately reversed himself:* Dr. Muhammed Saeed El-Nabulsi, interview with the author, November 7, 2007.

31 *In the next five years:* Petra Bank application to the Board of Governors of the Federal Reserve System to form a corporation to do business in the United States, April 7, 1983; Andrew Gowers, "Jordan Reels from Another Banking Blow," *Financial Times*, September 26, 1989.

32 *He gave what amounted:* Nabulsi interview, November 4, 2007.

32 *In all, they borrowed:* Chalabi says most of the loans were used to pay the college tuition costs of their children. He says he extended the loans with discounts of some 40 percent.

32 *Prince Hassan and his wife:* Nabulsi interview, November 4, 2007.

32 *Regardless, Chalabi says:* On his deathbed in 1999, King Hussein abruptly changed the line of succession, passing over his brother, Hassan, for his son, Abdullah II.

34 *At the invitation of Peter Galbraith:* The son of John Kenneth Galbraith, one of the leading economists of the twentieth century, Peter Galbraith also helped uncover Saddam Hussein's gassing of the Kurds. After the U.S. invasion of Iraq in 2003, Galbraith served as an adviser to the Kurdistan Regional Government in northern Iraq.

CHAPTER FIVE

36 *During the cleric's telling:* Nasser al-Sadoun, interview with the author, November 7, 2007.

37 *He therefore arranged:* This information is based on multiple interviews with

a source who personally reviewed the records of Petra Bank and the other Chalabi family-owned financial institutions. The source agreed to talk only on background—meaning that I could use the information but not identify the source by name in this book.

38   *The king assented:* Dr. Muhammed Saeed El-Nabulsi, interview with the author, November 7, 2007.

40   *Accompanying them:* Daghistani has asked me not to disclose the name of the prince, who was so close to her she called her "auntie."

42   *He laid it out:* Jim Hoagland, "Hussein Needs All His Survivor Skills Now," *Washington Post,* September 14, 1989.

42   *In addition, the official points out:* The central bank's former governor, Nabulsi, also cited half a billion dollars as the amount of Petra Bank's debts.

43   *He also dispatched:* Glenn Golonka was the loan and marketing officer. Glenn Golonka, interview with the author, July 20, 2009.

CHAPTER SIX

47   *It was a truly radical proposition:* Iran, a Middle Eastern country with a predominantly Shia Muslim population, is not an Arab country. It is Persian.

54   *To do otherwise, they feared:* Richard N. Haass, *War of Necessity, War of Choice: A Memoir of Two Iraq Wars* (New York: Simon & Schuster), 126–31.

54   *In addition, such a scenario:* Ibid., 126–31.

54   *What was Tehran's sway:* Ibid., 134.

55   *As the rest of the world:* Richard Boucher, U.S. State Department spokesman, March 6, 1991.

57   *"It is morally and politically unacceptable":* Quoted in George Lardner Jr., "Solarz Wants U.N. to Demand That Saddam Resign," *Washington Post,* April 11, 1991.

57   *Solarz has no recollection:* Stephen Solarz, interview with the author, February 2008.

57   *Solarz agreed to open some doors:* Solarz died in 2010.

58   *It was the heart:* Arthur M. Schlesinger Jr., *A Thousand Days: John F. Kennedy in the White House* (New York: Mariner Books, 2002), 128. Schlesinger was actually referring to the "New York establishment."

58   *two while still in office:* Those two were Bill Clinton and George W. Bush.

59   *When the Iraqi uprising:* Bruce Riedel (a career CIA officer who was assigned to the National Security Council during the 1991 Gulf War), interview with the author, November 15, 2007.

CHAPTER SEVEN

62   *"The United States government":* Whitley Bruner, interview with the author, December 19, 2009.

63   *Ahmad Chalabi's name popped up:* The CIA's first encounter with Chalabi occurred in 1968 in Beirut.

64   *"Give me a fucking break":* Frank Anderson, interview with the author, July 14, 2009.

66   *"We had great visibility":* John Maguire, interview with the author, July 9, 2009.

69   *"They didn't like Saddam":* Bruner interview, December 19, 2009.

69   *"I saw them as an asset":* Ahmad Chalabi, interview with the author, May 11, 2008.

73   *"I'm meeting you only because":* Ibid.

73   *Haass, for his part:* Richard N. Haass, *War of Necessity, War of Choice: A Memoir of Two Iraq Wars* (New York: Simon & Schuster), 256.

73   *On November 13, 1991:* Ahmad Chalabi, "An Iraq Without Saddam Is Still Possible," *Wall Street Journal*, November 13, 1991.

73   *At the time, Iran:* Founded in 1982 during the Iran-Iraq War, the Supreme Council for the Islamic Revolution in Iraq (SCIRI) brought together under one banner many of Iraq's various Shiite groups. It was based in Tehran and supported the ideologies of Iran's Ayatollah Khomeini.

73   *His name has surfaced:* "The Tower Commission Report," *Washington Post*, February 27, 1987. Hussein Niknam's name also shows up in redacted form in Lee H. Hamilton and Daniel K. Inouye, *Report of the Congressional Committees Investigating the Iran/Contra Affair* (Washington: U.S. House of Representatives Select Committee to Investigate Covert Arms Transactions with Iran, 1988).

74   *They, along with the kidnappings:* Robert Fisk, "Ties That Bind the Hostages," *Independent*, August 30, 1989.

74   *From his association with Mughniyah:* Hussein Niknam was reported to be meeting Ahmed Jibril, the founder and leader of the Popular Front for the Liberation of Palestine–General Command. Jibril was the first old-guard Palestinian militant to embrace the Islamic Republic of Iran and such Iranian-backed terrorist groups as Hezbollah—noteworthy for the rare bridging of the Sunni/Shiite divide among the various Sunni-led Palestinian movements and the Shiites of Iran. "UT 772: Bomb, or Gun-Running?" *Middle East Defense News*, October 2, 1989.

78   *At the meeting, on July 29, 1992:* Statement issued by Margaret Tutwiler, then State Department spokesman, following Secretary of State James Baker's meeting with the Iraqi National Congress, July 29, 1992. *U.S. Department of State Dispatch*, August 3, 1992.

79   *Northern Iraq may have been:* David Mack, interview with the author, November 16, 2007. Now retired, Mack served as the deputy assistant secretary of state for Near Eastern affairs and as U.S. ambassador to the United Arab Emirates.

CHAPTER EIGHT

83   *The fact that de Gaulle:* At the beginning of World War II, Charles de Gaulle
      was a colonel; in 1940 he was promoted to "provisional brigadier general." A
      brigadier general is a one-star general.

86   *State feared the possible fragmentation:* Martin Indyk, *Innocent Abroad: An
      Intimate Account of American Peace Diplomacy in the Middle East* (New York:
      Simon & Schuster, 2009), 30–43.

87   *The Clinton team's assumption:* Ibid.

88   *The* marja *are religious scholars*: The word *marja* ("model") is an abbrevia-
      tion of the longer *marja al-taqlid* ("model of imitation").

91   *For example, he was often "unavailable":* Whitley Bruner, interview with the
      author, December 19, 2009.

92   *"It bristled with":* David L. Phillips, *Losing Iraq* (Boulder: Westview Press,
      2005), 4.

92   *"fish out of water":* David Mack, interview with the author, November 16,
      2007.

92   *"You're gonna have your hands full":* Bob Baer, interview with the author,
      May 17, 2009.

CHAPTER NINE

94   *"The DO is the only arm":* Robert Baer, *See No Evil: The True Story of a
      Ground Soldier in the CIA's War on Terrorism* (New York: Random House,
      2002), 32.

95   *In his undercover work:* With an estimated budget of more than $1 billion,
      William Casey oversaw covert assistance to the Mujahideen resistance in
      Afghanistan and the Solidarity movement in Poland; he also worked closely
      with anticommunist guerrilla movements in Central America.

95   *"screamed at the top of his lungs":* Baer, *See No Evil*, 94.

96   *It was during this tumult:* Robert Baer, interview with the author, May 17,
      2009.

97   *a Bay of Pigs–style fiasco:* In April 1961, a CIA-trained force of Cuban exiles
      invaded Cuba, landing at the Bay of Pigs on the island's southern coast, in
      an attempt to overthrow the government of Fidel Castro. When the United
      States did not provide air cover, Cuban forces routed the rebels and handed
      President John F. Kennedy a deeply embarrassing failure. Kennedy was so
      angry at the agency that he told aides he wished he could "splinter the CIA
      into a thousand pieces and scatter it into the wind."

99   *Chalabi predicted that:* Since the same units had fought to keep Saddam in
      power during the Kurdish and Shiite revolts of 1991, Clinton administra-
      tion officials were dubious of Chalabi's predictions. In December 1993, one
      month after Chalabi proposed this end-game scenario, a National Intel-
      ligence Estimate concluded that Chalabi's INC did "not have the politi-

cal or military clout to bring Saddam down or play an important role in a post-Saddam government." John Prados, *Safe for Democracy: The Secret Wars of the CIA* (Lanham, MD: Ivan R. Dee, 2006), 600.

99 *As for the southern front:* It's impossible to confirm independently the actual size of the Badr Brigade, but its estimated strength at the time ranged from about ten thousand to fifty thousand, all Iraqi exiles, defectors, and refugees.

101 *"We need your full support":* By 1995, the National Security Agency had cracked Iran's system of encryption and was able to "read" Tehran's most sensitive communications, according to multiple former and current U.S. intelligence sources. Two of those sources discussed the contents of the intercept describing the Iranian intelligence agents' meeting with Chalabi. In addition, Baer's account was independently confirmed by the *Washington Post.* Walter Pincus and Bradley Graham, "Coded Cable in 1995 Used Chalabi's Name: Intercepted Iranian Message Involved Plot to Kill Hussein," *Washington Post,* June 4, 2004.

103 *The three largest armies:* Martin Indyk, *Innocent Abroad: An Intimate Account of American Peace Diplomacy in the Middle East* (New York: Simon & Schuster, 2009), 161.

103 *"There was intense anger":* Kenneth Pollack, interview with the author, August 2, 2010.

104 *And now, Chalabi—through Bob Baer:* Indyk, *Innocent Abroad,* 162.

104 *Tony Lake, the president's national security adviser:* Tony Lake, interview with the author, January 2002.

104 *He had been assuring:* Baer interview, May 17, 2009.

105 *"What will you do?":* Ahmad Chalabi, interview with the author, May 12, 2008.

106 *a gruesome assassination attempt:* In February 1978, an ax-wielding intruder attacked Ayad Allawi as he was sleeping in bed. The intruder left him for dead, lying in a pool of blood. Separately, Allawi happens to be a cousin of Ahmad Chalabi and a lifelong rival. Like Chalabi, he is a Shiite, but one with close ties to the Sunni officers corps. After the U.S. invasion of Iraq in 2003, Allawi became Iraq's interim prime minister, the country's first head of government since Saddam.

CHAPTER TEN

108 *"This cannot happen again":* Senate Select Committee on Intelligence, *The Use by the Intelligence Community of Information provided by the Iraqi National Congress* (Washington, DC: U.S. Government Printing Office, September 8, 2006), 19.

109 *"a radio broadcast that was not broadcasting":* John Maguire, interview with the author, December 2009.

115   *"There was a breakdown":* Senate Intelligence Committee, *Use by the Intelligence Community,* 25.

115   *In fact, since the 2003 invasion:* In 2003, a colonel in the Iraqi Intelligence Service (ISS) came forward and surrendered to his American counterparts Iraq's entire file on the foiled coup attempt. The ISS officer did so, John Maguire told me, because he wanted to apologize for the brutal torturing and murder of General al-Shahwani's three sons. "He thought it was dishonorable," Maguire explained. From the file, the CIA learned the identity of the man who betrayed the plot, an Egyptian smuggler whom the CIA used once in 1994 to bootleg communications equipment from Jordan into Baghdad. Two years later, the Egyptian was arrested at the Iraqi border attempting to bring hashish into the country. "To save his own skin," Maguire learned from the Iraqi file, "the courier confessed to all these things he had done in the past. Iraq's intelligence service ran his stuff to the ground and eventually linked that courier to one of Gen. Shahwani's sons."

CHAPTER ELEVEN

117   *He hadn't seen much:* Tamara Chalabi, *Late for Tea at the Deer Palace: The Lost Dreams of My Iraqi Family* (New York: Harper, 2011), 371.

119   *More to the point:* Kenneth M. Pollack, *The Threatening Storm: The Case for Invading Iraq* (New York: Random House, 2002), 86–87.

120   *As Brooke well knew:* Four years before the election, in November 1972, Hamilton Jordan wrote a seventy-page memo outlining the master plan for taking the White House. "Carter followed it, step by step, and won," the *Atlanta Journal-Constitution* noted in its May 20, 2008, obituary of Jordan, who died that month from cancer. Drew Jubera and Tom Bennett, "Hamilton Jordan: 1944–2008," *Atlanta Journal-Constitution,* May 21, 2008.

120   *He had tipped the balance:* Joe Holley and Martin Weil, "Architect of Carter Presidency," *Washington Post,* May 21, 2008.

120   *a 62 percent approval rating:* CNN reported on January 16, 1997, "A new CNN/USA Today/Gallup poll finds President Bill Clinton's approval rating riding high as he prepares to begin his second term. A full 62 percent, an all-time high for Clinton, approve of the way he is doing his job, with only 32 percent disapproving."

121   *"It was literally":* Duane R. Clarridge, interview with the author, January 5, 2008.

121   *his Christmas Eve 1992 presidential pardon:* Duane Clarridge was indicted in November 1991 on seven counts of perjury and false statements. On Christmas Eve 1992, with less than a month left in office, President George H. W. Bush pardoned him.

122 *He immediately tapped:* In later years, Clarridge would form a private spy agency, fielding operatives in Afghanistan and Pakistan. Mark Mazzetti, "Former Spy with Agenda Operates a Private C.I.A.," *New York Times*, January 23, 2011.

122 *"chief instrument":* Steven R. Weisman, "The Influence of William Clark," *New York Times*, August 14, 1983.

126 *They figured that:* Clarridge interview, October 31, 2010.

126 *Clark didn't attend:* David Laux had also been the equivalent of the U.S. ambassador to Taiwan from 1986 to 1990.

CHAPTER THIRTEEN

136 *"I was blown away by it":* Richard Perle, interview with the author, January 20, 2011.

137 *The vote was a significant victory:* For an excellent account of President George W. Bush's inner circle of advisers and the formative influences on them, see James Mann, *Rise of the Vulcans: The History of Bush's War Cabinet* (New York: Penguin, 2004). Regarding "Star Wars," historians at the Missile Defense Agency traced the moniker "Star Wars" to a March 24, 1983, article in the *Washington Post*, quoting Senator Edward Kennedy as describing President Reagan's Strategic Defense Initiative as "reckless Star Wars schemes." See Lou Cannon, "President Seeks Futuristic Defense Against Missiles," *Washington Post*, March 24, 1983.

138 *But, even as they moved:* Irving Kristol, *Neoconservatism: The Autobiography of an Idea* (New York: Simon & Schuster, 1995), x.

138 *In the meantime, Perle:* Mann, *Rise of the Vulcans*, 33.

138 *In 1975, for example:* Jacob Heilbrunn, *They Knew They Were Right: The Rise of the Neocons* (New York: Random House, 2009), 232.

138 *Kissinger would later write:* Henry Kissinger, *Years of Renewal* (New York: Simon & Schuster, 2000), 114.

138 *"Lewis became Jackson's guru":* Quoted in Peter Waldman, "A Historian's Take on Islam Steers U.S. in Terrorism Fight," *Wall Street Journal*, February 6, 2004.

139 *"There's an element of that":* Quoted in George Packer, *The Assassins' Gate* (New York: Farrar, Strauss and Giroux, 2005), 29.

139 *"If Albert were still around":* Paul Wolfowitz, interview with the author, February 8, 2011.

139 *"The importance of Persian Gulf oil":* Paul Wolfowitz, *Capabilities for Limited Contingencies in the Persian Gulf* (Washington, DC: Pentagon, 1979), 1. The full study was first provided to authors Michael R. Gordon and General Bernard E. Trainor for their book *The Generals' War: The Inside Story of the Conflict in the Gulf* (Boston: Little, Brown, 1995), 6–9, 480, and to James Mann for *Rise of the Vulcans*, 80–82.

139   *But Wolfowitz thought:* Mann, *Rise of the Vulcans*, 80–81.

140   *Wolfowitz's limited contingency study:* Ibid., 80.

140   *"There is no doubt that it is Iraq":* Richard N. Perle, "The real stakes in the Persian Gulf," *U.S. News & World Report*, October 26, 1987.

CHAPTER FOURTEEN

144   *"aesthetically pleasing":* Quoted in Mark Matthews, "U.S. Aim Is to 'Contain' Hussein," *Baltimore Sun*, February 4, 1998.

144   *Some neoconservatives argued:* William Kristol and Robert Kagan were the leading advocates of a U.S. invasion. William Kristol and Robert Kagan, "Saddam Must Go," *Weekly Standard*, November 17, 1997.

144   *"Politically it was a nonstarter":* Richard Perle, interview with the author, January 17, 2011.

146   *"If we are serious":* Paul Wolfowitz and Zalmay M. Khalilzad, "Overthrow Him," *Weekly Standard*, December 1, 1997.

147   *"By 1997, the Iraqis knew":* Charles Duelfer, interview with the author, February 8, 2011. In 2004, Charles Duelfer also became leader of the Iraq Survey Group, the fact-finding mission sent to Iraq to hunt for Saddam's nonexistent stockpiles of weapons of mass destruction.

147   *"The safety of American troops":* Project for a New American Century, Letter to President William J. Clinton, January 26, 1998.

148   *"open support for the Iraqi National Congress":* Richard Perle, "No More Halfway Measures," *Washington Post*, February 8, 1998.

148   *"to persuade Republican leaders":* Martin Sieff, "Iraqi Exile Group Seeks Backing as Alternative to Saddam," *Washington Times*, February 20, 1998.

148   *"I believe Secretary Perle's analysis":* Senator Chuck Hagel, "Establishing a Clear Objective in Iraq," *Congressional Record* Vol. 144, No. 8, February 9, 1998.

148   *"The time for talk":* Quoted in John Diamond, "GOP Says Bombing Iraq Not Enough," Associated Press, February 9, 1998; Helen Dewar, "Republicans Increase Pressure for Inside Job Against Saddam," *Washington Post*, February 10, 1998.

148   *Appearing that week:* ABC News, *Nightline*, "Could an Attack on Iraq Do More Harm Than Good?" February 11, 1998.

149   *He used the plane ride:* See also Seth Gitell, "Senate Swinging Behind Struggle to Liberate Iraq as Islamic Radicals Issue Warning Yanks Will Die," *Forward*, March 6, 1998.

149   *"The neocons came to visit me":* Samuel R. Berger, HBO History Makers Series, Council on Foreign Relations, September 11, 2006.

149   *"[W]e have had experiences":* The transcript of the February 20, 1998, town hall meeting on Iraq at Ohio State University is available at http://www.fas.org/news/iraq/1998/02/20/98022006_tpo.html.

150   *"For me, personally"*: Stephen Rademaker, interview with the author, November 10, 2010.

CHAPTER FIFTEEN

153   *Annan also consented:* Kenneth M. Pollack, *The Threatening Storm: The Case for Invading Iraq* (New York: Random House, 2002), 89–90.

155   *"I am here as an elected representative"*: Ahmad Chalabi, Testimony to the Senate Foreign Relations Subcommittee on Near Eastern and South Asian Affairs, March 2, 1998.

156   *For the first time:* Seth Gitell, "Senate Swinging Behind Struggle to Liberate Iraq as Islamic Radicals Issue Warning Yanks Will Die," *Forward*, March 6, 1998.

157   *"The GOP will be tempted"*: Jim Hoagland, "From Pariah to Iraq's Hope," *Washington Post*, March 5, 1998.

157   *"All that was required"*: Francis Brooke, interview with the author, January 15, 2008.

157   *There were a handful:* Lieberman became an "Independent Democrat" in 2007.

158   *"This is a smoking gun"*: Quoted in Jim Hoagland and Vernon Loeb, "Tests Show Nerve Gas in Iraqi Weapons," *Washington Post*, June 23, 1998.

158   *"That conclusion we drew"*: Charles Duelfer, interview with the author, February 8, 2011. Duelfer says one possible explanation for the lab results cited in the *Washington Post* article was that some amount of VX had been loaded and unloaded on a test basis in a few warheads in 1990, but "this was a crude and never-perfected capability." In addition, two years earlier, in 1988, Iraq had used a rudimentary form of VX in three gravity, or aerial, bombs that it dropped over Iran. But, Duelfer says, that was regarded as an "experiment" as opposed to the successful "weaponization" of VX.

160   *Saddam then ordered:* Pollack, *Threatening Storm*, 90.

CHAPTER SIXTEEN

162   *"a major step forward"*: Quoted in Tom Bowman, "General Voices Doubt on Anti-Hussein Bill," *Baltimore Sun*, October 22, 1998.

162   *Meanwhile, Richard Perle:* Perle had said earlier in the year that "[t]he Iraqi opposition is kind of like an MRE [meal ready to eat, or U.S. Army field ration]. The ingredients are there and you just have to add water, in this case U.S. support." Richard J. Newman et al., "Stalking Saddam," *U.S. News and World Report*, February 23, 1998.

163   *"It was the siren song"*: Anthony Zinni, interview with the author, December 6, 2007. Zinni was commander in chief of the United States Central Command from 1997 to 2000.

164 *"We in the State Department":* Frank Ricciardone, interview with the author, November 7, 2007. Ricciardone was the U.S. ambassador to Egypt at the time of my interview with him, which took place in Cairo. He is currently the U.S. ambassador to Turkey.

165 *Then, in early 1999:* Kenneth M. Pollack, *The Threatening Storm: The Case for Invading Iraq* (New York: Random House, 2002), 94–96.

167 *Angered by Zinni's "open scorn":* John Lancaster, "A Nominee's Long Road to 'No,'" *Washington Post,* October 3, 2000.

168 *Chalabi managed to wrangle:* Elaine Sciolino, "Iraqi Opponent Says He's Leaving Iran to Plan Takeover," *New York Times,* January 28, 2003. The money for the Tehran and Damascus offices was earmarked in 1999 but not released until 2001.

168 *So there'd be no regime change:* Pollack, *Threatening Storm,* 99.

169 *the future secretary of defense:* Actually, Donald Rumsfeld was the future and past secretary of defense: he held the position under both Gerald Ford (1975 to 1977) and George W. Bush (2001 to 2006).

CHAPTER SEVENTEEN

174 *The vast majority of terrorism experts:* See Peter Bergen, "Armchair Provocateur. Laurie Mylroie: The Neocons' Favorite Conspiracy Theorist," *Washington Monthly,* December 2003.

174 *Such was the menagerie:* Chalabi first told me about the January 21, 2001, meeting during my visit to Baghdad in May of 2008. We discussed the details of the meeting several times during that trip. Later, his aide, Francis Brooke, told me that he attended the meeting, and confirmed Chalabi's account of it. Richard Perle confirmed that the meeting took place in his house, though he could not recall who exactly attended. Harold Rhode said he didn't recall the meeting specifically, but had no reason to doubt that it occurred. John Hannah doesn't recall anything about the meeting either, but, like Rhode, he doesn't dispute that it occurred. "It sounds reasonable to believe that it happened," he told a source close to him. Wolfowitz told me he had "no recollection" of the meeting, though he did not deny that it occurred. "I just don't remember it," he said. Feith, on the other hand, asserted, "I'm reasonably confident that I was not at that meeting. It doesn't sound familiar. I think I would remember it. But I can't be certain. I think I wasn't. But I'm happy to be corrected." Khalilzad declined to be interviewed for the book, and Laurie Mylroie did not respond to my numerous attempts to reach her.

175 *He foresaw strong resistance:* Among those who worried Richard Perle was Bruce Riedel, a career CIA analyst assigned to the National Security Council, where he had served as a special assistant to Bill Clinton and senior director for Near East Affairs. Riedel had known and dealt with Chalabi

since the 1990s—and was no fan. Similarly, Riedel believed an INC-led insurrection was doomed to failure.

177   *"The INC enjoys more support":* Andrew Parasiliti of the Middle East Institute, quoted in Daniel Byman, Kenneth Pollack, and Gideon Rose, "The Rollback Fantasy," *Foreign Affairs,* January–February 1999.

178   *The occupied areas:* Duane R. "Dewey" Clarridge, interview with the author, February, 2002.

179   *By contrast, Saddam's elite Republican Guard:* By way of another contrast, during the March 2011, uprisings in Libya, Colonel Muammar el-Qaddafi had an army of fifty thousand soldiers, only ten thousand of whom he trusted enough to deploy against the rebels.

179   *"U.S. air support could not protect":* Byman, Pollack, and Rose, "Rollback Fantasy." One of the authors, Ken Pollack, was intimately familiar with the Iraqi opposition and its war plans from his stint at the National Security Council during the Clinton administration.

180   *But Wolfowitz thought:* Paul Wolfowitz and Stephen J. Solarz, "Letter to the Editor," *Foreign Affairs,* March–April, 1999.

181   *"Our sense was":* Interview with the author, State Department, Washington, D.C., August 26, 2008.

181   *"They really carried":* Richard L. Armitage, interview with the author, December 19, 2007.

182   *Nor did they view:* Douglas J. Feith, *War and Decision: Inside the Pentagon at the Dawn of the War on Terrorism* (New York: HarperCollins, 2008), 200–201.

182   *"I have been working with Zal":* Richard Perle, "Urgent Fax Message to SECDEF," February 19, 2001 (3:47 p.m.).

183   *The Pentagon's candidate:* In 1998, Randy Scheunemann had championed passage of the Iraq Liberation Act in the Senate.

183   *The move was part:* Eli J. Lake, "Pentagon Seeks to Take Over Iraq Policy," United Press International, March 21, 2001.

CHAPTER EIGHTEEN

186   *In March 2001:* "Insider Notes," United Press International, March 21, 2001.

187   *The hope was that:* Joyce Battle, *The Iraq War—Part I: The U.S. Prepares for Conflict, 2001* (Washington, DC: National Security Archive, September 22, 2010), available at http://www.gwu.edu/~nsarchiv/NSAEBB/NSAEBB326/index.htm; Douglas J. Feith, *War and Decision: Inside the Pentagon at the Dawn of the War on Terrorism* (New York: HarperCollins, 2008), 206–11.

187   *"needed to be able to do the fight":* Paul Wolfowitz, interview with the author, February 8, 2011.

187   *To Secretary of State Colin Powell:* Bob Woodward, *Plan of Attack* (New York: Simon & Schuster, 2004), 22.

187   *In the case of Iraq:* Karen DeYoung, *Soldier: The Life of Colin Powell* (New York: Random House, 2006), 345; Woodward, *Plan of Attack*, 22.

188   *He urged National Security Adviser Condoleezza Rice:* Feith, *War and Decision*, 206–11.

188   *Later that month:* Ibid., 209.

188   *"This is not as easy":* Woodward, *Plan of Attack*, 21–22; Battle, *The Iraq War*.

189   *But as he eventually would say:* "9/11 Before & After," *60 Minutes*, CBS News, March 21, 2004; Richard A. Clarke, *Against All Enemies: Inside America's War on Terror* (New York: Free Press, 2004), 231–32.

190   *Saddam had long regarded:* Senate Select Committee on Intelligence, *Postwar Findings About Iraq's WMD Programs and Links to Terrorism and How They Compare with Prewar Assessments* (Washington, DC: U.S. Government Printing Office, September 8, 2006), 105–13.

190   *as senior regimes figures would later tell:* Charles Duelfer, *Hide and Seek: The Search for Truth in Iraq* (New York: PublicAffairs, 2002), 191–92.

191   *"with almost a sharp physical pain":* Clarke, *Against All Enemies*, 30.

191   *"There aren't any":* "9/11 Before & After," *60 Minutes*.

191   *Iraq must have helped them:* Clarke, *Against All Enemies*, 30.

192   *"Such as my friend here":* Richard Perle, Ahmad Chalabi, and Bernard Lewis, interviews with the author. See also Bryan Burrough, Evgenia Peretz, David Rose, and David Wise, "The Path to War," *Vanity Fair*, May 2004.

192   *Both Wolfowitz and Feith:* See, among others, Battle, *The Iraq War*; Michael Isikoff and David Corn, *Hubris: The Inside Story of Spin, Scandal, and the Selling of the Iraq War* (New York: Crown, 2006), 80; Michael R. Gordon and General Bernard Trainor, *Cobra II: The Inside Story of the Invasion and Occupation of Iraq* (New York: Random House, 2006).

193   *"[S]keptics fear American hawks":* David Rose and Ed Vulliamy, "Iraq 'Behind US Anthrax Outbreaks,'" *Guardian*, October 14, 2001.

193   *"second wave of terrorist attacks":* President George W. Bush, "Radio Address by the President to the Nation," November 7, 2001.

CHAPTER NINETEEN

196   *"Veteran reporters and creaking commentators":* William Safire, "Advance the Story," *New York Times*, October 22, 2001.

197   *"I want you to find":* "9/11 Before & After," *60 Minutes*, CBS News, March 21, 2004; Richard A. Clarke, *Against All Enemies: Inside America's War on Terror* (New York: Free Press, 2004), 32.

199   *They gave Saeed a polygraph test:* Senate Select Committee on Intelligence,

The Use by the Intelligence Community of Information provided by the Iraqi National Congress (Washington, DC: U.S. Government Printing Office, September 8, 2006), 40.

199   *The debriefing in Thailand:* Ibid.

199   *"If verified":* Judith Miller, "Iraqi Tells of Renovations at Sites for Chemical and Nuclear Arms," *New York Times*, December 20, 2001.

199   *They were searching:* James Risen, "How Pair's Finding on Terror Led to Clash on Shaping Intelligence," *New York Times*, April 28, 2004.

199   *The unit then reported:* Mike Maloof, interview with the author, January 11, 2008; Risen, "How Pair's Finding."

200   *By this time:* Senate Select Committee on Intelligence, *Use by the Intelligence Community*, 69, 115, 133.

200   *"isn't worth the paper":* Warren P. Strobel and Jonathan S. Landay, "Infighting Among U.S. Intelligence Agencies Fuels Dispute over Iraq," Knight Ridder, October 24, 2002.

204   *Francis Brooke told us:* Francis Brooke, interview with the author, January 2002.

205   *"These guys beat me up":* Richard L. Armitage, interview with the author, December 19, 2007.

205   *"Right off the bat":* John Maguire, interview with the author, July 31, 2010.

207   *When Secretary of State Colin Powell:* Senate Select Committee on Intelligence, *Use by the Intelligence Community*, 113.

CHAPTER TWENTY

212   *The U.S. message:* Douglas J. Feith, *War and Decision: Inside the Pentagon at the Dawn of the War on Terrorism* (New York: HarperCollins, 2008), 280–83.

213   *Instead, the State Department proposed:* Ibid., 277–79.

213   *"It was clear they were pushing":* Richard L. Armitage, interview with the author, December 19, 2007.

213   *"I remember sitting":* Interview with the author, State Department, Washington, D.C., August 26, 2008.

214   *"I never heard anyone":* Feith, *War and Decision*, 255. Feith also wrote, "I do not know what might exist in the file cabinets of every official in the Defense Department, but of the thousands of pages of material that senior Defense Department officials wrote for interagency meetings on post-Saddam Iraqi governance, I know of *not one* supporting the charge that the Pentagon had 'anointed' Chalabi as leader of Iraq."

215   *And on their flight:* Charles Glass, *The Northern Front: A Wartime Diary* (London: Saqi Books, 2006), 92.

215–16 *"When the Iranians like you":* Charles Glass, "Chronicle of a War Foretold:

On the Move with Ahmad Chalabi, the Man Who Would Be King," *Harper's Magazine*, July 1, 2003.

216 *"We are a proud nation":* Ahmad Chalabi, "Iraq for the Iraqis," *Wall Street Journal*, February 19, 2003.

218 *"Ahmad told me":* Aras Habib Karim, interview with the author, June 24, 2007.

CHAPTER TWENTY-ONE

219 *"It makes a lot of difference":* Francis Brooke, interview with the author, January 15, 2008.

220 *"We were in touch":* Harold Rhode, interview with the author, April 19, 2010.

221 *"People in the White House":* Bruce Riedel, interview with the author, December 3, 2007.

221 *"We were telling people":* Rob Richer, interviews with the author, September 21, 2007, and May 20, 2011.

222 *But, now, in the heat of battle:* Michael R. Gordon and General Bernard Trainor, *Cobra II: The Inside Story of the Invasion and Occupation of Iraq* (New York: Random House, 2006), 314–17.

222 *"You're flying Iranian agents":* Bruce Riedel, interview with the author, December 3, 2007.

223 *And on the morning of April 5, 2003:* See Gordon and Trainor, *Cobra II*, 314–17; Charles Glass, *The Northern Front: A Wartime Diary* (London: Saqi Books, 2006), 229–59.

223 *"Ya Hussein!":* Glass, *Northern Front*, 257.

CHAPTER TWENTY-TWO

227 *"Feith called me that night":* Jay Garner, interview with book researcher Tammy Kupperman Thorpe, December 7, 2007.

227 *Shortly thereafter, Wolfowitz organized:* Wolfowitz denies directing the CIA to give Chalabi an STU. But two former agency officials, including Rob Richer, the then director of clandestine services for the Agency's Near East Division, confirm it.

229 *"It was a statement":* Rob Richer, interviews with the author, September 21, 2007, and May 20, 2011.

229 *"Our president refused":* Richard L. Armitage, interview with the author, December 19, 2007.

230 *"Ahmad is positioning":* Christopher Dickey, "The Master Operator," *Newsweek*, March 8, 2004.

230 *In one instance:* That defector was the Mukhabarat major Mohammad Harith, who appeared on *60 Minutes* and whose fabricated testimony made it into Secretary of State Colin Powell's UN speech providing the rationale for war.

231   *"We are heroes in error"*: Jack Fairweather and Anton La Guardia, "Chalabi Stands By Faulty Intelligence That Toppled Saddam's Regime," *London Daily Telegraph*, February 19, 2004.

231   *"really frosted"*: L. Paul Bremer with Malcolm McConnell, *My Year in Iraq* (New York: Simon & Schuster, 2006), 291.

231   *"He was a big factor"*: Interview with the author, Baghdad, June 19, 2007.

232   *"So he was printing old money"*: Interview with the author, Baghdad, September 13, 2008.

233   *"The Iraqi Mukhabarat"*: Interview with the author, November 10, 2007.

CHAPTER TWENTY-THREE

235   *Quds was to Iraq's Shia militias:* Rick Francona, "Iranian Qods Force in Iraq: Treat Them Like al-Qaida," MSNBC.com, January 26, 2007; Lionel Beehner and Greg Bruno, "Iran's Involvement in Iraq," Council on Foreign Relations, March 3, 2008.

235   *"You'd see all of these dead bodies"*: John Maguire, interview with the author, May 21, 2011.

235   *"We'd lose thirty guys"*: There were 1,214 casualties in April 2004.

236   *"This was huge, just huge"*: Interview with the author, May 2011.

238   *He wrote down:* I was joined by my then colleague Adam Ciralsky.

238   *"top Bush administration officials"*: Mark Hosenball, "Intelligence: A Double Game," *Newsweek*, May 10, 2004.

238   *"What the hell is this?"*: Rob Richer, interview with the author, May 20, 2011.

239   *It was left to three-star general Michael Hayden*: Air Force Lieutenant General Michael Hayden was promoted to four-star general on April 21, 2005. A year later, George W. Bush appointed him director of the CIA.

241   *It would be "inappropriate"*: Jonathan S. Landay, "Iraqi Group Linked to Questionable Intelligence Loses U.S. Funding," Knight Ridder, May 19, 2004; Michael Isikoff and Mark Hosenball, "Rethinking the Chalabi Connection," *Newsweek*, May 19, 2004.

241   *Down the road:* Romesh Ratnesar et al., "From Friend to Foe," *Time*, May 31, 2004.

241   *"This was a manufactured charge"*: Ahmad Chalabi, interview with the author, December 11, 2010.

241   *"There's all this stuff"*: Quoted in Ratnesar et al., "From Friend to Foe."

242   *"the laugh test"*: Quoted in David Johnson and James Risen, "Polygraph Testing Starts at Pentagon in Chalabi Inquiry," *New York Times*, June 3, 2004.

242   *The bureau sent a small army*: Ibid.

243   *"They strapped their wagon"*: John Maguire, interview with the author, May 21, 2011.

243   *"Ahmad Chalabi is not a controllable asset"*: Bruce Riedel, interview with the author, December 3, 2007.

CHAPTER TWENTY-FOUR

245   *"They thought they could"*: Ahmad Chalabi, interview with the author, September 2005.

247   *"Ahmad thought that since we delivered"*: Nabeel Musawi, interview with the author, December 21, 2007.

248   *"I would be blamed"*: Ahmad Chalabi, interview with the author, May 31, 2008.

248   *"thrown his weight"*: Dexter Filkins, "Where Plan A Left Ahmad Chalabi," *New York Times*, November 5, 2006.

249   *"It's not even that I'm angry"*: Tamara Daghistani, interview with the author, May 6, 2008.

250   *Would the Iranians support him:* Filkins, "Where Plan A."

250   *"He got angry a lot"*: Aras Habib Karim, interview with the author, Baghdad, July 2007.

252   *Chalabi said at the time*: Ibid.

252   *"Why is it that the U.S. can't"*: Interview with the author, 2010.

253   *"It was a huge"*: Senior U.S. military commander, interview with the author, May 8, 2008.

254   *"He's way smarter"*: Ryan Crocker, interview with the author, May 15, 2008.

254   *"He was dead to us"*: Col. Steven Boylan, interview with the author, June 6, 2011.

255   *"This is the second time"*: Ahmad Chalabi, interview with the author, May 2008.

CHAPTER TWENTY-FIVE

256   *Everything outside that compound:* Orville Schell, "In the Twilight Zone," Salon.com, March 17, 2006.

256   *"Ahmad set up"*: Francis Brooke, interview with the author, January 19, 2008.

258   *I was among Chalabi's guests:* A night in the Yellow Zone could sometimes resemble the cantina scene from *Star Wars* in terms of the kind of characters who passed through Chalabi's compound. During my several trips there while researching this book, I ran into, among others, the former Defense Intelligence Agency officer who, during a drunken stupor, was suspected of having leaked to Chalabi's chief of intelligence the fact that the United States had cracked Iran's secret communications codes. I shared a few beers and a bottle of scotch with the DIA officer, who went by the name of Harry Covert when I met him. There also was Laurie Mylroie, the conspiracy theorist who argues that Saddam Hussein was behind both

the 1993 and 2001 terrorist attacks on the World Trade Center, as well as the 2001 anthrax attacks. Mylroie was staying at the compound, where she told me she was sifting through Chalabi's cache of seized Mukhabarat documents in search of evidence, which she never found, to support her theories. I also got to know Albert Huddleston there. He is a Texas oilman and staunch supporter of George W. Bush. During the 2004 presidential election, Huddleston contributed $100,000 to the Swift Boat Veterans for Truth, the controversial political group that targeted John Kerry's campaign by publicizing unproven allegations about Kerry's military service in Vietnam. Huddleston, who was in Baghdad trying to land an oil servicing contract, often spoke of his father-in-law, billionaire Nelson Bunker Hunt, who tried to corner the world's silver market in the 1980s.

258   *"American culture is like pornography":* Ahmad Chalabi, interview with the author, May 12, 2008.

260   *"I think he would have been," Perle says:* Richard Perle, interview with the author, July 7, 2007; reconfirmed June 3, 2011.

260   *"What I hadn't":* Paul Wolfowitz, interview with the author, June 2008.

261   *"Imagine how much stronger":* Kenneth Pollack, interview with the author, August 2, 2010.

262   *And from an Iraqi point of view:* Leslie H. Gelb, "Neoconner," *New York Times Book Review*, April 27, 2008.

SELECT BIBLIOGRAPHY

DOCUMENTS

Occupying Iraq: A History of the Coalition Provisional Authority, RAND National Security Research Division, 2009.

Report of the Select Committee on Intelligence on Postwar Findings About Iraq's WMD Programs and Links to Terrorism and How They Compare with Prewar Assessments, September 8, 2006.

Report of the Select Committee on Intelligence on the Use by the Intelligence Community of Information Provided by the Iraqi National Congress, September 8, 2006.

BOOKS

Ajami, Fouad. *The Arab Predicament*. New York: Cambridge University Press, 1992.

————. *The Dream Palace of the Arabs: A Generation's Odyssey*. New York: Pantheon, 1998.

————. *The Foreigner's Gift: The Americans, the Arabs, and the Iraqis in Iraq*. New York: Simon and Schuster, 2006.

————. *The Vanished Imam: Musa al Sadr and the Shia of Lebanon*. Ithaca, New York: Cornell University Press, 1986.

Allawi, Ali A. *The Occupation of Iraq: Winning the War, Losing the Peace*. New Haven: Yale University Press, 2008.

Baer, Robert. *See No Evil: The True Story of a Ground Soldier in the CIA's War on Terrorism*. New York: Crown, 2002.

Bush, George W. *Decision Points*. New York: Crown, 2010.

Chalabi, Tamara. *Late for Tea at the Deer Palace: The Lost Dreams of My Iraqi Family*. New York: Harper, 2011.

Clarridge, Duane R. *A Spy for All Seasons: My Life in the CIA*. New York: Scribner, 1997.

Cockburn, Andrew, and Patrick Coburn. *Out of the Ashes: The Resurrection of Saddam Hussein*. New York: HarperCollins, 1999.

Coll, Steve. *Ghost Wars: The Secret History of the CIA, Afghanistan, and Bin Laden, from the Soviet Invasion to September 10, 2001*. New York: Penguin, 2004.

DeYoung, Karen. *The Life of Colin Powell*. New York: Knopf, 2006.

Duelfer, Charles. *Hide and Seek: The Search for Truth in Iraq*. New York: PublicAffairs, 2009.

Filkins, Dexter. *The Forever War*. New York: Knopf, 2008.

Galbraith, Peter W., *The End of Iraq*. New York: Simon and Schuster, 2006.

Gordon, Michael, and General Bernard Trainor. *Cobra II: The Inside Story of the Invasion and Occupation of Iraq*. New York: Pantheon, 2006.

Haass, Richard N. *War of Necessity, War of Choice: A Memoir of Two Iraq Wars*. New York: Simon and Schuster, 2009.

Indyk, Martin. *Innocent Abroad: An Intimate Account of American Peace Diplomacy in the Middle East*. New York: Simon and Schuster, 2009.

Lewis, Bernard. *The Middle East: 2000 Years of History from the Rise of Christianity to the Present Day*. London: Weidenfeld & Nicolson, 1995.

————. *What Went Wrong?* New York: Harper Perennial, 2003.

Makiya, Kanan. *Republic of Fear: The Politics of Modern Iraq*. Berkeley and Los Angeles: University of California Press, 1989.

Mann, James. *Rise of the Vulcans: The History of Bush's War Cabinet*. New York: Viking, 2004.

Marr, Phebe. *The Modern History of Iraq*. Boulder, Co.: Westview Press, 2004.

Mylroie, Laurie. *Study of Revenge: The First World Trade Center Attack and Saddam Hussein's War Against America*. Washington, D.C.: AEI, 2001.

Nasr, Vali. *The Shia Revival*. New York & London: W. W. Norton, 2007.

Packer, George. *The Assassins' Gate: America in Iraq*. New York: *Farrar, Straus & Giroux*, 2005.

Pollack, Kenneth M. *The Persian Puzzle: The Conflict Between Iran and America*. New York: Random House, 2004.

————. *The Threatening Storm: The Case for Invading Iraq*. New York: Random House, 2002.

Risen, James. *State of War: The Secret History of the CIA and the Bush Administration*. New York: Free Press, 2006.

Rumsfeld, Donald. *Known and Unknown: A Memoir*. New York: Sentinel, 2011.

Takeyh, Ray. *Guardians of the Revolution: Iran and the World in the Age of the Ayatollahs*. Oxford and New York: Oxford University Press, 2009.

Tripp, Charles. *A History of Iraq*. Cambridge, U.K.: Cambridge University Press, 2000.

Weschler, Lawrence. *Calamities of Exile*. Chicago: University of Chicago Press, 1998.

Woodward, Bob. *Bush at War*. New York: Simon and Schuster, 2002.

—————. *Plan of Attack*. New York: Simon and Schuster, 2004.

Zimmerman, Warren. *First Great Triumph: How Five Americans Made Their Country a World Power*. New York: Farrar, Straus and Giroux, 2002.

ARTICLES

Buruma, Ian. "Lost in Translation: The Two Minds of Bernard Lewis," *The New Yorker*, June 14, 2004.

Byman, Daniel, et al. "The End of the Chalabi Affair?" *Foreign Affairs*, May 26, 2004.

Gelb, Leslie H. "Neoconner," *New York Times Book Review*, April 27, 2008.

Sanger, David E. "The Struggle for Iraq: The Exile; A Seat of Honor Lost to Open Political Warfare," *New York Times*, May 21, 2004.

INDEX

ABOUT THE AUTHOR

RICHARD BONIN is a veteran producer at CBS News' *60 Minutes*. In his twenty-eight years there, he has broken numerous stories and traveled to war zones from Central America to Afghanistan and the Middle East. He has also interviewed a range of newsmakers from Ronald Reagan to Richard A. Clarke, the former White House counterterrorism czar who blew the whistle on President George W. Bush's mishandling of the terrorist threat prior to September 11, 2001. Bonin has won five Emmys, including one for his reporting on 9/11, and an Overseas Press Club Award for his work in Iraq. He lives in Washington, D.C. This is his first book.